CW00347858

Rodney Tyler is a 44-year-old journalist and author. After graduating he spent a period on local newspapers before joining the *Daily Mail* in 1966. For the next 16 years he was a writer and executive on a number of national newspapers. It was during this time that he met and got to know Margaret Thatcher personally. He contributes articles to leading newspapers and magazines on a wide range of topics, but his special interest is politics, particularly the personalities. In 1986 he was invited to become acting Political Editor of the *News of the World*, the year in which he co-wrote Sir Ian MacGregor's best-selling autobiography *The Enemies Within*.

CAMPAIGN!

THE SELLING OF THE PRIME MINISTER

Rodney Tyler

GRAFTON BOOKS
A Division of the Collins Publishing Group

LONDON GLASGOW
TORONTO SYDNEY AUCKLAND

Grafton Books
A Division of the Collins Publishing Group
8 Grafton Street, London WIX 3LA

Published by Grafton Books 1987

British Library Cataloguing in Publication Data
Tyler, Rodney
   Campaign!: the selling of the Prime Minister.
    1. Great Britain, *Parliament*—Elections, 1987
   I. Title
   324.941'0858   JN956
   ISBN 0-246-13257-4
   ISBN 0-246-13277-9 (Pbk)

Printed in Great Britain by
Robert Hartnoll (1985) Ltd
Bodmin, Cornwall

Photoset in Linotron Sabon by
Rowland Phototypesetting Ltd
Bury St Edmunds, Suffolk

Contents

Acknowledgements

The people who co-operated with me in the preparation of this book come from different sections of the Conservative Party and hold many differing views on its direction and the conduct of the election campaign. Some are politicians – MPs or members of the Cabinet – some are party workers and some employed to help the party fight the election. But whatever their backgrounds or their differing views, they all wanted a Tory victory and a third Thatcher term.

I set out to write this book from the viewpoint, gained while reporting the 1983 campaign from the outside, that the Tory party was rather like a family which, in times of stress, suffered tensions and bouts of ill-feeling which soon subsided. I was not to know that I was going to witness, from within, one of the most bitterly criticised of all Tory election campaigns. The family squabble nearly ended in divorce. But this book has tried not to take sides and to stick to its original intention – that is, to be a narrative.

This is first and foremost the inside story of the campaign. It does not pretend to deep psephology or heavy political analysis – that is for others far better qualified than I. What I have tried to do is to tell the tale of the Tory Campaign 1987 from the viewpoint of those who fought it, whichever 'side' they were on. Nevertheless it does contain real criticisms of parts of the organisation, some of the events and a number of the people. I hope these are fair and are taken as constructively as they are meant.

For most of the people involved at the centre of the campaign it was fascinating, occasionally frightening and fatiguing beyond belief. It was a roller-coaster of tremendous exhilaration, which, at the end of the ride, could have dumped them unceremoniously in Opposition. That is what gave it more than a frisson of fear. It was a serious business. For some it became almost life or death. Now that it is over the rows and rages are acquiring a rosy glow with each day that passes – for some it will soon be as though it had never happened – but it is no exaggeration to say that others will never forget what they went through to win.

There were thousands who worked for that victory in the constituencies, hundreds in Conservative Central Office, dozens who played key roles, a handful who directed it. And Her. This book is their story.

I am eternally grateful to the Prime Minister for agreeing to the interview which forms the bulk of the last chapter. It is no secret that I am a great admirer of hers and it is in that context that any criticisms I have are made. The story was told to me over a period of four months by more than 20 of those most closely involved in the campaign. I hope I have rewarded their endless patience by getting it right, and, where I have erred, I hope they will forgive me. I dedicate this book to them.

I was helped to travel by Sheila Howe and Roger Boaden of CCO. I was helped to write, more than they know, by Sally Louis, Gail Bracket and Bettina Gonsalves, and was kept sane by the inmates of Centrehurst and above all by Maggie and Rachel. They also deserve the credit.

Rodney Tyler
London
21 June 1987

Prologue

The Prime Minister, the Right Honourable Mrs Margaret Thatcher, wearing a light grey suit and a blouse tied in a bow at the neck over a double strand of pearls, came bustling into the Cabinet room a few seconds after eleven o'clock on Monday 11 May 1987, her handbag as usual over her left arm, which she also used to clutch her bundle of files and papers. She hurried around the table to the only empty space – in the middle, facing the window overlooking the walled garden of Number 10 Downing Street. She sat down with Viscount Whitelaw, her deputy, on her left and Sir Robert Armstrong, the head of the Civil Service, on her right.

The expectant buzz of conversation which had preceded her entry – in which members of the Cabinet had joked among themselves that it was going to be 4 June after all, or 18 June, or even October, as Lord Young laughingly claimed on the basis of 'inside' information – died away as she took her seat. They all knew why they had been summoned – there could be no other reason for the calls that had gone out to their offices shortly before nine that morning. She neither teased them nor kept them waiting.

'I have been taking advice from some of my colleagues as to when the right time would be to call the election,' she said. 'I have looked at the opinion polls and the results of the local government elections and also at the state of the current programme of legislation and what we still have to do. I have concluded, in fact, that we have a lot to do and that what we must do first, therefore, is to get the election behind us. I have looked at the other dates, the fourth and the eighteenth of June, but there are strong arguments against them both. I have decided that June the eleventh is therefore the day.'

There was a short silence before a chorus of murmured assent and one or two 'hear hears' broke out. Mrs Thatcher looked around the table and smiled at the response. For more than five months she had been having secret meetings to discuss the strategy for the General Election, for more than three months she had been aware that the best date before the autumn would be 11 June, for nearly two months she had been taking a direct hand in the preparations and for a month, she was assured, all had been ready. But she had waited, as she had said she would, for the results of the local elections held the previous Thursday, then spent most of the weekend thinking about it and discussing it.

Some of the people she had talked to were predictable – Norman Tebbit, her Party Chairman, and John Wakeham, her Chief Whip – others much less so. The truth was that she wanted a whole range of opinions, not so much about the date, for that decision was hers and hers alone, but about the strategy, the tactics, the mood of the country and the 'feel' of the situation. One person she wanted to chat to had been more or less smuggled into Chequers on Saturday evening to avoid the embarrassment knowledge of his presence might cause. On Sunday her Strategy Group of senior ministers – known variously as 'The A-Team' and 'The Seven Dwarfs' – had gone over all the options with her. And finally she had driven back to Downing Street in the fading light of Sunday evening, promising to 'sleep on it'.

Now the die was cast. For a few seconds she allowed her Cabinet to express their relief and approval before assuring them that she too was anxious for battle and reminding them there was much to do. They quickly discussed plans to concertina the legislative programme into the next few days – which bills could be kept and which would be lost. Then she reminded them all that they must on no account give anything away before she had been to the Palace to seek Dissolution from the Queen and, after just 55 minutes, the meeting broke up. In a slightly embarrassed gaggle the ministers made their way out into Downing Street and walked the gauntlet of the massed TV cameras, photographers and reporters – all shouting the question none of them was allowed to answer.

The statement from Downing Street came two hours later. The nation had 31 days to make up its mind. The politicians had 31 days to persuade us. Mrs Thatcher had 31 days to a truly historic victory – or to a catastrophic defeat. The campaign was on.

1 | The Year of Living Dangerously

It was an extraordinary turnaround in fortunes from the moment on 27 January 1986 when Mrs Thatcher secretly confided to a close associate that she might have to resign, to the occasion, almost a year later, when she found herself, also in great secrecy, chairing a meeting at which she was told how she might win the next general election. Remarkable too in that this time there had been no 'Falklands factor', such as came to her aid after a disastrous year in 1981, to assist her steady rise in the polls. It was the more extraordinary because she was now entering uncharted waters. No Prime Minister this century had secured a third mandate in succession from the electorate – and the winning of it, if she did, could carry her through eventually into second place behind Sir Robert Walpole as the longest-serving single-stretch Prime Minister ever.

In the nature of things, governments run out of steam; Prime Ministers sag under the sheer unrelenting pressure of the job; mistakes are made, scandals erupt and somehow a consensus slowly arises that it is 'time for a change'. By the end of a second term, sometimes even long before it, the party in power, whichever one it is, is traditionally bereft of ideas, will and judgement and ready for the knacker's yard. No matter how mighty the achievements of the incumbent at Number 10, the electorate has time and again shown itself capable of dumping him unceremoniously on the steps of that famous doorway, while the furniture van backs up to the rear of the building to remove his personal effects from the flat upstairs. It happened to Churchill, in thanks for winning the war. It happened to Attlee, in thanks for creating the Welfare State. It happened to

Lord Home, to Harold Wilson, to Edward Heath and finally to James Callaghan – though he spared himself the embarrassment of the removals men by not actually living in Downing Street in the first place. And all because the people felt it was 'time for a change'. That, at least, is the broadest, and sometimes the most charitable, general explanation for their departures.

There were times in the early months of 1986 when it looked very much as though a similar fate was in store for Mrs Thatcher. Twice, in the party's own secret polls carried out by Gallup, its ratings slumped to 27 per cent. For most of the period it was running third behind both Labour and the Alliance. As for the Prime Minister, her own 'satisfaction' rating was frequently in the twenties, less than half that of each of the other party leaders, and her government's 'approval' rating sank below 25 per cent three times, reaching 23 per cent in the aftermath of the American raid on Libya. There was no hiding the mess the Tories and their leader were in. Most worrying of all were the signs of massive disaffection among the 6.2 million 'new' voters – the under-twenty-fives who had come of age since Mrs Thatcher came to power in 1979.

It is necessary to chronicle briefly the events which led to this massive slump in personal and party fortunes in order to examine the devastating effect they had within the party and the anxieties and hostilities they aroused, the nature of the woman who was on the receiving end of so many of these pressures, why she and the concept of 'Thatcherism' attract so many criticisms, and how she and her party managed such a dramatic improvement in their fortunes. For by January 1987, it was the prospect of Mrs Thatcher going on into a third or even fourth term that galvanised interest in the forthcoming campaign and raised it to a level, not only of historic interest, but of personal and political antagonism rarely witnessed before in this country.

The January 1986 unemployment statistics for the previous month showed the largest rise – 135,000 – since the darkest days of the first Thatcher administration. Eight out of every ten people in the country believed the issue was the most important one facing the government and very little appeared to be happening to improve matters.

Then the Westland row, which had started in the last months

of 1985 as an argument between the Department of Trade and the Ministry of Defence over whether an American or European rescue package for the ailing helicopter company was the better solution, reached its climax. Soon it led to the resignation of both protagonists, Leon Brittan and Michael Heseltine, and a far bigger row over how a letter from Sir Michael Havers, the Attorney-General, came to be leaked to the press – and who in Downing Street was involved in that decision.

Hard on the heels of that crisis – and fuelled partly by its anti-American component – came the row over parts of British Leyland being sold off to foreign companies such as Ford and General Motors. The DTI, under Paul Channon, its new and rather inexperienced Secretary of State, had to go into a swift reversal of its plans. The outcry was largely bogus – there was very little evidence that jobs would be lost and indeed a considerable benefit could have accrued – but such was the state of jitters in the government by now that a reversal of this so obviously 'Thatcherite' policy was hailed as a great victory by the opposition parties and a further nail in the Prime Minister's coffin.

In the early days of April the last of the major upsets hit Mrs Thatcher and her government with the decision, taken by the Prime Minister and only a tiny group of her close colleagues, to allow President Reagan to use British bases for his air raid on Libya. The outcry this time was fourfold: that the decision had been taken without proper consultation or debate; that it involved us in someone else's clumsy sledgehammer efforts to crack a tiny nut; that that someone else was American; and that the shadow of fear, which always passes over the population when the machinery of war is used in anger, had been unnecessarily cast over Britain.

It is hardly surprising that both her personal and party popularity collapsed – nor indeed that this, in turn, led to considerable anxieties within both Conservative Central Office and the Parliamentary Party. Twice in the space of three months – at the end of January and in April–May – there arose speculation that Mrs Thatcher might go, whether by falling or being pushed: it was said that senior Tories had given her 'six months to get her act together'. On the eve of the crucial Westland debate she herself felt shaky enough to doubt her future (though some around her later sought to dismiss this as late evening anxieties of the sort that had disappeared by the following morning). It is certainly true that if Leon Brittan had chosen to, he could have brought her to the brink of downfall, by naming the real culprits inside Number 10. Instead, he chose to remain silent.

In the aftermath of the Libyan affair there was again press speculation of a plot to get rid of Mrs Thatcher before the next general election. The truth of all these stories is elusive, but it appears unlikely that any formal plot existed. Presuming that her opponents in the party would be unable to persuade her that it was time to go, the machinery for getting rid of her – at the annual party conference in October – was too cumbersome, too distant and too damaging to party morale ever to be seriously considered. There were, however, those – including some quite near to her – who were none too anxious to conceal their hopes that she might herself decide to step down.

Whether the government had lost its grip or not and whether, at its head, the Prime Minister had lost control of her Cabinet or not, was in many ways irrelevant. What was important was that it was perceived in that way by many Tory backbenchers, party workers, the media and the public at large. Some put it down to 'mid-term blues', others saw it as a natural reaction to the enormous strains of the 12-month-long miners' strike the year before; whatever the reasons, the loss of confidence by, and in, her was palpable. Ironically, she was seen to be both weak and ineffectual in letting things get out of hand, and at the same time dogmatic and overbearing in pressing her increasingly reluctant Cabinet to her point of view. The nation's leader had weakened drastically in the nation's eyes and the nation's government was seen to be involved in noisy internecine squabbles.

There are two things the public do not expect of the Tory Party in government: first, that it should appear divided and, second, that it should appear incompetent. There is a feeling that Conservatives, if nothing else, at least run a tight ship. And there are two things the public have come to expect of Mrs Thatcher as leader of the Tory Party: that she is firm and that she is resolute. Now, not only was the party seen to be letting its supporters down, but its leader's finest qualities of firmness and resolution were seen as nothing more than bossiness and stubbornness.

Another factor was also at work. There comes a moment in the history of many administrations when the pressures, the unpopularity and the sense of isolation begin to snowball into a sort of collective paranoia among the close circle around the leader. Enemies, real or imagined, abound outside the trusted few. The press is hostile, the TV biased; colleagues are disloyal, and even old friends fall under suspicion. In these circumstances those closest to the Prime Minister form their wagons into a protective circle and the downward spiral begins. The leader sees fewer and fewer people from the outside and therefore receives fewer and fewer opinions other than those formulated and agreed on the inside. The leader's view of the world becomes distorted, which in turn serves to increase the isolation. The Prime Minister becomes the Prisoner of Downing Street. It can happen to anyone: it happened to Harold Wilson and to Edward Heath. It nearly happened in this period to Mrs Thatcher, for a number of reasons varying from her own unique position as our first woman Prime Minister, to her own personality and style, to the nature of her beliefs, and that of the team she has around her.

So what exactly had gone wrong? In 1979, the very fact that Margaret Thatcher was a woman was deemed to be something which could count against her in the election. Now she had won two elections, taken Britain through a small but alarming war, seen inflation become a distant memory and held fast through the longest and most bitter industrial dispute this country has ever seen: demonstrably her sex makes not a jot of difference to her ability as a politician. She is, and has been for more than twelve years, the best 'man' the Tories have.

But the reality of life in the upper levels of the Conservative Party is such that while we, the public, have changed considerably in our attitudes towards women – particularly those in positions of power – there are still some senior Tory politicians who have not yet come to terms with the fact that their leader is a woman. When things are going well they will grumble occasionally to their colleagues in a chummy sort of way and grin ruefully about one another's latest encounter with 'She Who Must Be Obeyed'.

But let things take a turn for the worse and all their uncompre-
hending bitterness and frustration comes pouring out. There are,
of course, notable exceptions: men like Norman Tebbit, Cecil
Parkinson, Sir Geoffrey Howe and Lord Young (perhaps because
they are all self-made men and/or have strong wives) have few
inhibitions in dealing with her on a day-to-day basis. But for
some other leading Tories, it is not too great an exaggeration to
say that the last time they were addressed by a woman as they
occasionally are by her was by their nannies. The products of a
traditional English upper-middle-class upbringing, proceeding as
they do from the nursery, to the single-sex boarding school, to
university and/or the army, then into politics and a repetition of
their parents' marriages, are not best suited to facing and dealing
with a single-minded, determined and often aggressive woman,
whose mind can function like a rat-trap, who often knows their
subject as well as, if not better than, they do, who has very
firm and positive views about what should be done, who will
argue those views forcibly and indefatigably and who, indeed,
sometimes indulges in a verbal scrap simply as a means of
clearing her and everyone else's mind as to exactly what the
issues are.

Faced with a real crisis, such men have tended to lack either
the will or the means to communicate their anxieties to her.
Their failure is compounded by the fact that after thirteen years a
significant number of them still do not understand Mrs Thatcher
herself or have any sympathy with her aims – or both. It is truly
extraordinary because neither the woman nor the objectives have
fundamentally changed in all that time.

The private Mrs Thatcher is, admittedly, a considerable contrast to her tough, abrasive image. She is still the same bustling,
busy, protective wife and mother she always was. Her marriage
is the bedrock on which all her drive and success is based. It is
surprising to an outsider – although not to those who know her
– to hear her describe her love for Denis Thatcher as: 'a golden
thread, which runs through the days, through the weeks, through
the months, through the years'. He is her husband, her friend, her
companion and – often most important of all – her sounding-
board. He can say the unsayable to her; she can shout at him
and tell him not to be silly and he does not feel threatened,

because he does not have a job to lose. And in the morning he is still there, encouraging and backing her all the way.

She is totally loyal to her staff – even to those who have not always served her well – and is immediately concerned with any of their personal problems. She regards a handful of them as being literally an extension of her family and was deeply upset, for example, when her former political secretary, Richard Ryder, married her diary secretary and closest confidante Caroline Stephens, and she was not invited to the wedding because they wanted it to be a small family occasion.

Certainly she is, and always has been, very direct in dealing with people. She looks them straight in the eye and asks them what they can do for her. She infinitely prefers 'can-do' people to prevaricators and chatterers. Once she has assured herself she has found the right person for the job she will leave them to get on with it. Those she is not happy with she will harry, sometimes to the point of exasperation. The civil servants who work best with her are those who bring her solutions, not problems. Not for nothing are Sir Gordon Reece, her PR and media adviser in 1979, and Tim Bell, her advertising man from Saatchi & Saatchi until 1984, still among her personal favourites: they are known in Downing Street and Conservative Central Office as 'the laughing boys' – for their constant optimism. Permanent pessimists do not last long in her company.

Nor has her approach to problems altered: here again it is we who have changed. By the late seventies we had come to expect chopping and changing from our leaders, the switching of policies to suit the needs of the moment and the hasty cobbling together of compromises – all of which went under the name of 'consensus politics'. Mrs Thatcher has given us something very different. Whereas Prime Ministers had traditionally sought office – and then sought to hold on to it – very much for the sake of being there, she saw being there as the platform on which to do things. The office changed many of her predecessors as they sought to twist and turn in order to hold on to it. She has remained fundamentally the same because she seeks, first and foremost, to change society, not herself.

She has never courted popularity or altered herself to appear what she is not. She excites great admiration for her fortitude

and forthrightness – but if things go wrong she knows these are
qualities which can work very much against her. She won in
1979, not just because it was time for a change, not just because
she was the 'housewives' champion', but because people sensed
then that she was the first politician for many years who was
not going to arrange an orderly retreat in the face of our terrifying
problems – she was going to meet them head on.

In October 1976 she published, through Conservative Central
Office, a booklet called 'The Right Approach'. It was the basis
of the election manifesto of 1979 and of 1983 and would no
doubt form that of the 1987 manifesto. It is a remarkable
document because it shows, not only the fundamental tenets of
what has become known as 'Thatcherism', but also how very
little either she or they have changed. It is worth quoting the
conclusion here – headlined 'A Free and Responsible Society':

We have set out in this document our analysis of the problems
facing Britain, some of the existing options, and our own
Conservative aims for the rest of the decade and beyond.
We have not offered extravagant promises, or doctrinaire,
simplistic solutions.

In our economy, and in every area of policy and public
administration, we want to re-establish balance and common
sense; this may seem a prosaic objective, but in Britain today
it is essential.

Our policies are designed to restore and defend individual
freedom and responsibility. We mean to protect the individual
from excessive interference by the State or by organisations
licensed by the State, to stop the drift of power away from the
people and their democratic institutions, and to give them
more power as citizens, as owners and as consumers.

We shall do this by better financial management, by reducing
the proportion of the nation's wealth consumed by the State,
by steadily easing the burden of Britain's debts, by lowering
taxes when we can, by encouraging home ownership, by taking
the first steps towards making this country a nation of worker
owners, by giving parents a greater say in the education of
their children.

In other words she wanted to see an end to consensus politics, a great recovery of Great Britain and, in time, the burial of socialism as a force in British politics. That was her view then, as it is now. It would be wrong to call this document an expression of her philosophy: that is far too grand a word. She is not a Philosopher Queen – more what the political commentator Paul Johnson calls 'a handbag economist'. She consumes the written material provided by the civil servants voraciously, but she is not a great reader of political thought. She could probably not talk with any great certainty or assurance about the intricacies of the works of Hayek, or any of the other gurus of the free market, but she knows someone who has, and she has probably reached the same conclusions without having read all the books. Her beliefs, to that extent, are instinctive and based firmly in common sense rather than high-flown ideology.

If then there is no great philosophy on which all her actions are founded, why all this talk of 'Thatcherism'? What makes it so special? After all we do not talk of Wilsonism, Macmillanism – or even Churchillism.

No other prime minister this century has come to office knowing, as she does, precisely what he wanted to do, why he wanted to do it and how he wanted to achieve it, and by doing so has had such a world-wide impact. It is both the style and the content which make Thatcherism – and in turn make it such a potent force. She has clear political aims, which are unchanging and which she expresses frequently – but then she pursues them with relentless energy and determination. She was wise enough to know, and to point out in 1976, that she could not deliver it all in one go. She knew then, and also pointed out, that there would be diversions on the way and that the sort of Britain she had in mind would take a long time to bring about. She must also have known that a fair measure of the resistance to her aims would come from within her own party and would further serve to isolate her. She once described herself as 'the Cabinet rebel' – implying that she was the one who wanted to get on and do things, while her colleagues wanted to enjoy the more traditional pastimes of high ministerial office – preserving, as far as possible, the status quo.

She is the first 20th-century prime minister to lead from the
front in this way. She is not chairman of her Cabinet, she is its
leader. She tells ministers what she expects from their departments. She is urgent to get things done. She pushes, she presses,
asks questions and demands explanations. Sometimes she irri-
tates them, individually or collectively. Sometimes she gets too
far out in front of them, or, as happened early in 1986, they feel
she has lost her grip and they defeat her. Remarkably, she appears
not to take setbacks too badly. There is a theory that she
uses men like Sir Geoffrey Howe, John Wakeham and William
Whitelaw deliberately to stop her doing things that would take
her too far ahead of the rest of the Cabinet.

A defeat, moreover, does not mean that a plan is abandoned,
it is merely shelved for the time being. The vision remains intact.
She is aware that the pace at which she wishes to travel is not
necessarily the same as that of her Cabinet, her backbenchers,
her party – or even, when it comes to it, the country who voted
her in. She is aware also that hers is neither an easy set of aims,
nor an easy style to live with. The combativeness which carried
her through the great battles – over inflation, the Falklands and
the miners – cannot be turned off like a tap. It is part of her and
it can irritate colleagues, supporters and voters alike. It can also
make enemies, and there remains within that top echelon of
government a number of men who are in no sense her friends.
Some are enemies because of the way she came to power within
the party, some because she is a woman, some because they find
her policies abhorrent, some find her style offensive – or any
mixture of these. Her victory in 1983 did much to silence them,
but they remained there afterwards and, if the going got tough
– as indeed it did in early 1986 – they were not going to help
make life any easier for her.

Her problems were also compounded, the sense of isolation
increased and the circle of wagons drawn in tighter as a result
of the far greater amount of criticism which was levelled at her
own staff during this period. Some, like Bernard Ingham, were
criticised directly over the Westland affair; others, more generally, for jointly contributing to the creation of a bunker mentality
within Number 10; all of them for not having the political
'antennae' to recognise the crisis in which they were becoming

THE YEAR OF LIVING DANGEROUSLY

enmeshed. It was by no means the first time such a state of collective paranoia had come about inside Number 10 – the very structure of the place is not conducive to openness. What made it worse was the fact that a number of its inhabitants at the time were not best equipped to cope with the stresses as they arose. It surprises many people to learn that the Prime Minister actually has very few powers and very few staff. She governs by virtue of the position she holds as leader of the party and head of the Cabinet, and at Number 10 itself there are only about 80 people in total, including secretaries, security men and cleaners. Their lives – and the Prime Minister's governmental life – are run by six senior civil servants, the most senior of which, the Principal Private Secretary, runs the Private Office. Nigel Wicks had only been in the job of PPS for three months when the Westland storm broke and the Prime Minister's Private Secretary Charles Powell, a diplomat, was not sufficiently experienced to cope with the crisis. Matters were not improved by the fact that the head of her Policy Unit, Professor Brian Griffiths, had also only just arrived in Downing Street, and the situation was further aggravated by the cloud of suspicion hanging over her Press Secretary Bernard Ingham.

He is a 48-year-old abrasive Yorkshireman of legendary, volcanic temper. He is extremely close to the Prime Minister – he has to be in order to speak 'for her' in his off-the-record briefings to the lobby journalists. Nevertheless, since he was a central figure in the leaking of the Westland letter and his influence is acknowledged to be far greater than that of a mere head of the press office, criticism and suspicion of him after Westland served to weaken further the position and reputation of the Prime Minister, although she stood by him with her customary loyalty.

One person who could, and did, try to help out at this time – because he has no governmental role – was Stephen Sherbourne, her Political Secretary, whose job it is to look after her links with the political world, especially with Conservative Central Office. A 41-year-old ex-teacher and former special adviser to Patrick Jenkin, he got the job after successfully holding down one of the most high-risk tasks during the 1983 election: that of briefing the Prime Minister before her morning press conferences. He often has to be the bearer of bad as well as good tidings in and out of the Prime Minister's office and, on more than one occasion, he has by timely intervention prevented dangerous situations from getting totally out of hand.

Nevertheless, events conspired to explode at a time when three of the key figures in Downing Street were relatively new and/or inexperienced and a fourth was under a cloud of suspicion for his role in them. And all the acumen of Sherbourne and the other politicians around the Prime Minister was not enough to compensate for the lack of political 'feel' among the civil servants around her at the time. They were simply not shrewd enough to hear what was happening correctly or understand it.

The raising of the psychological drawbridge around this tiny group which took place at this time did no one any good. It is not necessary to be a student of *Yes, Prime Minister* to know that it is in the nature of civil servants, when faced with a crisis, to do nothing. For them inertia has two advantages: it may just result in the problem going away, and since it involves no action it cannot provoke a reaction.

But this attitude in the area of public relations, at a time of growing public disillusionment with the conduct of government, further exacerbated the Prime Minister's slide from grace with the public. It is one thing, for example, not to warn Parliament of the intention to allow the Americans to use their bases in Britain for the raid on Libya, even not to tell all the Cabinet – that was a political decision, which had political repercussions. But, in the public's eyes, it was quite another to take the people by surprise. It was not a mistake that Reagan's press advisers made in the run-up to the raid.

Indeed for a while the do-nothing approach to the Prime Minister's position in the public eye, coupled with the bunker mentality which prevailed around her, threatened her whole future as much as the incidents which had given rise to it in the first place. If there was a reluctance to come out from behind the barricades, if the only means of the public knowing directly what was in the Prime Minister's mind was through the strident twice-weekly shouting match in the bear-pit of Westminster's question time, if the public's only indirect knowledge of what she was thinking or feeling had to be filtered through Bernard Ingham's aggressive briefings of the lobby journalists, and if the only other source of guidance on the state of Conservative thinking at the top came to the public via its party chairman Norman Tebbit, a man who would cheerfully admit to being not well-versed in the fine arts of smiling public relations, then is it any wonder that the public changed its collective mind in droves about her?

The great leader we had seen in the Falklands crisis came to be seen as a bossyboots; her resolute approach to the nation's difficulties became stubbornness; her forthrightness in doing what was necessary to put the country back on its feet became the harsh, uncaring attitude of a woman who had lost touch with the people. Hers had never been an easy creed to sell. She had offered no soft options. She had told the public there would be no easy way out. They had believed her and trusted her. Now they did no longer and few people, least of all within her own party, gave her long to last.

But Mrs Thatcher is nothing if not a fighter. There is within her a strength of purpose, a sense of mission and an inner resilience, none of which lends itself to giving up, however tough the going. She is lucky also in her friends. Just as her beliefs and style have made her enemies, so have they brought her the loyal allies who share her convictions, and who believe that the regeneration of Britain would be impossible without her combativeness and who, therefore, when the crisis was at its worst, set about doing all they could to sustain her. The battle for Maggie's ear – always a sharp tussle, involving the soap-operatic ingredients of jealousy, back-biting and self-advancement, became at times in these months a bitter conflict which tested loyalties to the limit. Some had to persist in their efforts to get to her through the protective barriers, some had easier access.

Lord Young, Ian Gow and a handful of others – including some of her own backbenchers – went in to see her at one time or another with the same basic message: 'You have not fought all this time for the things you believe in so much to see it all go down the drain now.' In one case an old and much trusted friend talked to her for an hour and a half, analysing what he thought had gone wrong and what she should do to put it right. He did not hold his anger back, nor did he pull any punches. Throughout the entire time she hardly said a word and when he left she just said: 'Thank you,' quietly.

For a while she withdrew from the field, in order to regroup her troops and start again. It was a tactic she had used before, notably in 1981 when the miners threatened confrontation and she was not ready to face them. She was quiet in Cabinet, listening rather than dominating and pushing them on. There was talk in the press of a new and chastened Mrs Thatcher – but by the end of the parliamentary session in July she was back in the thick of things again.

Her increasing confidence began to communicate itself to her backbenchers. Unlike Edward Heath, who had cut himself off from his supporters in the House of Commons as soon as he got to Number 10, Mrs Thatcher had always maintained channels of communication. Her backbenchers know they can get in to talk to her if they really need to; they often see her about the House, in the cafeterias and tearooms. They could see she was getting back her form and they, in turn, communicated that confidence to their party faithful each weekend when they returned to their constituencies.

Each July, at the end of the parliamentary session, the Prime Minister gives her backbench troops – the 1922 Committee – her 'end of term' report. She told them that 1986 had been a difficult year, but that they had turned the corner. Some members there thought that 'difficult' was an understatement – it had been catastrophic. But they were forced to share her conclusion: after all, the party was now only four points behind Labour in the polls and two points ahead of the Alliance. As they left for their break most were at least convinced that not all was lost.

It was all very well for the humble backbenchers to go off for their three-month holiday away from Westminster; no such luck attended the ministers – particularly not those in the Cabinet. There is a belief, borne out by the polls, that the government has an advantage over the opposition parties through the summer months. Initiatives can be announced to a press eager for news, the Whitehall machine can be pushed into action to give the impression of activity, whereas it is difficult for the other parties to make their mark on the media while the House itself is shut down. Accordingly, all hands were ordered on deck for a summer campaign aimed at getting the Tory party back to the top of the polls by the time of the party conferences in October.

Few ministers took more than a fortnight off: even the 'Tuscan Tories' – the lucky ones, including Douglas Hurd, who own or rent villas in Tuscany – were all back at their desks well before the end of August and a stream of major speeches and initiatives started pouring out of the Whitehall publicity machine. For example, Douglas Hurd (who had amused himself on holiday by writing a short story about a Prime Minister who is murdered in . . . Tuscany) announced a series of moves on prisons, immigration and law and order, and Norman Fowler, who had prudently strayed no further than the Isle of Wight with his family, announced the start of a pre-election blitz on the ever intractable problem of hospital waiting lists.

The Prime Minister went into hospital for a minor operation, and from there to Cornwall to recuperate with Sir David Wolfson, her former chief-of-staff at Number 10, and his wife Susan. On her return she went straight to Dulwich to supervise the move into the new house she and Denis Thatcher had bought and was to be found, at one stage, on her hands and knees scrubbing floors. However, she too was back at work by the third week in August, planning a tour of Scotland, where the Tory vote was slumping dramatically, and more importantly preparing what was widely predicted to be her last ministerial reshuffle before the election.

The man who guides her hand in this delicate manoeuvre is her Chief Whip, John Wakeham. Largely unknown before his appointment in 1983 – he had started his rise in 1979 as a Junior Whip, then served in the Industry Department before going to the Treasury – he had quickly established a reputation as a master of the black arts of his trade. He is on the record as saying that, as Chief Whip, his job is to 'stop Her Majesty's Government doing silly things'. He is the sounding-board in the House for what the government is up to. He smoothes the path ahead of the government's business by calming ruffled feathers with his charm and where necessary exerting discipline. He is the government's AWACS, giving early warning if it is moving too far ahead of the parliamentary party. In this last capacity he frequently has to step through from his office in Number 12 Downing Street to

Number 10 and bring the Prime Minister bad tidings. But he is known to be very good at handling her and has the patience and resilience required to talk her out of firmly held positions.

It is said that he should have warned Mrs Thatcher earlier of the impending Westland row – and taken steps to nip it in the bud – but equally it is said that his were the principal efforts that got her out of it. There is a special bond between them, beyond the fact that they naturally get on well (he is another self-made man): his wife Roberta was killed in the Brighton bomb outrage in 1984 and he was terribly injured. A year later he married Alison Ward, who had been his secretary and had helped looked after his two adopted sons and nurse him back to health. She had been Mrs Thatcher's secretary throughout the 1970s and was referred to by Denis Thatcher as 'my other daughter'. When they decided to marry Mrs Thatcher insisted that they hold their reception in Downing Street.

John Wakeham has one other job, which makes him the most influential, if not the most powerful, politician after the Prime Minister. He is the parliamentary party's talent scout and head-hunter. He spots the bright young men; on his recommendation they get their first job; and all subsequent preferments are in his power. It is said that it was he who twice talked the Prime Minister out of bringing Cecil Parkinson back into the govern-ment team – despite her clear preference for doing so – on the grounds that the party would not be ready to accept his return until he had passed the test of being re-elected by his constituents.

Parkinson's was indeed one of the names spoken of by many in the party, in the weeks of speculation leading up to the reshuffle, as one of the likeliest candidates for a role of assisting the Prime Minister within Number 10 in the presentation of both her and her policies. His outstanding success as chairman of the party in 1983 was based as much on his ability to get on with her as on his organisational skills, and although his fall from grace had been as spectacular as his rise, he had remained a personal friend and confidant throughout his 'exile'. At one stage later in the year it was mooted that he, Tim Bell and Gordon Reece should meet the Prime Minister at 8.50 each morning to go over the public – as opposed to lobby – presentation of her and the government. She was very keen on the idea, but a combination of Wakeham, Tebbit and Bernard Ingham firmly scotched the idea.

As it turned out there were no changes to the Cabinet team, but 33 middle and junior ministers found themselves moved – ten of them out of the government altogether. It was dubbed the 'Presentation Shuffle' for the number of newcomers who were known to be good media performers – including the redoubtable Edwina Currie, who was photographed on the day wearing a T-shirt saying 'Never underestimate the power of this woman' and filmed in her house waiting for the telephone call from Downing Street. As an exercise in media consciousness it owed a lot more to *chutzpah* than it did to humility.

For all that Mrs Thatcher was talked out of a return role for Cecil Parkinson, she had nevertheless taken notice of the desperate need for better presentation of the government's policies – and indeed for a greater sense of co-ordination and direction to be given to those policies as they emerged from their respective ministries into the light of day. Accordingly in June she had set up what she and her advisers called the Strategy Group – instantly and popularly renamed 'the A-Team' – which from September onwards was to meet most Monday mornings for the rest of the year. Under her chairmanship, it was attended by William Whitelaw, Norman Tebbit, as chairman of the party, Nigel Lawson, the Chancellor, Douglas Hurd, the Home Secretary, Sir Geoffrey Howe, the Foreign Secretary, and John Wakeham. Stephen Sherbourne, the political secretary at Number 10, also attended. Rather pointedly, John Biffen, the Leader of the House, who had upset Mrs Thatcher earlier in the year, was left out, as were all the spending ministers.

There are hugely varying accounts of what the Strategy Group was for and what it actually did for the rest of the year. Its purpose was fourfold: to discuss, identify and co-ordinate emergent government policy; to make sure that the policy was presented and explained properly; to lay the ground for the forthcoming election manifesto, keeping control of it firmly in the hands of the Prime Minister (there had been stories of Norman Tebbit trying to hijack the process); and, perhaps most important of all, to make sure everyone knew there was a group actually doing something about the sadly neglected area of presentation. Outsiders, who tended to sneer at it as being a talking shop at which nothing much concrete was achieved, tended to miss this last point. The very existence of the team did much to dispel the feeling in the party that Mrs Thatcher had become the Prisoner of Downing Street, surrounded by her praetorian guard of civil servants.

The A-Team also had a further role. With her eye already on 1987 as a possible election year, and aware that she had tended to isolate herself in the early months of 1986, Mrs Thatcher wanted to demonstrate that the formulation of policy for the third term would involve as wide a cross-section of people as possible. The deliberations of the A-Team were to play a central role in this in the New Year. However, during the autumn their discussions ranged over law and order, education, housing and the inner cities. It was from these that there began to emerge, in one form or another, many of the ideas which would eventually emerge in the manifesto at election time. Although fine details were not decided on, the value of the deliberations was to get a sense of the pace and direction in which the government should declare its intention to move in the third term.

Detail – and the sense of the whole parliamentary party being involved – was left to the Prime Minister's other creation at this time: the Policy Groups. Unlike the A-Team, these were specifically set up to prepare for the election and they provided the first indication that, whereas the whole tenor of the 1983 manifesto – and indeed the campaign itself – had been a low-key demonstration of a government whose first priority was to get the country right, this time it was going to be very different.

There were several reasons for this, the principal one being that you can go to the country once and say, 'We told you it was going to be a long haul. We're getting there; inflation is down, the economy is getting back on its feet. Britain's on the right track. Don't turn back', but you cannot do it twice. Although in the summer of 1986 it was still too early to say that things were coming right, the indicators were that by the summer of 1987 they could well be – and then a very different agenda could be proposed.

The eleven Policy Groups covered the principal areas of government activity: Managing the Economy, Working Britain,

Home Office and Inner Cities, National Health Service, Education and Training, Housing and Planning, Environment and Energy, Rural Britain, Family and Society, Young People, Foreign Affairs/Europe/Defence. There was some debate at first about who should chair each of the groups. It was powerfully argued that ministers, protected as they were by their civil service mandarins, would be unable to uncover any new policy initiatives – on the grounds that it would be a poor reflection on their departments that the policies had not been thought of long ago and already put in hand. To get round this it was suggested that a form of ministerial musical chairs should take place, each of the groups being headed by a minister from another department. The shudder of fear that ran through Whitehall at this idea was palpable and it was swiftly agreed that even the Treasury, traditionally the most perfect of all departments, would be able to come up with a few new ideas – especially with the prompting of the backbenchers recruited to assist.

Indeed, each of the chairmen was invited to recruit academic experts as well as backbenchers to assist their labours. In no time at all, all over Whitehall, breakfast meetings, working lunches and late suppers were convened while they deliberated against the deadline set for them – 22 December. Why that day? The Prime Minister thinks of public holidays as a chance to catch up on her reading and she regarded the Christmas break as as good a time as any to go through the eleven reports. (As it turned out, three of them – Rural, Foreign and Education – were delayed by other urgent business, so she took the 3000-page Sizewell Report – due to be published in the New Year – to Chequers to read as well over Christmas.)

The work of the A-Team and the Policy Groups was augmented from two other areas. Professor Brian Griffiths now had the Policy Unit at Number 10 firmly in hand and his work, particularly in assisting the Education Department, was becoming increasingly effective. He too would have an input into the manifesto – as would each of the individual ministers. Protocol decreed that if the policy groups were to be given their head to come up with radical proposals in each of their areas, then, largely to save embarrassment, but also to put the record straight if necessary, ministers should also be allowed to make their own presentations to the A-Team. A number of them chose to do this.

The whole structure was carefully and cleverly designed. Everyone felt he had a say and the Prime Minister had the choice of accepting, in whole or in part, the suggestions of the policy groups themselves, or those of the ministers who had chaired those policy groups but felt they had another side of the picture to present, or the A-Team's own verdict on those presentations – or of ignoring it all and setting her own agenda in conjunction with Brian Griffiths. In the meantime, the week-to-week work of the A-Team gave the vital impression that at last the government was back on its feet and going somewhere.

Conference season follows hard on the summer holidays. The TUC hold theirs at the beginning of September and, although increasingly peripheral to most areas of national debate, its extremist element can always be guaranteed to pull Labour down two or three points in the polls. The two wings of the Alliance, the Liberals and the SDP, hold theirs in late August and early September and, despite the most careful attempts to demonstrate how united their leaders were, managed to show such fundamental gulfs between the two parties – particularly on defence – that they slumped to below 20 per cent in the polls.

Labour, relaunched with a red rose logo and tremendous efforts behind the scenes to keep extremism at a minimum and demonstrate how reasonable its policies were, succeeded for a while in convincing some commentators that they were witnessing a rebirth of moderation in the party, but not for long: they too slipped in the polls to level pegging with the Tories. The same polls showed Neil Kinnock's own image begin to slip at about this time. It could have been the first public consciousness of what the commentators were already calling the 'Welsh Windbag', and his personal leadership rating fell steadily from 50 per cent in late September to the high thirties by Christmas.

Conservative worries about the Alliance were confirmed after the Labour Conference. The more the so-called 'loony Left' frightened potential voters away from Labour, the less the Tories were picking them up: they were now going over to the Alliance and would continue to do so, seeking the middle ground rather than shoring up the Tory vote. The greater the Tory onslaught on Labour, the more the Alliance benefited from it. The wide variation in policies between the two Alliance parties – or the sheer lack of them – did not appear to worry the voters. Messrs Steel and Owen succeeded in giving the impression that, in contrast to Labour and the Tories, their parties were full of nice people who deserved a chance. The 'third party' share of the vote in Britain had been rising steadily since the 1950s and in 1983 the Alliance was second to the Tory party in 268 of its 397 seats. Despite the recent slump in the Alliance vote, anxieties were being expressed that the Tories were in danger of leaving dealing with this threat too late and that Mrs Thatcher and Norman Tebbit were unsuited by experience, age and temperament properly to recognise, let alone deal with, the new phenomenon.

But for the moment that was forgotten as the Tory party conference, widely expected to be a rather gloomy affair – with the faithful still suffering from the effects of the disasters of earlier in the year – turned into a well-organised triumph, with minister after minister trumpeting the theme of 'The Next Move Forward'. It was clearly designed to be a collective effort, emphasising the party's progress towards the ideals of Thatcherism. All the fuzziness and lack of direction that had characterised so much of the last year was gone and the impression was given of a party that was beginning to get the economy right and planning where to go from here.

Indeed, the economy was showing signs of improvement – signs which were to increase steadily into the New Year. The government's well-publicised battle between the spending ministers and the Treasury, over whether money should be spent on tax cuts or public spending, was resolved in the autumn with less recourse than anticipated to the dreaded 'Star Chamber' Cabinet Committee, which traditionally referees these disputes. The first hints were there that in the spring the Chancellor might not only carry out his promise to increase public spending, but also squeeze a tax cut out of the system.

Many of the indicators seemed set fair. Manufacturing output was up by 1.2 per cent in the third quarter of the year – the largest increase for six years. Inflation was down to 3 per cent. October's trade surplus of £65 million followed two months of deficit. And the projected growth rate for the economy in 1987 was 2.7 per cent – up by 0.6 per cent on 1986. Anticipating tax cuts, Treasury figures forecast that real personal disposable income would rise in 1987 by 4 per cent. In industry productivity was rising; unit labour costs were falling – as were interest rates. Not only were things coming right, the economy was growing faster than any of Britain's major European competitors.

The most promising sign was in the unemployment figures. For most of the time she had been Prime Minister, Mrs Thatcher had had the albatross of three million-plus unemployed around her, and her government's, neck. Increasingly there was evidence that middle-class voters were troubled by the government's apparently uncaring attitude and were beginning to think of voting for the Alliance – on the grounds that the party would not deliver them into the hands of the socialists, but would at least take away the guilt they felt at voting Tory.

In her reshuffle in September 1985, Mrs Thatcher had given the task of dealing with unemployment to David Young – Lord Young of Graffham. Finchley Woman had chosen Finchley Man for the most important job in the government. The son of Jewish immigrants, he was educated in the Prime Minister's constituency, left school at 16 and by 24 was personal assistant to Sir Isaac Wolfson at Great Universal Stores. While still in his thirties, he made a fortune in the industrial property boom of the 1960s and lost a fair amount of it – though not all – in the crash of the 1970s. He slowly drifted towards the Tory party until in 1982 he was invited by Norman Tebbit to chair the Manpower Services Commission. Quiet, charming and a good listener, he brought formidable managerial skills to the job – as well as pushiness and influence in the corridors of power. In two years he transformed the MSC from a quango that everyone thought was about to be written off, to the force in the battle against unemployment it is today. In 1984 the Prime Minister had the idea of bringing him into Number 10 as chief-of-staff in charge of co-ordinating policy, but, as so often with such moves to change anything at the centre of power, she lost. Instead she put him in the Cabinet as Minister without Portfolio and gave him a peerage. Many thought that, not having a real civil service department under him, he would vanish from sight, but they reckoned without his tenacity.

He is a classic Thatcher do-er. She appointed him to the Department of Employment in 1985 after he had given her, for her summer reading, a paper which outlined a possible two-pronged policy for dealing with unemployment, based on the premiss that it was no use waiting for the economy to pick up, there was plenty to be doing in the meantime.

The first prong was to use the system for dealing with unemployment to revive people's incentive to work, particularly among the long-term unemployed. The existing system was geared towards containing the problem, not solving it. Unemployment offices had been separated from job centres, so there was no incentive, or obligation, for the unemployed to do anything more than pick up the cheque. This thinking eventually led to the Restart programme.

The second prong was to set out to publicise every single programme available to the unemployed, an idea which eventually turned into 'Action for Jobs'. Although it was aimed primarily at the unemployed, it also had a vital public relations component in it to help assuage the guilt in the tree-lined suburbs: everyone would realise that everything that could be done was being done.

As soon as David Young got the job he set about implementing his programme with his customary energy and directness. Within the department, heads were banged together and people charmed and cajoled into changing long-held attitudes. Any unpopularity he might have aroused dissipated when his civil servants saw that on their behalf he was prepared to bang heads outside the department too, and although his style of line management was alien to their ethos, they responded to it when they saw the success it could bring. By mid-1986 unemployment was ceasing to rise and in October it started to fall – and continued to do so for the rest of the year.

The effect of this turnaround was dramatic. It changed the backdrop against which all government policy was analysed. For almost as long as they had been in power, ministers of all departments had tended to be on the defensive in media interviews, because it was impossible for them to claim that things were improving without, at best, their arguments being undermined by the statistics of the rising numbers of jobless and, at worst, being accused of not caring. The fall in the total, slow though it was to start with, was the most important indication that the government had at last turned the corner.

It showed in the polls too. In the secret tracking study Gallup did for the Tories in the third week of December 1986 it showed their share of the vote at 41 per cent – the highest it had been all year. Mrs Thatcher's popularity rating was also approaching 40 per cent again. When asked, irrespective of how they would vote, who they thought would win the next election, 69 per cent said they thought the Tories would and only 10 per cent through Labour would. But in the main polls the Alliance were also back to nearly a quarter of the vote and the thought was lurking in the back of many Tory minds that, come election day, the greater threat might come from here and not from Labour. The nightmare of middle-class voters deserting to the Alliance, where they felt they might get roughly the same sort of policies without the rough edges of Toryism, haunted their Christmas dreams.

It now seemed quite likely to many of them that the next election would be decided by people who did not like Mrs Thatcher. There were those who disliked her and voted Labour or Alliance anyway, but now there were others who did not like her. Some of them would nevertheless vote for her, because their admiration for what she had achieved outweighed their distaste for what they saw as the harshness of the way she had achieved it. But there were now possibly others who had voted for her before, but would not vote for her again – they would go for the illusion of the Alliance, so that they could have most of the pleasure of Tory policies without any of the pain.

Mrs Thatcher enjoyed her Christmas. She loves having the family and friends like the Carringtons and the Parkinsons round her. On Christmas Eve her son Mark, newly-engaged, arrived home from America, where he works, and her daughter Carol was also just back from a journalistic assignment at Disneyworld in Florida. They had a lively party at Chequers, and 'Mum' made the evening by wearing a multi-coloured Disney sunshade with battery-operated flashing lights on it, which Carol had given her for fun.

It had indeed been a remarkable year for her. But after Christmas, as she settled down to her mountain of reading, it cannot have been an entirely comfortable feeling to know that her electoral fate might well lie in the hands of voters who disliked her. Nor that she had one other major worry central to her success at the polls – her Party Chairman, Norman Tebbit.

2 | Norman Tebbit meets Central Office

Along with the 15-inch-high pile of Mrs Thatcher's Christmas reading – comprising the eight finished documents of the Policy Groups and the Sizewell Report – was another, altogether slimmer, blue-bound folder containing only 110 pages. The file came from Norman Tebbit's office on the first floor of Conservative Central Office in Smith Square, just a short walk away from the Houses of Parliament and Downing Street. It had been prepared for him in the weeks leading up to Christmas by Michael Dobbs, his chief-of-staff, and its message to her from the two of them was: 'We're ready – whenever you are.'

This document was to provide the framework for discussion at the secret meeting with her which was planned for 8 January – secret because if word of it or its agenda were to leak out, it would immediately start a bout of premature election fever. For the document was a precise breakdown of how Central Office had planned for the next Tory victory and its state of readiness to go to the polls. Both Tebbit and Dobbs anxiously awaited the Prime Minister's verdict on it, because its five chapters represented the culmination of a year's hard and often thankless work on their part.

There was another, more crucial, reason for their anxiety. The delivery of the booklet to Number 10 a few days before Christmas had come at the end of a bad year for the relationship between Mrs Thatcher and Norman Tebbit and her verdict on it would largely set the seal on the way things would go between them in the vital months to come as the election approached. To say the relationship between them had been strained would be an understatement – it had very nearly ruptured one day at the end of July, when Tebbit had marched angrily into Downing Street with a file of press cuttings under his arm, on the point of resigning.

The relationship between a Conservative Prime Minister and his or her Party Chairman has never been an easy one, even though, by all accounts, this incident was exceptional. It is a particularly difficult bond to sustain amicably while the party is in power for, while the machinery of government in Whitehall takes all the credit for success, failure – as judged by the voters in by-elections – is deemed to be the fault of the incompetents in Smith Square. Edward Heath had problems, and Mrs Thatcher has had problems with three of the four of her incumbents at Conservative Central Office (CCO). It comes under increasing strain as the year and then the month of the election approaches. Lord Thorneycroft, for example, tried in 1979 to wheel Heath into the Tory campaign – a plan which she had to thwart. Nor was all sweetness and light between her and Cecil Parkinson in 1983, despite their mutually roseate memories of the campaign.

To the politician of whatever party, so much is at stake and the pressures so great, that tempers are bound to fray – the more so if you are a leader in the mould of Mrs Thatcher. All her aggression and forthrightness goes into winning. To many, particularly those at Smith Square, who have seen it all before and been doing it for twenty years or more, it is frankly impossible to understand the greater pressures which stem from the fact that here is a leader who not only wants to win, but feels she has a mission as well. There are few occasions when she drives herself harder than in the run-up to and during an election campaign. It can safely be said that there are none when she drives those around her harder. In 1983, after a particularly blistering session one evening, one of her closest political friends got dead drunk in his office and, late that night, was heard shouting: 'I can't take five more years of that woman.' The two of them are still very close – so much so that I suspect he has wiped the incident from his memory. Victory at the hustings, as in battle, has a fortunate habit of tampering with the memory.

Problems also arise from the very structure of the hierarchy of the Conservative Party, for Smith Square houses, in effect, two Conservative Parties. There, almost invisible, is the peak of the pyramid of the National Union of Conservative and Unionist Associations, known simply as the National Union. This is the voluntary Tory party – the Tory party of the thousands of canvassers in the field, the willing hands who organise the coffee mornings, the bring-and-buy fundraisers, at the base of its structure. Each of the members belongs to a constituency association, which selects its candidates for the election, in many cases appoints and pays for an agent to help the candidate and, with the agent's assistance, raises funds, about an eighth of which are forwarded up the line to CCO. The constituencies are divided into twelve areas, each with its own council, and from these come the members of the National Union executive – and its chairman, who is at present Sir Peter Lane, a city accountant. It is the National Union which holds the party's two annual conferences.

Highly visible, so that at times you could almost think the National Union did not exist, is the broad base of the inverted pyramid – the professionals who co-ordinate the party organisation and make sure it adequately serves both the voluntary and the parliamentary party. At their head is the chairman of the party, Norman Tebbit, his deputy, Peter Morrison, and the vice chairmen. Most of them are MPs and appointed from outside CCO by the Prime Minister, for periods varying between two and five years. The 180 or so real professionals man the departments of CCO, the principal ones of which are: Campaigning and Training, Research, International, Organisation (membership and elections), Press and Communications, and Special Services (computers). Finally there is the Treasurer's Department, which operates independently of all the rest with a staff of 18 under Lord McAlpine, the party's chief fundraiser – also appointed by the Prime Minister.

According to its many critics, it is a structure which is both unwieldy and resistant to change, designed to keep everyone happy rather than get things done. It has three people 'in charge' – the Prime Minister, the chairman of the party and the chairman of the National Union – each of whom can, and sometimes does, antagonise one or both of the others. Fund-raising and allocation of the global sums required to run it are separate from the executive powers responsible for running it, and those executive powers, as personified in the chairman, deputy and vice chairmen, can change as often as once every two years – leaving the poorly paid, mostly long-serving, full-time professionals often bewildered by conflicting sets of demands, methods and personalities. In turn their attitude to change is often understandably hostile and their resistance to it is legendary. There are more than 50 MPs in the House who have served in CCO, in addition to a number of members of the Cabinet; the ability of the departmental 'fiefdoms' to organise a lobby, and the power of that pressure, even on the Prime Minister, can be irresistible and they can make or break interlopers.

It is a system which grew up in another electoral age and, although it has had the facilities to deal with the realities of televised elections, centralised campaigns and the computer age tacked on to it, it has never had the thorough overhaul it needs. In peacetime, when things are good for the party, everyone papers over the cracks; when things go wrong and CCO gets the blame, it starts to creak at the seams and, as is the nature of politicans, it is the personalities, rather than the systems they have to operate, which become the targets.

To the outsider the Conservative Party seems like a most professional set-up – the most professional of all the party machines. Yet it, and indeed the entire party, has only the thinnest patina of professionalism. Perhaps we, the British, are happier without massive, vastly rich and well-organised political parties. We like them to retain, even at the highest level, more of the character of the local nature ramblers than of Nuremburg rallies.

For four years or more at a time, elected Ministers of State run massive departments, taking huge decisions on our behalf. Then up comes an election, and they revert back to their party, back to the people who put them there and to a sort of tennis club mentality. It is surprising to find this amateurish element in the very men and women who run the government. Just before the 1983 election, for example, the question of media monitoring – to pick up what was being said on all the TV and radio stations – was being considered by the election planning group and, rather than opt for the cost of a professional service, senior members of the Cabinet actually started to share out the tasks. Mrs Thatcher volunteered to cover the 'Today' programme on BBC Radio 4 from 6.30 a.m. on because she was always up then, and Sir Geoffrey Howe said he would do Capital Radio's night programmes, because he never went to bed before three or four in the morning and that was what he had on anyway.

For all its faults, its 12 areas and 650 constituency officers, once every four or five years the machinery at CCO creaks into life. In Smith Square the lights burn late; extra staff are taken on; it becomes the focus of the media and even the Cabinet listens to what its experts have to say. Twice, in 1979 and 1983, it won elections and little was done to change it. That there was a need to change it, all except its stoutest defenders would agree. That the time was not right to do so as election year dawned, was also not in question. But whether it could serve Norman Tebbit and, through him, Mrs Thatcher as well as would be required in 1987 was quite another matter.

Norman Tebbit was given the chairmanship of the party in the reshuffle of September 1985. It was said to be a great relief to the inmates of Smith Square to see the back of John Selwyn Gummer, who had held the post since Cecil Parkinson's departure in 1983 and for whose removal they were said to have been campaigning for some time. Tebbit was a contrast to Gummer; grammar-school educated, non-university, two years as a journalist then a period as a union officer (British Airline Pilots Association) – his CV was not exactly that of a grandee of the Tory party, and it was perhaps inevitable that he should find himself in sympathy with, close to, and then a fervent advocate of Mrs Thatcher and her views. Naturally abrasive, with a savage turn of phrase, he earned the sobriquet 'the Chingford Strangler'. His aggressiveness not only pleased the party faithful, who liked seeing one of theirs give as good as he got against Labour, but it had a purpose, too. He could say what the Prime Minister could not, diverting the attacks away from her on to himself: he became, in his own words, a 'lightning conductor' for her. In the two years before the 1983 election this worked particularly well in conjunction with Cecil Parkinson's moderate, smiling, charming presence in the media explaining Thatcherism. It was at his suggestion that Tebbit was included in the inner election group for 1983, which made Tebbit's opposition to Parkinson's own inclusion three years later the more surprising.

It is interesting that during all the period when Norman Tebbit and Mrs Thatcher were politically closest, between 1981 and 1985, they did not become closer friends. But he was a man who always kept his private life well away from the political arena – until the night of 13 October 1984, when the bomb in the Grand Hotel, Brighton, severely injured him and left his wife Margaret permanently paralysed. According to those who know him, the aftermath of the bomb was almost worse for him than the grim events themselves. He had a number of painful operations. His wife was in Stoke Mandeville Hospital for 18 months, during which time he had to cope with the return to political life, visiting her as often as possible and living by himself, doing all his own cooking and washing, in a lonely garret flat above the Admiralty. Although he was generously lent a house by the Duke of Westminster, the financial strain of having it adapted for his wife's eventual return home was enormous as was the personal burden of the realisation of what her paralysis would mean. She has to have nursing attendance 24 hours a day. It is extremely difficult to find nurses who will work in these conditions. And for him the problem is compounded by the fact that a complete night's sleep is impossible because she has to be turned over every two hours.

His friends say that this experience has made him a deeper, more thoughtful man – a man who cares more about values and law and order and the sort of society we live in. While he has still retained his total commitment to the success of the Thatcher government, his personal ambition is no longer what it was. He has, in a way, stepped back and is capable of seeing through the hurly-burly and taking the longer view. The shame, they say, is that while it has left him probably a better politician, it has removed from him the stable family base on which he relied so heavily for his political life. His enemies say it has left him obsessively secretive – even more than he was before: that he was always edgy and defensive and rather insensitive and now he is worse. Politics, particularly political gossip, is unforgiving and the hostile view was assiduously spread in the spring and summer of 1986 until that was how he came to be seen by more and more of his colleagues and by some inside Number 10.

This view of Norman Tebbit was not one that was shared by the Prime Minister when she made him Party Chairman. She had shown him and Mrs Tebbit enormous kindness ever since the bomb and had welcomed his return to work after he had recovered sufficiently. It is possible, however, that she was less kindly disposed to Michael Dobbs, whom Tebbit requested become joint deputy chairman of the party, alongside Jeffrey Archer.

Dobbs was one of the most intelligent people in and around the party structure. Still only in his thirties, he had long been recognised as one of the bright boys of the Thatcher era. An Oxford graduate, with a Ph.D. from Harvard, he had also worked as a journalist (on the Boston *Globe*) before returning to Britain in 1975, just as Mrs Thatcher became leader of the Tory party. For two years he worked in the research department, before becoming part of her private office team, principally briefing her before parliamentary appearances. It was a high-risk job, with a high failure rate, but he held it for two years and, in the 1979 campaign was one of the handful of close aides who travelled with her. Throughout this period he came to be a tremendous admirer of her and was disappointed, therefore, when he was not invited to join her team in Downing Street; shortly afterwards he left the party machine and joined Tim Bell, who, as chairman of Saatchi & Saatchi, had masterminded the Tories' successful advertising campaign. The two became close friends and formed a formidable working partnership, despite their contrasting personalities. Bell, who, it is said, is so charming that dogs cross the road to be patted by him, was the dynamic, inspired leader, while Dobbs – equally charming in his own way – smoothed the path ahead and the ruffled feathers behind and provided the essential solid back-up.

While working at Saatchi, Dobbs also found himself growing closer to, and increasingly helping, Norman Tebbit – first at the Department of Employment and then, after the 1983 election, at Trade and Industry. Bell left Saatchi at the end of 1984 and Dobbs was made a deputy chairman of the London end of the agency and, although not the Tory account handler, he still supervised the tiny amount of work the agency was doing for the party at the time. When Tebbit, now a close friend, asked him to go to Central Office he had three problems: first, would Saatchi release him to work at CCO full time until after the election? they would; second, who would pay his salary (since no one at Central Office earned half the amount he did)? Saatchi agreed to carry on paying his £60,000-plus salary; and third, since he was giving up at least two years of his life with Saatchi and at least two years of his ultimate ambition to enter Parliament, would his title at CCO be one which would mean something both there and on his CV afterwards?

This last point was where the difficulties arose. Mrs Thatcher would not make him a deputy chairman because, he was told, it would upset Jeffrey Archer and the existing vice chairmen. Hence the title of chief-of-staff to Norman Tebbit was suggested and, somewhat reluctantly, accepted by Dobbs. It meant, he realised, that he was going into an organisation which was notoriously resistant to change – especially changes wrought by outsiders – with no existing job to fill and a role which was so ill-defined as to mean anything from the chairman's managing director to his bag carrier. Dobbs is, however, nothing if not determined and he made up his mind to make a success of it, whatever the going. Nevertheless, given the nature of Central Office and the timing of first Norman Tebbit's, then his, arrival – as the government's fortunes began to slump – all the ingredients were now there for anyone who wanted to cause trouble.

In addition to its inherent weaknesses, CCO was still reeling from its encounter with the previous chairman John Selwyn Gummer, in which honours had come out about even. He had managed a few necessary reforms – among them splitting the formidable Organisation Department in two and instituting a full audit of all the constituencies. But he had been unable, or unwilling, to delegate, and he was sucked into the vortex of what rapidly became a hostile organisation. In the end they managed to discredit him and get rid of him before his reforms had a chance to bear fruit. Morale was low; the finances were in a bad way and some staff had been cut – others had left voluntarily.

Apart from an initial suggestion that they bring in management consultants to go over the building from top to bottom, which was met with extreme horror and abandoned, Tebbit and Dobbs set about making the most of the system as it was. Although

Jeffrey Archer was deputy chairman he did very little administration; he spent most of his time travelling the country, banging
the drum among the faithful. So the two men formed a rough
plan to proceed broadly on four fronts: to use the existing set-up,
control it more rigidly and improve it where and how they could;
to introduce and tack on to it new ideas and methods which they
considered would be useful come the election; to experiment
now with schemes which could turn out to be either vote-winners
or money-winners come the election; and – most crucial of all –
to prepare in the most comprehensive manner yet seen in Smith
Square for that election, whenever it came.

It was a series of aims which they both realised could not be
achieved without putting noses out of joint inside the building
and calling down criticisms from outside. It would be all too
easy, particularly in the atmosphere of defeat currently surrounding the government (at the beginning of 1986), to be accused of
complacency and letting the side down, because very little of
what they planned to do would at first be visible.

The events of Sunday 13 April 1986 have acquired a sort of
hallowed status of their own in the annals of the Tory party.
Their awfulness is still whispered about in hushed tones. Quite
inaccurately people say that that was the day *they* told *her* the
meaning of 'TBW' ('That Bloody Woman') and that she was it.
By 'they' they mean Tebbit and Dobbs. In fact the words themselves were never used – although others which meant the same
were. It may be speculated that the team from Central Office
went to Chequers that day with a totally different purpose in
mind for the meeting to that intended by the Prime Minister.
Their impression was that they were there to bring the Downing
Street team up to date on their research findings and to suggest
where they might go forward from that low point. It is possible
that the Prime Minister, with her new CCO 'team' installed now
for several months, was expecting a little more of the sort of
flash and dazzle she used to get from the eternal optimist Tim
Bell, when he was at Saatchi, rather than the grim message she
found herself receiving now from Dobbs – aided by John Sharkey,
the new Saatchi account director. It has even been suggested that
there had always been some personal lack of chemistry between

the Prime Minister and Dobbs, which surfaced that day in the absence of Bell, who had gone to become Chief Executive of Lowe, Howard-Spink, Bell.

It would probably surprise many people to know that Mrs Thatcher suffers many of the same insecurities as the rest of us. When she leaves the comfort and security of her 'bubble' in Downing Street and turns her mind to fighting elections, she finds she needs the security of known faces around her and becomes anxious to have her 'old boys' near – partly because they have proven track records and partly because she feels more comfortable with them. Whatever the differing expectations of the meeting at Chequers, it was clear that part of the problem was the absence of her old team. In any event, the meeting was a disaster and word of it soon spread – not always accurately and rarely kindly – throughout the party.

Preparations for the meeting had started at Saatchi nearly three months earlier with a form of research called 'Life in Britain' which was first used for political work by the agency in the run-up to the 1983 election. There are two principal problems with normal opinion polls that ask people how they intend to vote and what they consider the most important issues to be. The first is that how they answer is very much swayed by how the question is phrased: you would get the same answer to the two rather different questions 'Do you think all nuclear weapons should be banned?' and 'Do you think it is right to keep our nuclear weapons as long as the Eastern bloc has its nuclear arsenal?' Most people would say 'yes' to both questions – yet the first answer could be used by CND to back its case and the second by the Tory party to support its policy. The second problem is that experience has shown that presenting people with a list of possible most important issues – unemployment, defence, inflation etc. – and asking them to pick out one or two of them, results in a list of what people think the general public would consider the most important issues – not what they themselves feel are the most important things to them, nor indeed the things which will, in the end make them vote, or not vote, for any particular party.

Saatchi's 'Life in Britain' research was an attempt – used in similar forms by some of the other agencies and pollsters – to overcome these problems. Nine groups of between ten and a dozen floating voters were assembled in various parts of the country – most of them in the 25–45 age band, though there were two groups of under-twenty-fives and one of pensioners. Without being told who the research was for, they were asked by carefully trained market researchers how they felt about life in general and whether they were optimistic or pessimistic about the way things were going. The researchers then slowly led the groups round to politics, and the subjects' real feelings about politics, politicians and what concerned them most of all soon began to emerge very clearly.

The analysis of all these 'qualitative' sessions, which were also filmed on video and selected excerpts shown to the Prime Minister on the 13th, showed some marked changes from the groups Saatchi had interviewed in 1982. The images of the other three parties had stayed very much the same. Labour was still felt to be too left-wing, too dominated by the militants and the trade unions – but its leadership, under Neil Kinnock, was felt to be better. The SDP/Liberal Alliance appeal was still largely because it was in the middle and was not either of the other two parties. It had attractive leaders in David Owen and David Steel, but still nobody knew what it stood for. Essentially, as in 1982, the appeal of the Alliance was broad, but shallow. What had changed drastically was the view of the Tory party.

This work was, of course, being done in the aftermath of the Westland affair and as the row over British Leyland was rumbling on. Nevertheless, in 1982 the great strength of the Tory party had been its firm sense of leadership and direction, as personified in Mrs Thatcher. People had not worried too much then about where the leadership was taking them; they knew we were living in troubled times and they had simply wanted someone whom they could trust to know where to go. Mrs Thatcher dominated the results of the sessions in 1982 (it was post-Falklands), standing head and shoulders above all the other politicians; but now in early 1986 the party had lost that crucial factor. She was thought to have become more extreme, and both she and the party had lost their identification with the basic values of the voters. They were seen as just another government, stumbling along from crisis to crisis with no clear aims, no sense of direction any more and no leadership. The party had always been seen as incompetent in handling unemployment – now it could add education and the Health Service to that list.

All in all it was a fairly savage indictment from the public – one which was confirmed solidly before the meeting when each of the issues raised was tested 'quantitively' by standard polling techniques. That was the message: how best to deliver it? The chairman and his chief-of-staff decided there was absolutely no point in pulling their punches. Accordingly, Michael Dobbs and John Sharkey devised a model of a typical Tory couple with two children, living in the typically orderly suburbs which are the heartland of Tory support. They called them 'The Conservative Dilemma' – for, while the couple's whole instincts and history dictated they should vote Tory, they actually had very little reason now to do so. Their 'real' income had indeed gone up appreciably since 1983, but, because they had less and less faith in the Health Service, they were having to pay for private medical insurance; and because of standards in their children's schools they were having to scrape the money together for private education. Their mortgage rate had gone up, as had their rates. They were worried about the wife's safety on the streets, the grandmother's safety in her home and the children's safety from drug pushers at the school gates. It was no good the government telling them they were better off – because they did not *feel* better off. What was more, they did not feel the Tories any longer had it in their power to do anything about it.

The group assembled at 10.30 a.m. in the oak-panelled upstairs meeting room over the entrance hall at Chequers. Dobbs and Sharkey took their position at one end of the long table with their boards and video machine. Around the table sat Mrs Thatcher, William Whitelaw, Norman Tebbit, Nigel Lawson, Lord Young, John Wakeham and Stephen Sherbourne. At the beginning of the morning session the Prime Minister sat in almost total silence, which apparently acquired a flint-like quality as time went on. Then she became increasingly impatient, saying 'Yes, we know that' as each new point was raised. The meeting was well off the rails before lunch, with side discussions going on. For example, at one stage they spent half an hour talking about education policy, which was not covered in the presentation at all. Things were no better after lunch and there was considerable relief when at 4 p.m. tea was served and the meeting broke up.

In retrospect, some of those who were there believe the turning-point came when Dobbs pointed to the research which showed that Mrs Thatcher was strongly rated on three of the four attributes that it was most important for a party leader to have – strength, confidence and intelligence – but that on the fourth – forward-looking – she scored an even lower rating than the other three party leaders. In other words, she had lost her way. 'That,' said one, 'went down like a ton of bricks.'

Dobbs and Sharkey offered some creative work and suggestions as to how the sense of purpose about the government could be restored, but they were only themes: the decision about what exactly to do was a political one and not theirs to make, they pointed out. With hindsight, it was probably the timing of their message that was most wrong, and that was a factor over which they had no control. The Prime Minister had spent the last three months under almost constant attack and, although few other people in the room knew it (not even Norman Tebbit), she had just made the difficult decision to let President Reagan's jets use British bases to bomb Libya – which she must have known would cause further public outcry – and was, quite understandably, not in a mood to be told that she was what was wrong with the party and its slump in the polls.

Things were not made any better by the fact that relations between Norman Tebbit and the Prime Minister had been deteriorating steadily since the turn of the year. Perhaps it was the fact that at CCO he had not got the concrete brief of a Ministry behind him when he went to see her and, for the first time, his sphere of interest was as broadly political as hers and she resented this. Perhaps, as was later whispered, it was because she felt she had not received the support she could have expected from her Party Chairman over Westland and General Motors. Perhaps, even though it is part of the chairman's role to bring the Prime Minister the bad news in time of crisis, it was the style with which he did it that caused offence. Whatever the reason, there was already, apparently, some distance between them when she curtly dismissed the meeting at Chequers that afternoon.

The distance lengthened considerably two days later, when Tebbit let his anger at not being consulted over the raid on Libya be known, and within days fuel was added to the fire by reports that he had also been responsible for a 'disaster' at Chequers at the weekend in which the Saatchi people had called her 'TBW'. Almost certainly an element in this whispering campaign against Tebbit was inspired by those who had tried to damage her and failed, and now saw their chance to attack her by attacking him.

There was also an element in it which came from Downing Street. Mrs Thatcher was undoubtedly concerned about Tebbit's performance, frustrated that Central Office did not seem to be helping the situation, anxious, maybe, that he was not recovered enough to be in charge of the party – perhaps even angry at his apparent lack of support for her. There are, after all, times in any organisation when powerful figures at the top cease to get on well and, for a while, drift apart – especially if the one at the top finds the other 'difficult'. There were those in government who used this turn of events to isolate her further by encouraging it; there were those who used it as another sign that she had lost her grip and similarly encouraged it; and there were those who exaggerated it because they did not like Tebbit and wanted to get rid of him.

In the next four months they all had a field day. Word of the presentation at Chequers spread, along with rumours that Saatchi were about to be sacked: Norman Tebbit had to take the unusual step of issuing a statement that the agency would be handling the party's advertising until the next election. He was said to be trying to take over the whole of the election campaign because he now saw Mrs Thatcher as a liability, and he was allegedly claiming that he would be writing the manifesto and deciding its contents. The establishment of the A-Team was, therefore, seen as a rebuff for him, taking away his claim to the manifesto. It was said she could no longer stomach him and refused to see him except in Cabinet, when she had to. Certainly her feelings were not as strong as this, but the essential 'bi-laterals', as meetings between two people are called in Whitehall, were increasingly pushed to the bottom of the priorities when it came to making up her diary. This further isolated the two from

one another because, with less contact, each was less and less
aware of the other's thinking.

All summer the stories circulated, reaching a crescendo
towards the end of July when it emerged that Mrs Thatcher had
been seeing the research findings of another advertising agency
– Young & Rubicam – and it was presumed, wrongly it transpired, that she was on the point of removing Tebbit in the
autumn reshuffle. Seeing another agency is like seeing another
woman – or in her case man: it can cause great offence, as indeed
it did now. The Young & Rubicam research was based on an
assessment of voters' values and lifestyles, instead of the more
common socio-economic groups from A to E. The interviewer
asks each person up to 100 questions before placing him or her
in a category on the basis of the answers. Most of the Tory
supporters were in the 'belongers' category, which comprises
about 30–40 per cent of the electorate – the patriotic, home-
making family men or women with a sense of duty. This method
of looking at the voters in the country may have appealed to
Mrs Thatcher, especially in the light of her irritation with Saatchi;
however, the message from VALS, as it was known, was precisely
the same as the one Dobbs had delivered in April: that the
government was in desperate trouble.

Hard on the heels of Young & Rubicam came the first of the
season's crop of stories that Cecil Parkinson was to return, this
time in a role involving public relations at Number 10. Parkinson
and Tebbit are old friends – they grew up, politically, in the
same constituency party together. When Parkinson had to resign,
Tebbit stood by him and made his support very public. In fact
he had always regarded the Prime Minister, Parkinson and
himself as 'the three-hand team', which had achieved so much
and then been so badly damaged by his friend's downfall. But
the tenor of the stories was such as to further damage the Party
Chairman's position – for Cecil Parkinson was to return, it was
said, partly to help combat the abrasiveness of Norman Tebbit's
approach.

Finally, unable to contain his anger any longer and firmly
believing that some of these stories were being fuelled in Downing
Street, if not actually originating there, Tebbit marched through
the door of Number 10 one day at the end of July carrying a

folder of all the recent press cuttings, determined to find out what was going on and, if the Prime Minister was dissatisfied with him, to offer his resignation. His call could not have come at a worse (or, some would say, better) time. The Prime Minister was in the middle of the Commonwealth 'sanctions' conference, and due to go straight from there into hospital for the operation on her hand. It would be impossible for her to have the length of conversation with him that the nature of the business required for at least nine or ten days. But he was due to go on holiday to France on Sunday 10 August, and the situation demanded the air to be cleared before then. He left the cuttings and the problem with Stephen Sherbourne, who, with Michael Dobbs, spent much of the next ten days talking to their respective bosses, explaining the situation and calming things down.

During the morning of Saturday 9 August, as Tebbit was preparing to leave, the Prime Minister telephoned from Chequers, just as she too was about to depart to recuperate in Cornwall. She told him in essence that he was her Party Chairman, that she had no intention of removing him, and she acknowledged that the lack of meetings between them had been, to a great extent, responsible for their drifting apart and it was something she intended to put right – on a regular weekly basis – as soon as they returned from their respective breaks. He in turn assured her of his continued and total support and explained his side of what he felt had gone wrong between them. They talked for about 20 minutes, then wished each other well. With the agreement of them both, every newspaper in Fleet Street was told about the call that afternoon and their very public reconciliation was featured on the front pages of many of the Sunday papers.

It was a tremendous weight off Tebbit's mind – but why had it happened in the first place? The most satisfactory explanation is, I believe, that the Prime Minister was dissatisfied with the slow pace at which Tebbit appeared to be getting to grips with Central Office, as well as pin-pricked by his opposition to her on various issues during the spring. That, in the bunker mentality that existed at the time in Number 10, was presumed by some of those around her to be a major falling-out, and hence they over-reacted to fulfil what they imagined to be her wishes. It is unlikely that it was ever seriously in her mind to get rid of him. She is not a good 'sacker' and she could not have done so without major loss of face: to do so on the grounds of dissatisfaction would have been to admit that twice in the space of three years she had made a mistake with this most crucial of appointments, and to do so on the grounds of his health would have been to concede defeat to the IRA. She nevertheless retained some of her anxieties about the state of CCO, and the ability of her chairman and his chief-of-staff to get to grips with them, and decided that their team should be augmented with another deputy chairman.

Thus, out of the reconciliation came some good. Norman Tebbit, on his return, was able to concentrate fully with Michael Dobbs on the tasks they had set themselves. He managed to persuade the Prime Minister to let him have Peter Morrison as deputy in the autumn reshuffle over her nominee, the Deputy Chief Whip John Cope. The tall, charming old Etonian Morrison, son of Lord Margadale, and the grammar-school educated, self-made Tebbit had formed a good working partnership at the Department of Employment and now he fitted rapidly and effectively into the team. Many of the hostilities that Dobbs's arrival and position had aroused were now dissipated, since Morrison took over the organisation and implementation side of the operation, leaving Dobbs free to concentrate on policy and planning.

Contrary to the anxieties being expressed in Downing Street, Tebbit and Dobbs had not been inactive during the summer. In 1979, CCO had nodded in the direction of new technology, but without any proper awareness of its uses. For 1983, Cecil Parkinson and his deputy Michael Spicer had invested in Tigon hardware but, while their use had been more extensive, there was still no co-ordinated plan for employing computers. Elections are clearly out of the hustings age (as short a time ago as the 1950s there was no election coverage on television), but where they are going and what use they will make of new technology had not been properly assessed. The potential of direct mail, as a fundraiser as well as a vote-winner, was as yet largely untapped. The 1983 election was fought and won on national television, it was said; but what difference would the proliferation of local media make in the future to the chances of an individual candidate who knew how to use it? These were the sorts of questions Michael Dobbs set out to answer in a series of reports, innovations and experiments in the spring and summer of 1986.

He and Norman Tebbit set up a New Technology Department to rationalise the chaotic state of affairs they had found at CCO – where the company that supplied the existing computer had gone out of business, where there were three separate 'experts' on direct mail and five separate and incompatible word processing systems in use in the building. They brought Sir Christopher Lawson, marketing director in the 1983 campaign, out of retirement to organise and run the new set-up. They bought an ICL mainframe computer and set in motion a series of programmes to bring this aspect of the party up to date.

The most obvious of these was direct mail, which they saw as being a key tool in the electioneering of the next twenty years. The time is not too far away when, with techniques developing as they are at the moment, a political party will be able to use its computers to pinpoint very accurately the ten or 15 per cent of the population who are floating voters and to address each of them individually. For the moment the aim was to set up reliable systems for keeping in touch with the party's own members, and for contacting groups of people who might be interested in membership or contributing. Hence they purchased the mailing list of British Telecom shareholders and began a series of sample mailings to them.

BT became a fruitful area of operations – the more so because Tebbit's letter to the shareholders could tell them that it was Labour policy to repossess their voting rights, thus driving the share price down. From the first few mailings the party recruited 10,000 new members and received more than £100,000 in donations. By early 1987, from this and other mailshots, the party was heading towards a profit on the operation of a quarter of a million pounds and 20,000 new members. Michael Dobbs also began to examine how far the party might go in the use of direct mail in the election itself – for the law in this field is highly complex and in some areas simply not designed to take into account the development of computers.

New technology has also made it possible to produce an

election newspaper, which could be distributed around constituencies – with their own local news in it – during a campaign.
Dobbs had talks with the centre–right party in Germany, the
CDU, to see how they ran their newspaper operation. At this
time they were coming up to their first re-election and used some
of the experience of Saatchi in their campaign. The CDU slogan
'We're getting there' had distinct echoes of 'We're on the right
track. Don't turn back.' During the spring and summer the
Conservative Party also made a number of experimental political
broadcasts – some of which worked and some of which were
acknowledged to be disasters. And in the autumn it launched its
mail order 'Blue Rosette' business, again as a fundraiser and a
back-up service to make membership more attractive.

Seeing this activity from the outside, at a time when the
government was in deep trouble, gave the enemies of Norman
Tebbit and Central Office more ammunition. They were said to
be frittering their time away doing nothing of any use. Then
when the Labour party launched its 'Freedom and Fairness'
campaign, there was talk that they had allowed Neil Kinnock to
out-Saatchi Saatchi. When Labour's new, soft red rose appeared
on the front of the glossy brochure entitled 'Investing in People'
as its conference approached, there were still more criticisms.
Even Tebbit's friends began to ask what was going on at CCO.
And three by-election collapses in the Tory vote, each of more
than 16 per cent, confirmed their worst fears.

However, in his talk with the Prime Minister on 9 August, and
subsequently, Tebbit had persuaded her that CCO's apparent
inactivity masked a deliberate policy of waiting for the right
moment to relaunch the party – and that moment would come
at the party conference at Bournemouth in October. All through
the summer he and Dobbs sat tight, while the research was done
and the slogans tested on sample groups and the idea of 'The
Next Move Forward' emerged as the theme. The irony was that
the concept sprang very much from the research which had been
such a disaster when presented to the Prime Minister in April.
Follow-up surveys showed that the situation was still very much
the same and although the first indications of improvement were
beginning to show, what was needed was a renewal of the
government's sense of direction and purpose.

No conference in the history of the party was as thoroughly prepared as this one. Cabinet ministers were briefed well in advance on the need to co-ordinate their speeches under the umbrella theme and were asked to come to Bournemouth each with specific announcements to make indicating that the Government still had plenty of life left in it and plenty to do. Saatchi plastered the slogan everywhere – on banners, on information packs, on giveaways, on posters and leaflets and also, again for the first time, placed newspaper advertisements so that the public at large should be aware that the Tories were back in business again. It was also planned to be in deliberate contrast to the Labour conference the week before: clear policies and a definite sense of direction were offered, 'Freedom and Fairness' and 'Investing in People' dismissed as vague and shallow. It was a huge success for the Tories and one which was reflected in the steady improvement in the polls up to Christmas.

There was one crucial area of the work set in hand which would not bear fruit, or even show definite success or failure, until the election itself. The biggest potential point of friction between Central Office and the National Union is over the efficiency or otherwise of the constituency and area offices. It is also the point at which, somewhat unfairly, the worst of the criticism is aimed from outside at Central Office. Those in the centre are blamed for their inability to bring order to the chaos that is seen reigning outside. The truth of the matter is that CCO has very little power to direct either the area or constituency offices in what they do. This was the principal cause of the difficulty between John Selwyn Gummer and the National Union; his audit of every local party in the country was interpreted by many, not as an exercise in greater efficiency, but as a threat to their autonomy.

It is undoubtedly true that too many local associations are run on an exclusive, almost Masonic, basis, which takes no account of the increasing mobility of the very young executives which should be the lifeblood of the party: all too often they find themselves kept out by the established old guard. It is also undeniable that the calibre of Tory local councillors is declining, because the type of young man who might be attracted to set foot on the lower rungs of the political ladder is now simply kept too busy at his work to find the time for it. The Alliance have made great inroads into local government partly because of the large number of more 'leisured' housewives or public employees they attract as supporters, then candidates. The fall in the quality of Tory local government candidates has led, correspondingly, to a fall in the quality of constituency officers.

It is also true that the system of employing agents in the constituencies has great weaknesses. In 1983, Cecil Parkinson made great capital of the fact that 99 of his 103 'target seats' had a full-time agent in place by the time the election was called and that the Tories won 98 of those seats. But this, according to people inside the party, was papering over the cracks and it was fortunate that the national lead in the polls gave them such an easy run, because only a third of the agents were full-time *and* qualified. The other two-thirds was made up of trainees and retired agents brought back for the campaign. The central problem is that there is no national direction of where agents go, to make sure that they are concentrated in the most crucial seats. Agents are hired by the local party, and the best tend to go to the richest constituencies, which tend, in turn, to be the safest seats where they are needed least. A good agent can make all the difference in a marginal seat, especially at a time when the percentage of floating voters is very high.

Aware of the inherent weaknesses in the system and the trouble that Gummer had encountered, it was therefore with great delicacy that, in the early months of 1986, Dobbs and Tebbit embarked on the most important single aspect of all their early preparations for the election – the selection of, and investment in, their Target Seats, the 72 Tory-held marginals which they must hold on to in an election, if they were to achieve a majority of at least 58.

The selected seats were mostly their own marginals, with a handful of Tory seats which should have been safe, but which local circumstances, such as a popular member retiring, had rendered vulnerable. In about two-thirds of the seats the incumbent was defending against Labour in second place and in one-third against SDP. The process of selection was the most rigorous the party had ever done, involving lengthy consultations at all levels and a complete audit of all constituencies and took four months to complete. Each of the 72 constituencies was then given financial help for proper office accommodation, computers, computer training and assistance with campaigning. Encouragement was also given to recruit, where the constituency had none, as good an agent as possible, and all the agents were given extra training on special weekend courses to bring them up to the mark.

The effectiveness of the programme was beginning to be indicated by Christmas, when polls of the marginals began to show that the Tories were significantly ahead. The polls covered many more seats than the 72 chosen ones, but nevertheless CCO officials concluded that their efforts were making some difference. However, the Alliance surge which threatened early in 1987, and the possibility that this could put Owen and Steel into second place on election day, could have the effect of so drastically shifting the goalposts that the 72 chosen seats would become either safe or hopeless and a whole new set of marginals emerge. The party's only consolation in this was that it would have the same effect on all the other parties, wrecking everyone's target seat plans.

In the meantime they were convinced that one of the reasons for the success in the Tory target seats was the use of local direct mailing – particularly to first-time voters. There are companies which specialise in acquiring – perfectly legally and from publicly available sources – lists of people in certain categories: there is the list of doctors, with all their business addresses, which is compiled from the medical register and put on computer tape, or farmers, or BT shareholders, or vicars – or, as in this case, all young people new to the electoral register. Nearly three million of them were due to vote for the first time in 1987, so it was considered vital to canvass their support, the more so because the polls were showing the under-twenty-fives as one of the areas of lowest support for the Tories. Therefore CCO either sold cheaply, or gave, the tapes of first-time voters in their area to each of the 72 key constituencies and the first of a series of letters to them was written by each of the sitting MPs.

It was a long and tiring slog for those involved at CCO, much of it conducted under gunfire from their own side. The whispering campaign against Norman Tebbit had only abated, not stopped, with the telephone call in August. Not even the success of the party conference had silenced it. His attack, two weeks later, on the BBC over its coverage of Libya, then on the 'loony Left' councils, was deemed by his enemies to be further evidence that by the sheer tone of his onslaughts he was not fully fit for the office he held. Further criticisms began to surface of the quality of management at the top of CCO. The problem was said to be that he was isolated, cut off, behind his door, which was guarded jealously by his chief-of-staff, and that consequently decisions were being held up in the bottleneck and serious delays were building up. These anxieties were naturally communicated to the Prime Minister and used to feed her growing and perfectly natural anxiety, as 1987 approached, that the party might not make the best showing possible at the polls.

Morale inside CCO picked up considerably, however, after Tuesday 11 November, when Norman Tebbit took his entire top team round the corner to the St Ermin's Hotel, where, one by one, the department directors reviewed their progress and state of readiness. The chairman, delighted with what he heard, ordered them all to be finally ready (i.e. with everything they could prepare in advance) by Christmas Day. It was also good for the directors to see that they had not been working away in isolation – they could feel the whole operation coming together. If there was a day when a Tory victory in 1987 first seemed possible to those working for it, it was that day.

On the basis of the reports presented at that meeting, Dobbs then wrote the 110 pages of the blue book which went into one of the Prime Minister's Christmas boxes. For both him and his boss it had been a very difficult year but, as the government could claim at the end of it that unemployment had not started to fall by accident, so could they, that the public's perception of the government as being back on track, was no idle chance either.

It would not be until 8 January that Tebbit and he would find out which was uppermost in the PM's thoughts – her delight at their readiness, or her anxieties about their ability to carry it through.

3 | Battle is Planned

From the rear of the headquarters building of the Social Democratic Party in Cowley Street, Westminster, it is just possible to see into the back windows of Lord McAlpine's home round the corner in Great College Street. Just before 10.30 a.m. on Thursday 8 January 1987, a vigilant SDP staff member might have noticed an unusually large number of people making their way upstairs in the house to Lord McAlpine's first-floor sitting-room. He would have seen first Norman Tebbit, Peter Morrison, Robin Harris, head of the Conservative Research Department, and Michael Dobbs. Then, a few minutes later, shortly after a black Daimler had drawn up in the street, he would have seen Stephen Sherbourne and the Prime Minister climbing the stairs. He would not have needed too much intelligence to work out what was going on.

This was the first of four secret 'war councils' in the months leading up to the final announcement of the date of the election on 11 May. It was, in many ways, the day the election campaign itself started.

Mrs Thatcher bustled into the room and greeted everyone individually and warmly, then took a seat, opened her copy of Michael Dobbs's 'Blue Book' and got straight down to business. It was clear from the start that this was not going to be a repeat of the previous April's débâcle. She appeared impressed with much of the work that had been done and was, by and large, encouraging.

The first chapter of the book, 'The Grounds of Battle', offered a political overview of the situation: what was happening, what might change and what were the targets. The biggest weakness in the party's position was still the so-called 'caring issues' of unemployment, health and education. Unemployment was beginning to improve and research had shown that it was seen by many not to be the fault of the government. However, failure in the areas of health and education was rightly being laid at its door – although there were signs that Kenneth Baker's arrival at the DES earlier in the year was already having an impact. The government's biggest strength, according to the research, was its leadership. The good news was that at last both the Prime Minister and her party were thought to know where they were going again. Recent polling had shown that the party, for the first time for nearly a year, looked as if it wanted to win. The principal effort in the New Year, therefore, should be to reinforce this sense of direction and purpose and, at the same time, to avoid the type of banana skins which had caused the party to slip so badly in 1986.

By comparison, according to the book, Labour Party strategy was very conveniently coming apart at the seams. Despite its spring offensive in 1986 with the 'Freedom and Fairness' campaign and its red rose and high gloss, it was still seen to be too left-wing and unreliable on defence. It had done all that had been asked of it by Neil Kinnock, yet it had fallen behind at the polls. This, according to Tebbit and Dobbs, presented its leadership with a dilemma: either it had to stick with the policies and strategy it had and run the risk of sinking lower in the polls as the electorate became progressively more aware of the weaknesses, or it could embark on a new strategy at the risk of vast internal turmoil and dissent.

The Alliance, too, was described by Dobbs on the basis of research as in a difficult position. Long on image and short on substance, it had little option but to wait for a mistake or a mass defection from either of the other two parties and then hope to exploit that quickly before its lack of real policies could be exposed.

Chapter Two, 'The Order of Battle', dealt with the organisational readiness of the party within Central Office, department by department, including how far advanced were the various key election items such as the campaign guide, which is the candidates' 'bible' of facts on every conceivable topic produced by the Research Department. Its appearance is regarded among seasoned watchers as somewhat akin to the first flower of the election spring – despite the fact that in 1974 it did not appear until after the election was over and in 1977 it appeared ready for an election which did not happen until two years later. Mrs Thatcher was told that preparations for the guide were well in hand and it would be ready by late April, including any changes announced in the Budget.

Chapter Three, 'Pre-Campaign', covered the organisational targets for the run-up to the campaign, whenever that might be. It assumed that the first likely date would be in June, but at that stage did not in any sense try to suggest it. June was merely the first date by which they planned to have everything in place and ready to go – they could be ready earlier if required to do so. It outlined the campaigns that would be launched and the techniques for launching them, including the greater use of direct mail, particularly in the target seats. And it listed the principal events of the coming months – the Budget and the Prime Minister's visit to Moscow – and suggestions as to how best to profit by them.

Chapter Four, 'The Campaign', covered the election campaign itself, providing a rough framework for 'Thatcher tours', proposals for press conferences and who should man the key positions during the campaign. Most important is the selection of personnel to travel with the Prime Minister – they have to be a cheerful, comfortable, homogenous group capable of working 18 hours a day.

What is more, they must be completely loyal to both the Prime Minister and the chairman. It is only too easy, if something goes wrong out in the field, to blame the chairman and CCO and feed the Prime Minister's anxieties: a man with malice in mind can easily drive a wedge between them. Cecil Parkinson regarded this task of selection as one of the most crucial in 1983, for his own sake as well as Mrs Thatcher's. His efforts paid off. On one occasion something went wrong on the bus, and the PM ordered Michael Spicer to ring him on the radio telephone and tell him that she was going to change the plans. When he got through, Parkinson shouted, 'That's the most stupid thing I have ever heard of. Get her back to London and I'll talk her out of it.'

Spicer seemed to be behaving oddly, repeating what he had said the PM wanted. Parkinson again shouted, 'That's bloody stupid. I'll stop her – just get her back here' and rang off. Immediately they got back to London, Spicer warned him that the PM had overheard every word he had said. 'Oh my God,' cried Parkinson, 'what did she say then?' 'It's all right,' Spicer told him, 'she smiled sweetly and said: "If Cecil says not to do it – then we won't!"'

Other posts at CCO and in Number 10 have to be filled, such as the speech and article writers and even the team to have an answer ready for everyone from the League Against Cruel Sports to the Amateur Athletic Association should they ask questions on the party's policy. Chapter Four also suggested the sorts of issues that should be included in the campaign and a rough outline of the timing of them over the four and a half weeks from 'D–31', as it was known, to election day. It was important, for example, to see that potentially difficult issues were raised before the opposition parties could attack them and got out of the way long before polling day.

The last chapter offered a detailed timetable of all the major events of the year, all the key dates when government statistics would be announced, key party dates such as its two annual conferences (and those of the other parties), again, not as an attempt to select the date, but to provide Mrs Thatcher with as much information as possible on which to make her decision when the time came.

The document did not attempt to outline in any detail the 'low ground' issues on which the election would be fought – the party's individual policies which it would restate or put before the public for the first time. Those, it said, would be adequately covered in the manifesto, which promised even at this early stage to be quite robust. However, the whole drift of those policies would be forward-looking, would present a party that would be seen as still vigorous and full of ideas and initiative. The aim was to create a deliberate contrast to the other parties. The belief was that they would be looking backwards over the government's record, or over their own aims and policies which were still the same as at the last election. Thus the 'time for a change' factor would be reversed: the party of change would now be the one in office. The book did, however, encapsulate the 'high ground' of how the public would be encouraged to perceive both leader and party. Mrs Thatcher would be seen as the one who had brought us through the storm – the mother of the nation, the master mariner of the ship. We had come through the worst; there were still squalls ahead, but the ship was intact now and in good hands. Her leadership would be presented as leadership of substance and of achievement; by contrast Kinnock, Steel and Owen would seem like tinsel. A few slogans and themes including 'Sharing in Success' were raised for the first time and suggested as possibles for the campaign.

The Prime Minister was clearly satisfied. She went over each point in great detail, but found little to fault and agreed with many of the suggestions made. However, she rarely leaves a meeting without having had an argument. These episodes do not necessarily represent fundamental disagreement on her part, and being able to work out why she is arguing is often more important than the argument itself. For example, at the equivalent meeting in January 1983, David Boddy, then head of the CCO Press Department, outlined a number of TV options to her and then added innocently, 'And we have you scheduled for several Break-fast TV appearances.' He was subjected to a blistering attack for several minutes, during which he wondered what he had done wrong. He had in fact made no mistake at all beyond using the word 'scheduled', which caused her minor irritation at the thought of being pushed around. Those who knew her better realised that she was, in fact, clearing her own mind in order to focus totally for the first time on the issue of that year's election.

Thus when, after some time, the subject of the election tour came up in Lord McAlpine's sitting-room, her argument was not necessarily totally to do with the tour itself. It transpired that it was to do with several other things as well. It started on the topic of the number of marginal seats that had been pencilled in for her to visit. There is always a conflict in this sphere between those people in the area offices who slave away at trying to improve the party's standing in the 'tactical' seats and who know that a visit, however brief, from the Prime Minister could be worth that last vital thousand votes or so; those people in senior local party positions who see a prime ministerial visit as an opportunity for personal aggrandisement; and those who are concerned with the Prime Minister's overall presentation and who know that a series of progressions through cheering crowds of supporters are likely to make a much better impression on television each night than the howling mobs of Rentacrowd hecklers which would inevitably appear in some of the marginal constituencies.

In 1983 one of Mrs Thatcher's greatest irritations came one day when she found herself separated from the press and TV coach to be taken to the business premises of the chairman of the local party and proudly shown round. Later she angrily demanded of a somewhat mystified Cecil Parkinson how such time-wasting had come to be included in her programme.

In the age of media elections television and the press must come first and the slightest risk of crowd trouble will cause the Tory planners and security advisers to rule a place out, be it marginal or not. At this meeting Mrs Thatcher felt that the plans were wrong. There were far too many opportunities for trouble in them — and not enough of the cheering crowds. But this was only one of her worries. Although she was concerned about where she was being asked to go, this raised in her mind a greater worry about how she should go. She was only too aware, and did not need Michael Dobbs's document to tell her, that the more visible she was the better it would be for the campaign. But more visible also means more vulnerable and, especially since the Brighton bomb, this is a factor she has been forced to take more into account. She knew it would be disadvantageous to her to be whisked from well-guarded place to well-guarded place behind the bullet-proof glass of her Daimler. In her view, and it was one widely shared, the nature of the election would be such that it would not be long before the Labour Party would be saying she was scared to meet the people. She knows she must be seen as much as possible and meet as many people as possible at election time — besides, she actually likes it. But for those around her, as much as for her own sake, she has to make sure that if she is to be more visible and accessible, she must be as well protected as possible.

This was the second reason for the argument with Michael Dobbs — to clarify her, his and everyone else's thinking on the subject of the 'Battlebus', the vehicle she would use to move around on the ground for most of her tour. She wanted to make certain that it was not only going to be, as had been outlined, the most sophisticated vehicle of its kind possible in terms of the communications technology it would contain for her and her staff, but also the safest possible in case of the awful eventuality of a terrorist attack.

Whether there was another reason for the argument with Dobbs it is difficult to say. Certainly reports of the meeting circulated in the upper echelons of the party and, as had happened after the meeting in April, they painted neither him nor Norman Tebbit in a totally good light. Some believed that it was just one of her 'natural' arguments to help the meeting concentrate on the issue. Some were convinced that her real dissatisfaction was with her party chairman, but, having decided to stick with him, she could not be seen to attack him and chose his chief-of-staff instead. Others believed that the 'chemistry' between her and Dobbs was wrong – that his logical, almost pedestrian, style of presentation was ill-suited to her more mer-curial, instinctive mind; and that he suffered also, by comparison, from not being Tim Bell.

Whatever the reason, it opened up another long-standing area of debate between her and her CCO officers – that of the whole area of communications. Quite possibly this was at the root of all her querulousness that day. The suggestion was made to her that one of the key personnel on the bus, the travelling press officer, should be a Number 10 civil servant called Christine Wall, who had worked in Downing Street for some time as number three to Bernard Ingham. She had made something of a name for herself the previous summer when she had accompanied the Prime Minister to Cornwall. The young press officer, still in her twenties, had at first successfully kept the media at bay, then arranged the photo-call for them which resulted in pictures of Mrs Thatcher playing with the Wolfsons' dog on the beach appearing on every TV channel and in every newspaper.

The rule in Whitehall is that the Civil Service should not, for the most part, assist in party matters. There are, of course, grey areas to this ruling – the purpose of the large number of ministerial special advisers is to give political rather than governmental perspectives to their masters. But at election times civil servants must withdraw and deal only with governmental matters – or resign for the period of the election. The suggestion now put to the Prime Minister was that Christine Wall should be offered a full-time job at CCO with a view to her taking the travelling press job during the election. Mrs Thatcher dismissed the idea, adamant that it would not be appropriate for a civil servant to be approached in such a way. However, she did reluctantly agree that Dobbs and Stephen Sherbourne could at least discuss the matter with Christine Wall.

To understand Mrs Thatcher's anxieties about communications it is necessary first to go back to 1979. In that campaign she was not the first politician to use an advertising agency, but she was the first to grasp what could be the full impact of communications across the whole spectrum of the media. She knew that if she could find the right man, he could transform all her advertising – in posters, in newspaper advertisements, even the party political broadcasts. She understood that striking material would be talked about in its own right. She knew also that the right man could transform her impact on the press and in television interviews. She understood (as not many politicians did, or indeed do) that the *Sun*, the *Star* and the *Mirror*, were just as important – more so in fact – than *The Times, Telegraph* and *Guardian* and that ratings were often more important than prestige in granting interviews. She had found in Tim Bell and Gordon Reece two men who not only understood what she required almost instinctively, but also worked together without squabbling or vying for position.

Bell and the Saatchi team worked on the advertising and party political broadcast side, first positioning the Conservative Party as the party of freedom, opportunity, individual responsibility, prosperity and choice, then, with posters like the now famous 'Labour Isn't Working', attacking the government to make people dissatisfied with it and begin to think it was time for a change. Then, in the middle of the 'winter of discontent', they moved to the high ground when, in a PPB, she appealed as a stateswoman to the whole nation in a time of crisis. Reece, meanwhile, was using the press and television news to bring her out as 'the housewives' champion', undermining Labour's traditional working-class vote and pointing up by comparison James Callaghan's aloofness every time she went into a market and knew how much the price of apples had risen.

As the election results showed, it was an amazingly successful campaign, but it bred an enormous amount of resentment. For the first time, perhaps, politicians saw their traditional control over elections slipping. There was deep suspicion of these 'advertising johnnies', who suddenly seemed to be everywhere whispering in her ear. Some senior Tories very genuinely believe to this day that she would have won without the work of Reece and Bell and dismiss their efforts as a trivial matter of cosmetics. Others and many of her opponents go to the opposite extreme and attribute some sort of hocus-pocus to the process – as though the skills of the team were such as to fool a large percentage of the populace into voting for someone they did not really want.

Reece has been consistently credited with 'softening her image' to appeal to the voters. He is somehow supposed to have persuaded her to change her hairstyle and her voice – as though a can of hairspray and a touch of elocution would win an election. The truth is that when he was first consulted by her, not long after she became leader of the party in 1975, he had to stop her doing things that were not natural to her because people had told her that was the image she should project. Both the hair and the voice were her decision, the first for reasons purely unknown, except that every now and then women do change their hairstyles, the second because the lower the voice, the less the strain on it. Both Reece and Bell, far from working some form of sorcery on her, spent a good deal of time working out what was really her and making sure that was conveyed.

Neither claims to have done anything more than use their considerable skills in advertising and public relations to communicate what was asked of them. Theirs were not the opinions, merely the communication of them. Most people involved in political communication make the mistake of arguing with their client what is the right thing to say. Mrs Thatcher knew from the beginning what she wanted to say, Bell and Reece told her how to say it.

Nevertheless, many Tories were resentful of the media mystique which grew up around the pair of them and the influence they appeared to have over her. When the election was over and she disappeared behind the doors of Downing Street, their influence naturally waned. Whitehall press officers took over the job of the day-to-day presentation of the Prime Minister – and they are by and large a very different breed: to their many critics, the training and instinct of a government press officer is to be expert in lack of communication. There are many of them, and politicians too, who conspire in the belief that Parliament is the be all and end all of public utterance: if you have made a statement in the House, answered questions on it and had your press officer lobby-brief the correspondents on the thinking behind it, then you have told the whole country. This is not communication as the professionals see it, and over the years both Bell and Reece made many enemies by arguing that just because she was in Downing Street, it didn't mean that Mrs Thatcher should stop telling the people what she was up to.

In times of trouble one or other, or both, would be invited to see her. But there was little they could do, apart from cheer her up, to break the Whitehall stranglehold on her, particularly after 1983. Indeed, on more than one occasion Reece's very presence was regarded as an unnecessary intrusion by Bernard Ingham, who lost no time in saying so. Come the election, of course, and things are very different. She must emerge from the 'bubble' that surrounds all prime ministers and put herself in the hands of those party people whose job it is to get her re-elected.

Any person in a position of power will have a number of sycophants and hangers-on clustered around him or her. Talk of tight groups of cronies, kitchen cabinets and who has the ear of the PM at any one moment is the stuff of Westminster gossip. Mrs Thatcher has, by and large, been too busy to have a set group of people to relax and gossip with in the evenings. She is not a natural gossip. She prefers, as we have seen, to be surrounded by people who do things, rather than people who talk about them. But for all that she is remarkably free of cloying cronies, she is susceptible to another type of attention – noticeably at election times – which is a product partly of her own womanhood and partly of the inflated ego necessary for most men to carry off the role of politician. The whole team around her wants to win the election. Some, like Cecil Parkinson and Bell and Reece are sufficiently confident of themselves and their abilities to work hard and selflessly for the team. They might fight and have rows – as indeed they did in 1983 – but basically they worked together.

A significant number of others, in contrast, want to be the one who won the election. They are not the people who will join a team to see the team win and the captain carried shoulder-high from the field. They too want to be carried shoulder-high from the field – so that the captain will be forced to acknowledge they are as good as she is, that they got her where she is. It is an aspect of the state of mind, outlined earlier, that has not fully come to terms with the fact that she is a woman. And in order to be the one carried shoulder-high from the field they will quite happily knock down their own team-mates – presumably on the false statistical probability that doing so makes it more likely that they will get the accolade.

Her team in 1979 was remarkably free of this trait. Those closest to her – Airey Neave (in the early stages) and Sir Geoffrey Howe, Richard Ryder, then her political secretary, Lord Thorneycroft, her party chairman, and Tim Bell, Gordon Reece and Ronald Millar, her speechwriter – worked together as a team and she felt comfortable with them and confident in them.

In 1983 things were different. The party was so far ahead in the polls that the feeling grew that it would be silly to do anything at all in case it upset the voters. It was a very low-key, almost boring campaign. Unlike 1979, when their work had gone on all winter, the campaign lasted just four weeks. So reluctant was Mrs Thatcher to commit herself to a date – she wanted to keep all her options open until the weekend after the local election results on 2 May – that Saatchi were forbidden to do any work until the campaign was announced and Reece was forbidden to return from his job in America until the end of the first week, when the manifesto had been launched. Cecil Parkinson was a great contrast to Lord Thorneycroft; but he, like Mrs Thatcher, only to a slightly lesser extent, understood the need for communication and was a superb television performer in his own right.

Hence there was less for Bell and Reece to do and, although she wanted their reassuring presence around as in 1979, there were more people in the team this time who wanted to be the one who scored the winning goal and were happy to exclude the pair of them as much as possible, denigrating them in the process. When I asked a prominent member of the team what exactly Reece's role would be in the 1983 campaign, I was told, 'We'll find somewhere for him . . . in a cupboard.'

However their enemies, who believed finally they had removed them for good when the Guinness affair broke (both had worked for Guinness during the Distillers takeover, although neither was implicated in any way in any wrongdoing), had not taken two factors into account. If they are gone and there is no communicator like Cecil Parkinson at the centre of the campaign, a very large hole is left in terms of both communication skills and Mrs Thatcher's almost superstitious desire to gather her 'old boys' around her when it comes to election time. On a number of occasions from the summer of 1986 on she tried – and some of the more open-minded people around her also tried – to resurrect the old team in one form or another, only to be told that it was not possible, but she neither abandoned the idea nor ceased to worry that there might be a huge gap, come election time, in the communications area. It was her insecurity about this crucially important sphere of the campaign – which few people around her saw as being particularly vital – that was at the root of many of her anxieties.

Nor were matters improved by the very nature of Norman Tebbit's public persona. Arguments rage all the time around the government's ability, or nearly always otherwise, to 'sell' its message – particularly, as we have seen, when times are bad. Critics of the government blame Mrs Thatcher, or the Cabinet – or Bernard Ingham – for its poor performance in the polls. Some of them blame the chairman of the party for not 'doing something' about it. The fact is there is very little the chairman can do, without treading on the toes of people in Downing Street: he can, however, say a great deal. Cecil Parkinson's smiling, pleasant exposition of the Thatcher creed did much to soften the edges of the message in 1983, but Norman Tebbit's equally sincere endorsement of the product, three years later, was seen to put an unwanted, harsh, aggressive extra edge on what was already a creed somewhat devoid of soft options. It was a classic example of the Latitude of Acceptance theory – one of the two basic theories which govern all communications – which says

that the same observation made by two different people is bound
to have two different effects: and there could not be much more
different presenters than Parkinson and Tebbit. Tebbit's enemies
used this to try to undermine him with the Prime Minister. He
made a virtue of his function as 'lightning conductor', and
directed his attacks against the BBC and the 'loony Left', favourite targets among the Tory backwoodsmen, but it was hardly
the sort of thing that goes down well among the so-called
chattering classes or those who might just be put off by all that
aggression. Mrs Thatcher, wisely, kept silent on the subject, but
it must have further underlined in her mind the need for someone in the party to take control of the whole communications
issue.

In fact Tebbit and Dobbs had started to get to grips with the
problem as soon as they had arrived at CCO. It was clear that
Harvey Thomas, the jovial, bespectacled, born-again Christian,
who had been in charge of the physical arrangements for all Mrs
Thatcher's appearances in 1979 and 1983 – the selection of
venues and the decoration, sound, lighting and speech-reading
facilities in those halls – had been given the wrong job by John
Selwyn Gummer, when he made him Director of Communications in 1985. The amateur quality of areas of the party,
coupled with its lack of any proper management set-up, render
changes in it subject to the personalities involved rather than the
demands of particular jobs. Harvey Thomas was made Director
of Communications more because he was popular and well-liked
than because he could manage an area which, depending on its
incumbent, had at times covered everything from press and TV,
to marketing, direct mail and advertising.

Four moves were planned to overcome the problem: first, a
new Chief Information Officer was found to strengthen the Press
Department and give it the sort of lobby access it had lacked
since the death in 1984 of Tony Shrimsley. John Desborough,
ironically a *Mirror* lobby man, but who had fallen out with his
masters, was approved and signed up. Second, Harvey Thomas
was moved sideways with the title of Director of Presentations
and Promotions. Third, Sir Christopher Lawson, who had been
Marketing Director in 1983 – in charge of advertising, marketing
and direct mail (leaving press and television to Shrimsley) – was

persuaded back from retirement to take over New Technology (which would now cover marketing and direct mail, but not advertising).

The fourth move in the plan had foundered, principally on the Prime Minister's anxieties about the whole area of communications. Press was strengthened, marketing and direct mail were covered, but what of the overall control of the whole strategy for them and advertising and the media – television in particular? A good deal of time was spent approaching and talking to a number of people who might just fit the bill and one name – Michael Mander, former managing director of the Thomson Organisation – was actually put to the Prime Minister, who promptly turned it down on the grounds that he did not have the required television experience. The problem with most of the rest of the thirty or so names on the list was that they also did not have the experience required, and the few who had the experience could not afford to take the kind of drop in salary the job entailed. There was clearly not another Gordon Reece among them.

So the plan was changed to making the job a team effort. Norman Tebbit, Peter Morrison and Michael Dobbs would collectively oversee press and advertising and supervise the work of a new person, on a lower grade, who would work out and execute a strategy for television. And it was this stage, with the Prime Minister pressing to know what was being done, that the arrangements had reached by the time the meeting at Lord McAlpine's house took place on 8 January – hence much of the Prime Minister's anxiety and irritation.

The meeting was due to last for three hours – Mrs Thatcher had another engagement in the early afternoon at Downing Street – but so intense was the discussion that it was not until nearly 4 p.m. that she finally declared herself, with reservations, happy with CCO's progress and bustled out, confident, for the first time, that most of the machinery for victory was in place. 'Yes,' she said, 'we're on the way. Let's be cautiously optimistic,' – a favourite phrase of hers which can mean anything from exactly what it says to 'I'm dancing with joy – but it would be foolish of me to show it at the moment.'

Nevertheless her satisfaction did not stop her worrying about the problem and when, a few weeks later, Christine Wall's name was put to her again, in a slightly different context, she accepted it. The original idea to have her as travelling press officer on the bus came from Stephen Sherbourne. As a result of the 8 January meeting Dobbs suggested that, in view of the Prime Minister's distinct unease about TV, she might also take over and run that side of the operation under guidance from CCO.

Christine Wall's job, as soon as she could get to Smith Square, would be not only to prepare for her role on the bus but also to develop the whole strategy for Mrs Thatcher's TV campaign – what the aim of it would be, what the pace would be and which programmes she would appear on. The move had many advantages from everyone's point of view. It was a problem solved for Norman Tebbit – not an ideal solution, but one which, with their help, could be made to work at least until after the election. It appeared to keep the Prime Minister happy; and, as everyone noted with a certain amount of satisfaction, it would give the campaign a perfectly legitimate route into Bernard Ingham's thinking, which was acknowledged as being important in knowing how to keep the Prime Minister happy. Thus, with her confidence in the television front of the campaign bolstered, the heat was off the search for a communications supremo. The job could be done by the existing team, in effect, for the time being at least, by Dobbs.

The enemies of Parkinson, Reece and Bell were happy to note that the arrangement made the presence of the old team less necessary even on the periphery. However this did not stop Mrs Thatcher continuing to express anxieties that they be involved, come the day. It can be established beyond doubt that Mrs Thatcher wanted them, but who talked her out of it time and again, and why, is more elusive.

Those who put it around that there was some personal enmity between her and Tim Bell, for example, were clearly unaware of the meeting between them on the evening of 16 February when, at a party to mark Caroline Ryder leaving her job as the PM's diary secretary, the two talked for some considerable time. It was the third time they had met coincidentally, at various functions, in three weeks and Mrs Thatcher opened the conversation by bantering with Bell about his weight. 'I'd lose weight, Prime

Minister, if you had an election,' Bell replied. 'The work would soon get the weight off.' 'I can't hold an election just for you to slim!' she laughed. Bell's position was, in fact, the most difficult of the three, because he had left Saatchi to become deputy chairman of a rival agency amid some acrimony at Christmas 1984, but, at the Prime Minister's insistence, was supposed to have been retained by Saatchi to work on the Tory account. The arrangement was unsatisfactory, dependent as it was on the goodwill of all sides. Suspicion soon gained the upper hand and every whisper that the Prime Minister was unhappy with the agency was interpreted, wrongly, as an attack by Bell aimed at getting the account for himself. Equally every whisper that Bell was allegedly damaged by the Guinness scandal was amplified and used as a further argument for cutting him out of the arrangements. Dobbs, caught in the middle – on the one hand Bell's friend and protégé, on the other an employee of Saatchi – found himself in an increasingly invidious position and having to take sides.

Whereas Saatchi had gone through both 1979 and 1983 with a tiny operation centred essentially on the personality of Bell and his unique relationship with Mrs Thatcher, their approach to 1987 was of necessity more formal. In 1983, Bell, Dobbs and Dobbs's wife Amanda had handled the account, with the creative work done mostly by Jeremy Sinclair and Charles Saatchi himself. By the beginning of 1987, not only was their work for the Tories more extensive than ever before – they were doing more of the research, more design work, more production of the promotional material – but also, without Bell, a whole team had been formed to handle the account. John Sharkey had moved in as account director before Dobbs left to go to CCO. Now he had four executives under him in addition to the old creative team.

Early in the year the agency was allowed to start on some of the creative work for the campaign. The first work – coming as it did before the manifesto was completed – concentrated on general themes stressing the forward-looking nature of the government and portraying Neil Kinnock, not as a politician whose time had come, but one for whom it had gone ten years ago.

The Labour Party communications machine was also beginning to gear itself into election life in the early months of the
year. Instead of opting for one agency, the Kinnock team had
formed a Shadow Communications Agency – a team of twenty
or so volunteers from the advertising, marketing and media
worlds. There had been some talk in 1986 of abandoning the
team concept, but its work had so impressed Peter Mandelson,
the party's Director of Campaigns and Communications, that it
had been kept on. Like the Tories, Labour was seeking victory
in a number of key marginals – 132 – and putting much of
its effort, including its advertising work, into these. The PR
consultant Lynne Franks had also been recruited in 1986 to help
promote the leader and party. Neil Kinnock was photographed
appearing at such 'youthful' events as the opening of the film
Absolute Beginners and with groups of teenagers wearing T-
shirts with Labour slogans on them.

Neil Kinnock was clearly determined to avoid the disasters
which had plagued the Foot campaign four years earlier, when
the campaign machine was so large and cumbersome that outsiders had been able to sit in on its meetings unchallenged.
Now, with Larry Whitty, the party's general secretary, he was
determined to keep the numbers down to a manageable size of
about ten. A key figure in the group was to be the New Zealand-
born MP Bryan Gould, the campaign co-ordinator. It was with
his agreement that the decision was taken to concentrate almost
all the Labour leader's media appearances on television, on the
assumption that if the campaign was to be fought on television
then that was where Kinnock should be and, since the press were
almost universally hostile to the Labour leader, there was little
point in his dealing with them – with the exception, of course,
of the *Mirror*.

When the Tories learned of this plan in late January, they saw
it as potentially one of the biggest own goals of the election. They
now painted for themselves a picture of the Labour campaign:
Kinnock was going to be seen night after night traipsing round
old schools, old hospitals and old factories in run-down areas of
Britain – for to their mind there was little point in his visiting
anywhere that was modern or successful, on the grounds that
the credit for it would have to go to the Tories. What is more,

the Tories believed they would be able to claim that he was running away from the press, and hence from any really close questioning on the weaknesses of his policies, and that by opting for television only they could demonstrate that it was he who was avoiding the issues and trying to reduce politics to the level of cosmetics.

But what made the Tories really triumphant was the belief that the decision was based on a fundamental error. The election, they argued, might well be fought and won on television – but the pace of it was dictated by newspapers. It was still the press that picked up the issues and ran with them and television tended to follow. Much of what went into the following day's papers and television was developed from the morning press conferences – the free-for-all question-and-answer sessions that all party leaders traditionally conduct early each morning. Now, argued the Tories, if Neil Kinnock was planning to confine himself to television and ignore the morning press conferences, leaving them to the other members of his Shadow Cabinet, he would find himself, not leading the arguments, but trailing pathetically along in their wake. We should see.

The Alliance, too, decided not to appoint an advertising agency as such – relying instead on a team put together by Dave Abbott, their publicity consultant and chairman of the Abbot, Mead Vickers agency. Even this move reflected some of the divisions between the two parties that lay just beneath the surface. It was reliably reported at the time that David Owen had wanted a full-blown, modern, agency-led campaign befitting the party which he hoped after 1987 would take over the role of official Opposition and dominate the centre–left of British politics, but that the Liberals, ever conscious of their more anti-consumerist following, with its emphasis on community politics and abhorrence of all things slick and Saatchi-like, were violently against the idea.

The Alliance team also decided early on to concentrate their efforts principally in the 120 seats they had most chance of winning and to sell their two leaders as a joint package – or, as Mrs Thatcher put it, 'two ends of a pantomime horse' – touring the country together. Surprisingly, but perhaps prompted by their relative shortage of funds, they decided not to take the route of expensive press and poster advertising, opting instead to base their campaigns heavily on direct mailing. By the turn of the year, based on their ability to fight by-elections more effectively than the Tories, they were able to claim they were ahead of both the other parties in the use of computers. This was a claim which did not over-worry Smith Square: the Alliance was known to use a disproportionate amount of its resources fighting by-elections and, come the real thing, with the jam spread more thinly, the Tories believed their superiority would show through. In the by-elections of 1986–7 the Alliance also established a reputation for some very efficient 'dirty tricks' – such as putting out bogus literature in the name of the other parties – but these too were seen in CCO as being irritants which would largely evaporate in a general election.

Mrs Thatcher's confident, if slightly anxious, departure from the meeting at Lord McAlpine's house was the signal for Norman Tebbit and Michael Dobbs to go ahead with many of the plans they had laid for the early part of the campaign. Just as the work on the target seats had begun the year before, now it was time to set another stage of plans in motion. The direct mail operation, approved now by the Prime Minister after extensive tests, was moved up a gear and letters aimed at target groups from shareholders to company directors to young first-time voters began to leave CCO at the rate of a million a month. There had been some severe problems with the operation – some of Chris Lawson's original forecasts for it had been wildly optimistic – but if it ever was going to prove its worth as a fundraiser and support winner, now would be its chance to do so.

Agreement had also been given, for the first time, for an election newspaper. Dobbs had been impressed by the CDU's capacity, on the weekend before the German elections, to produce and deliver an eight-page newspaper to the vast majority of the electorate. After trials in the UK it was clearly impossible to emulate the German success; nevertheless it was decided to go for a four-page Tory paper and attempt to deliver it to every household in the 72 target constituencies.

Harvey Thomas and Roger Boaden, the two tour experts, began to travel the country looking for the right halls for the six massive rallies at which the Prime Minister would make her major set-piece speeches, for the market places and shopping centres where she would make her whistle-stop appearances and for the factories and shops which she would tour meeting the people. There would be many more meetings before this, most crucial, element of the Tory campaign would finally be settled.

The meeting had also finalised some of the key personnel for the campaign. Liaison between Central Office and Number 10, a job which can be a joy or a nightmare and which had been carried out highly efficiently by Sir John Eden in 1983, went to Sally Oppenheim, the MP for Gloucester who was retiring, and Sir Philip Holland, MP for Gedling in Nottinghamshire, also standing down, was to look after the PM's correspondence. William Whitelaw was to chair the Questions of Policy Group. John Whittingdale, Paul Channon's special adviser at the Department of Trade and Industry, was to be, for the second election in a row, the travelling 'brains' on the bus. His role was to have at his fingertips any fact or figure the Prime Minister might require in the three weeks of travelling. Not only had he done it without a fault in 1983, he had also won the Battlebus Scrabble Competition.

The pace was beginning to warm up; but January was still far enough away from any possible election date for Central Office to discreetly 'leak' a few potentially embarrassing items to the local and national press – matters which, if they were to come out as fresh in the excitement and hurly-burly of an election campaign, could cause considerable trouble. For example, the chairman of one of the London constituency parties had some years before been a member of the National Front. His repudiation of the NF and all it stood for was now placed firmly on record, lest the matter should be raised later and he, or they, be accused of trying to hide it.

For Michael Dobbs, however, there was one other, more pressing and infinitely more important matter to deal with after 8 January. Discreetly he began asking secretaries in CCO and special advisers in the government ministries to supply him with dates – dates when statistics would be coming out, dates when important meetings were to take place, and dates when the opposition parties had things planned. He began to research election law and the meaning of the mysterious 'dies non' – 'days that do not exist'. As each report came in it went into a file which was locked away in the top compartment of his office safe each night. Finally, towards the end of the month all the material was to hand, and he wrote a 20-page report to Norman Tebbit and the Prime Minister.

At his first weekly bilateral with Mrs Thatcher in February, Norman Tebbit took the report with him to Downing Street and, alone in the Prime Minister's study, the two of them had the first major discussion, not about who, how, what or why, but when.

4 | If Doomsday Comes

It is well known that after the Greenwich by-election in February there was a fair amount of blood-letting, blame-attaching and scapegoat-seeking within the Labour Party. What is not so well known is that very much the same angry recriminations reverberated through the Tory party. For, while there was an acknowledgement that the party might never have won the seat, there was considerable fury that it had not apparently tried harder. The anger was perhaps more savage because the victory of the SDP/Alliance candidate, Mrs Rosie Barnes, was yet further confirmation of a surge in Alliance support which had taken it from below 20 per cent in the October conference season (particularly after the disastrous Liberal Assembly) to level with, if not an inch ahead of, the Labour Party. This prospect of the surge gaining further momentum in Truro a fortnight later and turning into a spring bandwagon unleashed some of the darkest of Tory nightmares, and hence some of their most bitter bile.

Mrs Barnes polled 18,287 votes, to the Labour candidate Deirdre Wood's 11,676 and the Conservative John Antcliffe's 3,852. The drop in the Tory vote of 23.7 per cent was far and away the largest of that Parliament and, although much was made of the unsuitability and left-wing stance of Deirdre Wood, the Alliance took only one vote from Labour for every five from the Tories.

Much was also made of the Alliance tactics: the fact that an entire 'national' team of high-tech experts backed up by hundreds of volunteers was moved into the south-east London constituency to fight the seat; the fact that the 'targeting' of voters was done with a sophistication and to a degree never attempted in this country before – even take-away food shop owners were identified and direct mailed as a group; the fact that the candidate herself was a 'natural' for fighting a by-election – a personable mother of three, a political 'virgin' who had belonged to no other party before 1981, and a local resident, the wife of a local councillor, with children at local schools; the fact that the themes were simple (if devoid of content: 'Our heart is in the right place – but so is our head. We care but we are realistic too'); and the fact that heavy emphasis was placed first on getting the local bandwagon rolling – by telling everyone it was – then encouraging tactical voting on the grounds that the Tories could never win so their supporters might as well vote SDP to keep the awful Deirdre out. It was a stunningly successful by-election campaign, run professionally and it had the added advantage of being on Fleet Street's doorstep, so its impact nationally was vastly exaggerated. All three parties possibly broke election law by overspending: none of them was willing, naturally, to accuse any of the others for fear of the revelations that might result from an investigation.

For the Tories the result brought back memories of the year before, when they had lost Ryedale, only just held on to Derbyshire West, and done abysmally at Newcastle-under-Lyme – each with a lesser, but still catastrophic, collapse of their vote than they experienced in Greenwich. All their anxieties floated to the surface. Fairly or unfairly, the candidate was deemed to have been unsuitable; the candidate's 'friend' – Colin Moynihan, MP for Lewisham East, next door – had not been much help; the local party was moribund; the help from Central Office was pathetic; CCO had not really tried because they did not like the candidate and knew they were not going to win anyway; and the Alliance had trounced the Tories in direct mailing – an area in which both parties were planning to put great faith and even greater amounts of money come the general election; Norman Tebbit was not fit to be chairman of the party; he had lost control of CCO; and there was no line management there, nor proper preparations for the election campaign.

The Tories rarely wash their dirty linen in public, so few criticisms surfaced; but nevertheless they were expressed at all levels of the party, from the backbenchers to the Cabinet. CCO defended itself stoutly on the grounds that, unlike the Alliance, who send a whole national team in to take over and fight by-elections, the Tories have to blend a national and a local team together – and on this occasion it was not a blend that mixed particularly well. Any government with a majority of 141 is, they pointed out, going to fall victim to supporters being wooed away into tactical voting on the grounds that, however they vote, it is not going to remove that government. The Alliance campaign, they said, was based on the constant repetition of how well the party was doing, rather than on policies or any detailed examination of what it planned to do: it was a hype which would never bear the scrutiny of a general election. And what was more, they claimed, the fact that the national polls showed the Tory vote holding up in the upper thirties was an indication that the 'TBW' who had most influenced the voters at Greenwich was more likely this time to have been Deirdre Wood than Mrs Thatcher.

The principal reason why the row remained out of the media was that, in the week that followed the by-election, attention was most firmly focused in the opposite direction – towards the Labour Party. Many in the Tory camp, and not a few in Labour too, thought in its aftermath that Greenwich would be looked back upon as the point at which Labour lost the election. Not only did the party slump to third place in several of the polls, but Neil Kinnock's own personal rating, already damaged by the unseemly slanging match he was involved in with the Prime Minister in the middle of the month, fell a full ten points to around 30 per cent. In the inner councils of the Labour Party there was open talk of major efforts to improve his image and performance. To many voters the party, which had batted solidly through 1986 with little to show at the end of it, and which had started the year by looking increasingly vulnerable under the Tories' attack on its defence policies, now suddenly looked like a party in the grip of unattractive people like Deirdre Wood and with an ineffectual leader in Neil Kinnock.

From within CCO, the collapse of the Labour Party had been a process anticipated to take the best part of a vigorous general election campaign – not something which could happen in the space of two weeks with hardly a huff being puffed. For a while it took people aback. There was almost a sense of shock that Labour had been made to appear so vulnerable so quickly – the more so among those whose whole lives had been spent in attacking it. There is in almost every Tory politician – particularly among the more robust ones – a need for Socialism; to have the 'bad' against which the 'good' can shine. A lifetime's habit of having Labour as adversary in the House of Commons, and merely taking the argument out to the country for an airing at election time, was now threatened. With great unease the Tories began to evaluate the unthinkable: the collapse of Labour would lead to a rise in the Alliance. Indeed there were signs that this was so already. What would it mean? How much would the goalposts shift? Would the Alliance rise be permanent? Was this a bandwagon, which, if allowed to roll on, could eventually threaten them? Would what was beginning to look like a cosy cruise to June now have to be October? Above all, what should they now do to handle the Alliance problem?

No party since the war has held power in Britain with more than half of the vote. The difference between the two major parties has always been small enough, and the presence of all the smaller parties just large enough, to prevent this happening. Mrs Thatcher's victory in 1983 was, apart from the two very close polls of 1974, the lowest winning percentage for 30 years – yet it yielded her a 141-seat majority. The principal reason for this (and for the two 1974 results) is the steady growth of the third party in British politics in the last 20 years. From the Liberals being dismissed in the 1950s and early 1960s as the Celtic fringe, the Alliance is now considered not just as the third party, but one which was only 2.2 per cent behind Labour at the 1983 election and which by early in 1987 was showing every likelihood of doing even better this time. The old straightforward Tory/Labour wars, with a swingometer brought out at election time to measure the numbers of victories and casualties on the field of battle, had become a thing of the past. It was always dangerous to believe that elections were fought on class lines, since many trade unionists must have voted Tory, but nevertheless there were clearer lines and stronger party allegiances thirty years ago than there are now.

It is these changes, coupled with the huge demographic alterations in post-war Britain, which have made interpreting the polls and, therefore, working out what the effect of the Alliance might be, such a hazardous process. Put simply, what has happened is this. In the 1950s and early 1960s what was known as a 'cube' law governed the number of seats which changed hands at election time. Presuming that the two main parties started off at 50 per cent each, a 2 per cent swing would give an 8 per cent change in seats. This meant that the party with the largest percentage of votes got a clear – if somewhat exaggerated – majority in the House of Commons. The complexities of the law need not concern us beyond the fact that it has slowly changed until now, in the 1980s, a 2 per cent swing yields only a little more than a 2 per cent change in seats, so a party needs to have a much greater percentage of the vote than its nearest rival to achieve a clear majority.

The reason for this is that the number of marginal seats has declined rapidly. Whereas there were 166 marginals in 1955, there were only 80 in 1983 and would probably be only 60 in 1987. This has come about because the spread of Labour and Tory voters used to be far more even across the constituencies than it is now. Before the mass of people owned cars, the middle classes lived in city centres, but now Labour has the inner cities and the middle classes have moved out to the suburbs, which the Tories dominate along with the rural areas. Where inner city populations have moved to New Towns, the tearing up of physical roots has also often meant the tearing up of old political allegiances, and many of these are now Tory – or Alliance – seats too. The new political map of Britain after 1983 gave the Tories 85 per cent of the seats in the south and the Midlands. Apart from Central London and South Wales, Labour had only two seats south of Coventry. Labour's large holdings were in the cities of the north and Scotland. Glasgow had seven Tory MPs in 1955 – in 1983 it had none. Nor did Central Liverpool or Manchester.

There are two areas, however, apart from the big cities, which remained even as the 1987 election approached, remarkably unaffected electorally by this change, the north-west, particularly Lancashire, and the Midlands, particularly to the west and east of Birmingham. Partly because there had always been a stronger tradition of working-class Tory voting and partly because there had been less movement of the population in these areas, they had changed less, and therefore it was in them that many of the marginal seats were concentrated. Almost all of them were either Conservative-held with Labour in second place or vice versa. A 3 per cent swing between these two parties in either direction at the election would cause 30 seats in these areas alone to change hands, a point we will return to in a moment.

The rise of the Alliance had hardly affected these seats at all, for although it was second to the Tories in 262 of the 397 seats they won in 1983, the vast majority of these were the safe Tory seats, not the marginals. But a general breakthrough into second place could change the pattern drastically – especially if it were at the expense of Tory votes.

The Alliance went into 1983 strong on idealism, weak on practicalities and almost non-existent on meaningful policies. Subsequently its idealism did not dim, nor, according to its critics, did its policies improve much – they were still, to the Tories and Labour alike, a hopeless hotch-potch, cobbled together out of convenience rather than conviction. However, its ability to fight had made enormous strides. Out in the constituencies, while Labour had been squabbling among themselves and the Tories had been concentrating in their own inimitable fashion on 'being Tories' and fundraising, the Alliance was on the streets digging its way into the fabric of society, establishing a base through what they call 'community politics'.

The 1985 county council elections showed exactly how well they had prepared the ground. The Alliance made huge gains right across the country, particularly in the traditionally Tory shires of the south and west. They either gained control or took the balance of power in Cornwall, Devonshire, Wiltshire, Gloucestershire, Hampshire, Sussex and Cambridgeshire. There was a further reason why they managed to capture so many of the shires: they managed to convince a substantial proportion of the electorate that, because of Tory policies, it was they who were subsidising vast and often crazy spending by the left-wing councils in the cities. It was perceived that huge increases in the rates – of up to 20 per cent – were going directly to fund the sort of nonsenses they had come to associate with Brent and Haringey.

These Alliance successes served not only to point up the increasing weaknesses of the Tory party at local government level, but also to give the Alliance a political base from which to fight the 1987 general election. Some Alliance councillors would, of course, have been in place long enough for disillusion with them to have set in, but overall they now had a base in many areas which would make them a greater threat.

Until early in 1987 the evidence was that most of the Tory fall in the polls since 1983 had been picked up by the Alliance, but the polls were fluctuating so wildly that it was difficult to pin down exactly what was happening. It is clear that in March, however, the Alliance began to pick up from Labour, in spite of continuing variations.

The politician or expert who could produce a formula for why people vote one way or another might not die a rich man, but he would have found the key to staying in power forever. As we have seen, if people are asked what are the most important issues, they will give an entirely different set of answers to the ones they give when asked what affects them most. Unemployment was clearly the most 'important' issue in 1983 and the Tories clearly had the worst policies for dealing with it, in the view of the electorate – yet the Tories romped home. What little evidence there is points to the fact that people vote according to how they feel about the parties, rather than what they think about the issues. People switch their vote for a variety of reasons: on impulse, on the feeling that it is time for a change, because they feel the quality of their lives would be better with another party – whatever the reason, they first switch emotionally and then go looking for the policies of the party they have just come to, because they want in the end to vote for something.

The Alliance clearly benefited from these varied reasons for changing votes between 1983 and the spring of 1987, most of all, perhaps, from the feeling that it was time for a change from Mrs Thatcher herself and that her dominating personality was something some people no longer admired enough to vote for her. This feeling was perhaps most strongly felt among what the political commentator Alan Wakins called the 'cultivated classes'

– which he saw as the intellectual bedrock of the Alliance – and which, concentrated as they were in the teaching, social work and communicating professions, tended to have an influence far outweighing their actual numbers.

In early March, the added impact of the number of voters clearly losing patience with Labour and switching to the Alliance, brought it level with, and in one or two polls even in front of, the socialists. The end of the 'cube' relationship of votes to seats had meant, as we have seen, that as long as the leading party was five percentage points ahead of the next one down, it would hold an overall majority. In practice this meant that the Tories could not afford to go under 38 per cent of the vote and really needed to be well above this before they could start thinking of an election, for in the last two elections they had lost five or more points during the campaign.

In simple statistical terms, it did not matter who was second. If, for example, the Tories gained 40 per cent of the vote and 2 per cent went elsewhere, as it traditionally does, then the remaining 58 per cent could be split any way as long as neither of the other two parties went above 35.

There were, however, three factors which caused the Tory nightmares after the Greenwich by-election. First, the obvious one that it would be the start of a bandwagon which would take the Alliance through past the magic 35 per cent barrier. The second was the possibility, increasingly talked about, of tactical voting.

The idea of uniting the anti-Thatcher vote in every constituency in the land was, of course, very appealing to those who could not see any other way of getting the Tories out. Indeed, it was a motley collection of just such people who launched TV 87 at the beginning of February – with the aim of encouraging a mass vote to keep the Tories out in 100 key constituencies. Tactical voting had been used by the Alliance in by-elections, to persuade Tories to vote to keep Labour out and Labour supporters to vote to keep the Tories out. The prospect of using it as a party-sponsored weapon in a general election campaign was, however, seen by the Tories as a pipe dream – unless the Alliance wished to see Labour get in. The problem, as they saw it, was that no overall message could be applicable to every constituency in the land and it was far too complex a message to be tailored to local demands. How many voters would understand a politician who said: 'If you are in a Tory constituency where Labour is second then vote for them, but if you are in a constituency where we are second then vote for us'?

Nevertheless, the Alliance themselves made no bones about their intention to use their direct mail facilities at a local level to encourage tactical voting during the general election campaign – particularly in their 130 target seats, where the skills they used so effectively in Greenwich would, they hoped, bring in votes from Labour to keep Tories out or from Tories to keep Labour out. And the thought that tactical voting might occur spontaneously, even among a tiny percentage of the electorate, could still be damaging to the Tories; it was definitely one of the factors causing sleepless nights as the Alliance surge began.

But it was the third factor which really caused the alarm bells to ring. Early in the year the Tories had commissioned from Gallup a secret in-depth poll of six of their target seats – each a critical constituency to hold on to if they were to win. Among the mass of information about local and national issues and breakdown by age, sex and social class were some staggering statistics pointing to the volatility of the electorate. Of those who had voted Tory at the last election, 8 per cent now firmly intended to vote Alliance, but 29 per cent of those who said they still intended to vote Tory, said that they were 'very likely, or fairly likely' to consider voting Alliance at the next election. It was this factor, coupled with the speed of change of the polls and the huge swings involved, which meant that nothing could now be taken for granted.

If volatility and tactical voting were causing nightmares among the party at large, there was one crumb of comfort in all this which was spotted by a few senior people in CCO and explored carefully and quietly throughout March and April until a position was reached when they could begin to calculate that there could actually be an advantage to be gained in certain circumstances from an Alliance surge in the election. 'It is amazing that no one has so far spotted it,' one senior Tory told me in early April. 'We have certainly kept very quiet about it. But it has shaped our thinking considerably.'

There have been not only urban/suburban/rural changes over the last thirty years, but also regional changes. Wales is more Conservative, Scotland less so, the south and south-east more so, the north and north-east less so. It emerged from the polls in the spring of 1987 that there have been further and significant regional variations since 1983. A Marplan poll for the Press Association in April, which gave the Tories 40 per cent, Labour 30 and Alliance 27, confirmed these regional changes. And on a rough calculation, it was claimed, a region-by-region breakdown would give the Tories a 100-seat majority – twice that which they would get if the calculation was made simply on the overall national figures.

Some of the regional variations were quite startling. London was about the same as the 1983 figure; but in the rest of the south-east the Tories were 5 per cent down to the Alliance. The Tories had lost 2 per cent to each of the other parties in the south-west, but were 2 per cent up in East Anglia. In both the East and West Midlands they were up – by 1 and 2 per cent respectively. In Wales they were up by 6 per cent, but in the north-west they were down by the same amount, the loss being evenly spread over the Alliance and Labour. In Yorkshire and Humberside they were 3 per cent down, and in the north and in Scotland 4 per cent down – the bulk of the switch going to Labour in each case.

In other words, Labour was picking up, by and large, where it did not really matter. Solid Labour seats were becoming more so. Only in the north-west, of the crucial areas, were the Tories in any serious danger – and much of that swing was likely to be in the already firmly Labour city centres. In any case there were signs that overall the Alliance were picking up as much as Labour.

Other polls at this time showed a further factor, partly attributable to the regional variations but partly also a sign of the better groundwork by the Tories than by the other parties in more narrowly contested seats. In these marginals the Tories were overall doing better than the other parties.

When all these snippets and clues were put together – and remembering the fact that Labour was second in nearly all the crucial seats in the north-west and the Midlands – an interesting scenario emerged. Suppose, as began to happen in March and April, that the Tories were to move steadily up above 40 per cent and manage to hold it there. And suppose that, as happened in 1983 and after Greenwich, the Alliance came surging up at the expense of Labour. Would this make the Tories too unhappy? The answer, worked out in CCO, was almost certainly not. In fact it would make them very happy.

They called it the 'Two-for-One' factor and the piece of arithmetic on which it was based was simple: take three seats, one in the south, where in 1983 the vote was Tory 40 per cent, Alliance 35 per cent and Labour 20 per cent; one in the Midlands, where in 1983 Labour had 40 per cent, Tory 35 per cent and Alliance 20 per cent; one in the north, where in 1983 Labour had 42 per cent, Tory 35 per cent and Alliance 22 per cent. Now suppose (for the sake of simple arithmetic) there is a 10 per cent shift to Alliance from Labour. Take 10 per cent off each of the Labour votes above and add it on to the Alliance vote. The effect is startling: the Tories lose the seat in the south to the Alliance, but gain two in the north from Labour.

The figures here are deliberately exaggerated to show the effect of what they calculated could happen in an election on a widespread scale and at a roughly corresponding rate. The Tories could end up with only one seat lost for every two gained. 'We might well find ourselves losing a few in the suburbs of London and in the south-west, but does that matter if we are picking up twice as many elsewhere?' one senior CCO figure told me, and the figures confirm his theory. If the switch were straight Labour to Alliance of 5 per cent – without taking Marplan's regional advantages into account – the Alliance would gain 12 seats, but the Tories 25. A straight 10 per cent switch would give the Alliance 25 more seats, but the Tories 57.

A signpost of how this effect might work could be seen, but went largely unnoticed, in the two by-elections held in mid-March. First, in the Parliamentary by-election in Truro, the young Matthew Taylor kept the seat for the Liberals. The Tory share of the vote fell by only 6.6 per cent and Labour came nowhere. Much of that swing to the Liberals was put down to the sympathy vote after the death of David Penhaligon, the sitting member. However, a week earlier, in the Euro by-election in Midlands West, which covers eight Parliamentary constituencies, the Tories had come within 500 votes of overthrowing the Labour majority – a significant rise in their share of the poll and a key pointer to their general election hopes in the region. The Alliance did better in this poll than they had done last time. In other words the Alliance had done better in both polls at the expense of Labour – and, as a result, had very nearly given the Tories a Euro-seat.

The signs were noted in CCO, but what was not known was how this 'Two-for-One' factor would be assisted by the helpful regional variations which had shown up and by the better Tory vote in the marginals. Or how it might be hindered by the slight drop in the Tory vote to the Alliance which could be expected anyway. As April drew to a close, however, Michael Dobbs began to work on a vast model which would take all these factors into account, and which would, when the time came to decide whether to go in June or not, be unique in being able to predict more accurately than any other system available to any pollster or rival political party what exactly was likely to happen across the country.

Whatever quiet confidence there may have been at CCO at these encouraging signs, there was no such calm within the party at large. In 1983 the problem of the Alliance had also reared its head but, under the guidance of Cecil Parkinson, it had been disposed of by ignoring it. Several advertisements had been prepared by Saatchi – including one which made cheeky reference to Roy Jenkins's fondness for claret – but they had stayed on the shelf.

In the wake of Greenwich and Truro, and with some of the polls showing the Alliance leaders moving temporarily into second place, such complacency could no longer be contemplated. But how to deal with the threat? The Alliance are traditionally difficult for the Tories to attack because they are, in effect, three separate targets: Liberal, SDP and Alliance. For example, nearly half the Liberal candidates at the general election would be supporters of CND, yet the difference on unilateral disarmament was the very reason why David Owen and his colleagues left the Labour Party in the first place. The two parties had fundamental differences on many issues and, as the Tories saw it, a third policy, cobbled together as the 'Alliance', was an attempt to reconcile them.

The Tories' problem was further compounded by the public perception of the Alliance as being fundamentally 'nice' people. You might think Mrs Thatcher very effective as a Prime Minister, but you would not want to have her to dinner. You might think Neil Kinnock nowhere near as effective, and you might have him to dinner. David Owen was not only effective, you would also have him to dinner. That was how the public saw them – but it was not how the politicians saw them. The leaders of the Conservative Party, particularly the Prime Minister and Norman Tebbit, had spent their entire lives attacking the Labour Party and found themselves, initially at least in the spring of 1987, temperamentally unsuited to do anything but attack the Alliance in the same terms.

However, the belief in CCO and the upper levels of the party was that all was not lost. If the Tories were losing some votes to the Alliance, then it was a safe presumption that they were going either because of the 'time for a change' factor or because distaste for Mrs Thatcher's style was overcoming people's admiration for her achievements. A strong restatement of her leadership, of her beliefs, her vision and the policies she still hoped to introduce would, it was thought, soon put this right. Indeed the emergence of the Prime Minister as leader, as visionary and as a politician with a lot still to do, was to be one of the phenomena of the spring. So successful was she to be that she virtually hijacked the 'time for a change' factor and made it the Tory party's own. It was the others, as the polls showed, who began to look tired and old.

For the Tories, having established their own clear sense of purpose, it then became easier to point to the lack of direction in the Alliance by questioning them closely on their policies. If, and when, they moved into second place, it would become even more imperative for them to have clear policies. In effect, the belief was, they would trap themselves: by claiming the right to be taken more seriously, they would find that they were indeed given more credit and, accordingly, challenged more firmly on everything they planned to do. However, the danger of the Alliance had always been thought to be that the more it was taken seriously, the more exposure it got and the more its share of the polls went up. Therefore the Tories now had to tread a very fine line between attacking, but attacking in the right tone (it was no use calling them all socialists or heaping abuse on them as they were used to doing with Labour), and not attacking so much that it took the electorate's eye off the main ball. Norman Tebbit's pursuit of David Steel from Truro to London, and his final 'Newsnight' confrontation with him on his policies was reckoned, in the party, to have been a major vote-winner: nevertheless, it took a while to get what seemed to be the correct balance; and it was not achieved without a certain amount of over-stepping the mark and back-pedalling. Nor was it achieved without a good deal of criticism – especially in the panicky days at the end of March when David Owen seemed to be putting the pressure on for a May election. To the Tories there was every reason why he should want to move on quickly from Greenwich and Truro to the main event: it would maintain the momentum of the two parliamentary by-elections and preserve the illusion of substance in the Alliance policies and, with the destruction of the Labour party, it would deliver the consequent realignment of the centre–left of the political spectrum into his hands.

The last thing he wanted, those at CCO were certain, was time for the Tory vote to go down below 38 per cent with the consequence that there was a hung Parliament. A deal with either party could only, in the long term, cause him more headaches than it cured – as the Liberals had found out after 1979. It was in his interests, as well as those of the Tories, to beat Labour thoroughly. This was a point made embarrassingly publicly by Neville Sandelson – a former MP, founder member of the SDP and close colleague of David Owen. He actively encouraged SDP supporters to vote Tory – in hope of a trouncing of Labour that would leave the SDP as the focus of the subsequent regrouping of the centre–left. The Tories felt that Owen must secretly agree with this and therefore, from his perspective, it was best to press for an election now.

There were many in the party who felt that not even Mrs Thatcher got either the tone or the content quite right in her first major attack on the Alliance – at the party's Central Council (its other annual conference) towards the end of March. She attacked

Labour as being full-blooded socialists, the SDP as half-hearted socialists and the Liberals as half-baked socialists. 'What of the Labour Party in exile?' she asked. 'By which of course I mean the Liberals and the SDP? In the last year or so in the House of Commons they have voted eight times more often with Labour than with us. Not much doubt where their sympathies lie.'

This pattern and tone was amplified somewhat a few days later by Norman Tebbit when he opened an exhibition in Central Office aimed at reminding the world that it was the tenth anniversary of the Lib–Lab pact and strongly implying that the Liberals were responsible for the 'winter of discontent'. Fellow MPs who had admired his performance against Steel were frankly incredulous that such crude methods were being used in what should have been a skilled piece of surgery to separate former or potential voters from the Alliance and reattach them to the Tories. The political commentator Bruce Anderson reminded the Tories of an Iain Macleod saying about the Liberals, which was the sort of tone they should now be using with the Alliance: 'The Liberals have some good ideas and some new ideas. The only trouble is none of their good ideas are new. And none of their new ideas are any good.' It was this sort of light, ironic tone which many in the party thought was needed – the sort of tone that, if you could not hear John Biffen saying it, then you should not say it, Anderson concluded, summing up their views admirably.

Amidst the bickering, the Tebbit camp made it clear that there was at least a method in what was being interpreted as their madness. They pointed out that it was no use continuing to treat the Alliance as the old party of protest and dismissing it out of hand right up until the day, five days before the election, when it suddenly appeared in second place in the polls. By that time it would be too late to start taking it seriously. Any change of approach at the last minute would, quite rightly, be seen as a panic reaction and almost certainly accelerate the Alliance bandwagon, instead of halting it in its tracks. The time, they argued, had come to take the third party seriously, and to start questioning what its policies were. After all, the story of the election, as far as the media were concerned, was quite likely to be the story of who came second. It was, to most people in newspapers and television, a foregone conclusion that Mrs Thatcher would win, and the only point of remaining interest was already emerging as the future of the Labour Party in the wake of its third defeat. It was necessary, therefore, to have on record a clear line of attack on both of the other parties, laid down and established well before the last week of the campaign.

Nobody argued with that: it was essential to start separating the leaders of the Alliance from their supporters – particularly those who had drifted there from the Tory party. And the only way to do this was to start questioning their policies, so that the supporters would start doubting the policies themselves. What was wrong, it was widely agreed, was the tone of the attack.

Whether this would improve, whether others than the party chairman would be encouraged to spearhead an attack on the Alliance; whether Norman Tebbit would be discouraged from joining the fray again; even whether it would have been better to have ignored the Alliance altogether on the grounds that the historic collapse of the Labour Party, so long prophesied, was not quite yet ready for its denouement – all remained to be seen.

What was in no doubt was that the party should be prepared for an Alliance surge in the last days of the campaign – it would be foolish to be caught out. It was therefore, in great secrecy, that alongside the plans for the press conferences and themes to be tackled towards the end of the election campaign – all of which were expected to be a triumphal climax – Michael Dobbs sat down to construct another, altogether different, hypothesis.

It was one for where the backs were against the wall; one to deal with the ultimate Tory nightmare – of an Alliance bandwagon which had rolled right over Labour and was heading out of control for the Tories. It was Greenwich happening nationally. It was the Doomsday Scenario.

5 | The October Men and the June Woman

At 9 a.m. on Tuesday 17 March there began a series of meetings in Central Office and in Downing Street which were to transform the management of the Tory election campaign, changing the direction and nature of parts of it out of all recognition. The meetings were hurried – the Budget Cabinet was due to start at 10.30 a.m. – but nevertheless decisive.

First, Lord Young called on Norman Tebbit at CCO to tell him, as a matter of courtesy, that he was formally going to offer the Prime Minister his help in the campaign. The chat was friendly if noncommittal; both men knew that there was little point in being otherwise until it was seen what Mrs Thatcher would offer her Secretary of State for Employment. Lord Young was then driven to Downing Street, where he was due to see the Prime Minister at 9.30 for one of their regular bi-laterals. He was immediately shown into her study on the first floor, where she was waiting, and for the next twenty minutes the two discussed the role she wanted him to play in the forthcoming election. She then asked him to say nothing about it until she had had a chance to tell Norman Tebbit, which she said would be after the Cabinet meeting. However, a few minutes later Young was called back to her study, where he found the Party Chairman with her, and she immediately said: 'Norman, I have been talking to David and I would like him to help.' She then outlined what she had in mind.

She made it clear that she thought Lord Young could assist with several of the crucial areas of the campaign about which she still had worries. To start with she wanted him to get to grips with the programme for 'Thatcher tours', which had become a continuing saga of dissatisfaction between Number 10 and CCO. This, however, was only the beginning and over the next few weeks it was to emerge that, in effect, the Prime Minister had decided to divide the campaign in two. Norman Tebbit and Central Office would continue to run the fight to get the Tories re-elected in the country and he would continue to be the figurehead of that fight as Party Chairman. But her side of it would increasingly be run by Lord Young, who would also occasionally act as a buffer between her and Central Office, passing on her wishes and assisting in the execution of them.

David Young's insertion into the campaign at this point could have been a stunning blow to the chairman, as nasty an affront as it is possible to imagine. But, surprisingly, he welcomed it warmly at the time, although in the next few days there was some initial standoffishness between them, as a result of which Lord Young went out of his way to make it clear, first to the chairman that his presence in CCO did not require a title or status, but was merely that of adviser and lubricator of the system, and second to the media that it was Norman Tebbit's idea. There was one immediate advantage to Tebbit in welcoming Lord Young's arrival: it could just help take the heat off him. For some time now relations between the Prime Minister and himself had, once again, not been the most cordial. He was finding it increasingly difficult to induce her to focus on making many of the decisions necessary to get the early stages of the campaign under way, while she was becoming less satisfied with the work coming out of CCO. According to critics across the whole spectrum of the party – and there were plenty of them – it was emerging that not only did Norman Tebbit not have the management style required to get the best out of Smith Square, but Michael Dobbs, for all that he was a highly paid executive of Saatchi, lacked the necessary political skills. It was no way to run the place, the critics said, to do everything so secretively behind closed doors. The running of a political campaign had, by its very nature, to be an open process with everyone at its centre, knowing what everyone else was doing and feeling free to join in the debate. Logjams of untaken decisions had built up and the preparations for the election were in danger of falling damagingly behind.

In a long talk about the difficulties between the Prime Minister and Party Chairman, one close acquaintance of Mrs Thatcher told me at the time: 'The problem is that she knows she should have moved Norman last autumn, while there was still time. But now it is too late and she is having to live with the consequences of her inaction – and that, in itself, is making her more irritable. She feels Norman still has marvellous qualities, but he is not, and may never have been, a good manager – not many politicians are good managers anyway. Whatever the reasons, the fact is that, here and now, she feels he just is not capable of running Central Office the way she wants. But she feels guilty about him and reluctant to blame him. Every time she thinks about it, she thinks of Margaret Tebbit and wonders how she would feel if it was Denis who was a quadraplegic. A man would have eased Norman out; but she couldn't bring herself to do it. There are many strengths, being a woman, that she brings to the office of Prime Minister, but this – if you can call it one – is one of the weaknesses.

'She fears she might lose the election if she does nothing, but does not see much she can do. Norman insists that he and Dobbs can run it themselves, and that they don't need any of the "old team" around. She thinks it's all in danger of falling apart and feels vulnerable without the support of people she knows and trusts to tell her the truth. It's getting to the stage now, that if she wants to consult anyone else about the election, they almost have to be sneaked in past the dustbins at dead of night for fear of Norman finding out. It may be that Norman is right, that there is no need to have anyone else involved, that they are on top of it all at CCO, that the bottlenecks are inevitable and only temporary – but at election times it's all hands on deck and you get help from anyone who has something to offer. To turn everyone away like this, is a hell of a risk to take *and* it makes her feel very exposed.'

Her solution to the problem, as she outlined it to Lord Young and Norman Tebbit on Budget Day, came, ironically, at the instigation of one of the very people the chairman believed best kept out of the campaign – Tim Bell. Two weeks earlier, on Monday 2 March, Lord Young had had dinner at the White Tower with his Special Adviser, Howell James, and Bell. The three had been friends for some time – Young had recommended Bell to Ian MacGregor during the miners' strike; Bell had recommended James to Young when he first became Minister without Portfolio. James, despite his natural ebullience and popular broadcasting past as one-time head of promotions and publicity at Capital Radio – before cutting his teeth on such nightmare causes as PR chief at TV-AM for its first two years – had taken to Whitehall like the proverbial duck to water and he and Lord Young had formed a very close professional relationship.

Over dinner the three men gossiped about the issues of the day and the problems of the coming election. David Young already knew that the March fall in unemployment was likely to be one of the biggest yet – and that his department was on target to drop below three million in the summer. This meant he could devote a little more time to political work outside the department and he speculated how best his talents could be used in the campaign – especially since he had no seat to fight.

He sounded Bell out about what he should do and found his suggestion that he offer the Prime Minister his services wherever she could best deploy them accorded with what he already had in mind. In the next week he did so, reinforcing the message with a telephone call to her at Chequers on Sunday 15 March giving her the first news that the fall in unemployment for the month would be more than 70,000. She gave him no indication then what she might have in mind, although they did discuss her general anxieties about the state of the preparations.

All three parties to the conversation two days later could see the benefit of 'selling' Lord Young's appointment as Norman Tebbit's idea. Indeed, on reflection, the advantages of it to the chairman were not just in deflecting the heat from him – there were many more: Lord Young was an old friend of his – it was Tebbit who brought him into the MSC, where they had not only worked well together but, with Peter Morrison, had formed a formidable trio. As a peer he was, in terms of ambition if nothing else, no threat to Tebbit; he could never be Prime Minister. He clearly did have the time to spare and his formidable management ability might just fit in well, help get things moving and ease the CCO team over some of the rocky ground ahead. It would, of course, help everyone to have, next to the Prime Minister, someone with whom she felt comfortable – particularly someone Tebbit could trust. Provided it was seen to be his idea and not something pressed upon him, it could only benefit the campaign, which, if it was successful and the Tories were re-elected, would, as it traditionally does, make a hero of the Party Chairman.

Nevertheless, the need to 'sell' the idea as Norman Tebbit's reveals something of the level of insecurity that nearly all senior politicians suffer. It is not just a phenomenon of the Tory party; the jostling and constant vying for position is endemic at the top of all parties. The rivalry and backstabbing among the Tories only seems worse currently for two reasons: firstly, the leader is a woman – so the battle for favour has a sexual component. There is real jealousy of the men like Cecil Parkinson and Tim Bell, who appear to have an ability with her that others lack. Secondly, she has been leader for more than twelve years and therefore a logjam of aspirants has built up beneath her.

Most politicians enter the business with the idea in mind that they might one day become Prime Minister. To get above the 'snow-line' and into a ministerial post, or even the Cabinet, does nothing to assuage ambition, in fact it fuels it. What is more, the level of egotism required to get on in politics is such that the higher the politician goes the worse the infighting becomes. Egos and reputations take dreadful batterings as every move of one politician is analysed by his enemies (which is most of the rest) for flaws and signs of weakness. A lot of it is very hurtful; much is grossly unfair – if not untrue; but they all do it to one another so, in a sense, they all deserve it.

Mrs Thatcher is known to be a tough infighter herself on occasion, but is for the most part above the fray. Below her, however, there is a constant swirl of rumour – the currency of politics – and gossip as to who is 'in', who is 'out', whose star is shining, who has weakened his chances, who has been offended or even humiliated by the very sort of thing which, if it were not presented properly, could be deemed now to have happened to the Party Chairman.

In fact there are two levels at which the entire Tory campaign could be judged. The public relations version is that it was a team effort, in which players performed under great stress and occasionally fell out, but mostly worked together; in the political version, everyone, while ostensibly playing the team game, was busy also kicking members of his own side and trying to be in the spotlight as much of the time as possible, if not actually scoring the goals. With a few notable exceptions it was rapidly emerging that the latter version was more true than the former. But for the moment Norman Tebbit was 'squared'; Lord Young was the only person who could never be a threat to him, and everyone was happy.

For the Prime Minister particularly, the inclusion of her Secretary of State for Employment in the campaign was the perfect solution to several of the problems which had been causing her anxiety – most notably that she now had someone with whom she felt at ease, to handle that most tricky of assignments, her own personal campaign. This, in itself, reveals some of her insecurities and need for reassurance. Lord Young immediately took a close personal interest in the arrangements for her tour, and was soon asked also to take charge of the design, presentation and launch of the manifesto, and then to arrange his own input into the party political broadcasts during the campaign. If she could not have Cecil Parkinson back and involved centrally – a move which even he had lately been cautioning as unwise and potentially demeaning for Tebbit in his present mood and at this late hour (although Parkinson still saw the Prime Minister from time to time and was pencilled in for extensive television and a major speaking tour during the campaign) – then she had possibly done just as well with David Young. His undoubted ability as a practical manager had caused great culture shock, but then great admiration, at the Department of Employment. If there were failures at Central Office, and if they were not terminal, then at least he would have a chance of being able to get to grips with them. His intense concentration on the problem in hand might, at first, cause offence in Smith Square, but his capacity to make light of his own intensity and to encourage those around him to even greater efforts, might also be just the approach the place needed.

One person who was not at all happy with David Young's appointment, when he first heard of it, was Michael Dobbs; but this was only short-lived and came about because of a mishearing on a carphone. Immediately after the Budget Cabinet meeting

Tebbit rang CCO from his car to tell Peter Morrison and Dobbs the news. He was put through to Morrison, who called Dobbs in to his office to hear what was said. Dobbs mistook his boss talking about David Young for another David, for whom he has more than a mild loathing, and he interrupted Tebbit to say: 'I don't want to be difficult, but he is not coming here to work as part of this team – because if he does one member of this team – me – is not going to be here. There is no way I will work with him.' It took five minutes of arguing to realise that they were talking at cross purposes.

There was genuine and more long-lasting anxiety at all levels of the parliamentary party. The 'sell' had not totally worked there and to many MPs the conclusion was inescapable that Lord Young had been brought in because of some inherent weakness in either the personnel or the plans at CCO. It was pointed out that it had not been thought necessary in either 1979 or 1983 to graft on to the campaign at the last moment anyone of his stature and that therefore there must be some problem of which they were not aware. Others doubted whether even Young's considerable managerial skills would be able to make much difference to the inherent problems within Smith Square. While he might well be invaluable in keeping the Prime Minister happy and soothing her anxieties, he could do little at this late hour to tackle the creaking machinery of the party election juggernaut, which they feared could collapse if the pressure really came on during the campaign. Some but not all of their criticisms were echoed in anxieties within CCO, particularly that Lord Young's arrival on the scene might not in itself do anything to help get the machinery through the stresses and strains of a rough campaign. There were those who began to worry that the party might have been better off if Central Office had after all been reorganised in 1986 and a proper system of line management instituted.

Anxieties within the party as an election approaches are of course perfectly natural, but the fears at this time ran deeper than they had in 1983, principally the fear that time was running out if there was to be an election in the summer. While the position of the Prime Minister and the government had improved enormously over the last year, they were still nowhere near where they needed to be if they were to tackle a four-week campaign with any confidence. The feeling among many, in both Westminster and Smith Square, was that there was not only a dangerous complacency about the Alliance in the upper levels of the government, not only was Central Office not ready, but also that Mrs Thatcher and her ministers should be making much greater efforts to sell her leadership qualities and their achievements to the country as a whole. There were those who could see real dangers in the belief, widely held, that Neil Kinnock would fall apart at the first whiff of grape-shot, that the Alliance were just a bunch of socialists and that all the country was simply longing for the chance to vote the Tories back into power. The polls, it was pointed out, still did not show the party consistently over the 40 per cent needed to be confident of a working majority, and they were certainly nothing like the high forties that the party had been scoring in March 1983.

Some, but by no means all, of these fears were allayed by three events in the rest of March and early April, which the Tories would describe as 'goals' and one which they would call a Labour 'own goal'. Together they did much to change the public perception of the Prime Minister and the government and, by their anticipated effect on the polls, caused the balance of opinion within the party to swing heavily towards an early election.

First: the dramatic drop in unemployment, predicted by Lord Young in his Sunday telephone call to the Prime Minister at Chequers and well signposted in the press over the next few days, gave a glimpse to the party, for the first time, that it might be able to go into the election with the rate hovering around or even below three million. As we have seen, the effect that this would have on the debate about all the government's policies would be enormous. In February, Lord Young, who was still by instinct an October man (he wanted to go into an election campaign with unemployment below three million and falling), had sent Mrs Thatcher a graph showing the anticipated fall in the jobless total through the year. The three million mark was due to be passed on 18 June – too late for 11 June, which was already seen as the best date in that month. Nevertheless the impact of the drop – for the sixth month running – was enormous.

Second: Nigel Lawson's Budget – delivered in the afternoon

of 17 March, the day Mrs Thatcher, Norman Tebbit and Lord Young had had their meeting – was, to the Tories, a major indication that the economic revival of the country was well and truly under way. A measure of that recovery could be seen in the ability of the Chancellor to introduce what he called a 'remarkable hat-trick' of measures: he cut taxes, reduced borrowing and increased public expenditure, all in one Budget. It had been an extraordinary turnaround in fortunes for him, too, since the previous autumn, when he had been faced with a sterling crisis and a sudden lack of confidence in his abilities. Now his enemies were ruefully talking of 'Lawson's Luck', with all the factors coming right at the right time. After so long waiting for the corner to be turned, suddenly he seemed to have the ability to do so much that would be so attractive to the electorate. The tax cuts would not show up in pay packets until mid-May, but this was seen to be an advantage for those who were already beginning to clamour for a June election – especially since they might well coincide with a cut in the mortgage rate. However, it was the increases in public spending – confirming the figures worked out the previous autumn – which drew most quiet satisfaction within the party; they meant that candidates would not have to go to the hustings with an empty cupboard to show in the crucial areas of the Health Service and education. The government's claim to have spent 25 per cent more in real terms on the NHS since 1979 could be seen to be part of a continuing commitment to tackle its problems.

It was the third Tory 'goal' – a solo dribble from deep in her own half – which was far and away the most spectacular. The Prime Minister's extraordinary trip to Russia at the end of March had a stunning impact both in Britain and in the host country. Weeks afterwards the Russians were still arguing over the live television interview she gave in which she trounced their interviewers, who were clearly used to being much more formal with their guests and not at all used to the combative, outspoken woman they came up against.

But it was not so much the hours of talks – during which she and Mikhail Gorbachev frequently argued themselves to a standstill – nor the prearranged and carefully stage-managed meeting with Russian dissidents, nor the electrifying effect of her presence on Russian crowds who flocked to see her and to meet her on her walkabouts, nor her TV interview, nor any of the other individual things she did which was the reason for the huge impact the visit had. Nor indeed was it that no Prime Minister – or, for that matter any head of state anywhere – had put as much preparation into a visit to another country as she put into this one. (She had one all-day briefing of mind-numbing complexity and many other lesser sessions, as well as reading mountains of documents including all Gorbachev's speeches.) The reason why the visit captured the imagination as it did was not even a mathematical aggregate of the impact of all these things, but more that they were all spun together by her into what was clearly a personal *tour de force*. Journalists with no liking at all for her came back from Moscow saying that they had never witnessed anything like it. It was clear she had had a profound effect on Gorbachev, which was matched by her words – that she understood him and could trust him. It was clear also she had had an equally profound effect on the world's media.

There was another factor which Tories and many others believed raised the trip's status to that of the historic. Mrs Thatcher was in Moscow, not as the Prime Minister of, say, the Britain of the late 1970s – the leader of a nation which had many years before pioneered the nuclear club, but had since fallen far behind in almost every measure of international prestige imaginable and was hanging on by its fingertips to its position at the conference tables of the world – but as the leader of a nation which was demonstrably back on its feet again, as the longest serving and most experienced leader of any major nation in the world, as the spokeswoman for Western Europe and, as the friend and confidante of President Reagan, speaking power-fully and persuasively for the West.

Suddenly the slightly over-the-top slogan Central Office were having 'tested' among groups as a possible for the election campaign itself did not seem so far-fetched. There was a feeling that it really was 'Great to be Great Again'. Britain was back on the map – and that to jubilant Tories was the true impact of what she achieved in her five-day visit. In an uncertain world Britain was once again providing, through Mrs Thatcher, the certain leadership that was needed.

Whatever the truth of the alleged media distortion and precisely however many minutes it was that Neil Kinnock had spent
with President Reagan the week before, his American visit could
not help but look weak by comparison; and the subsequent
bickering over who exactly did and said what on the trip was
seen in Smith Square as most definitely an 'own goal'. Kinnock,
they thought, was made to look second, if not third, division.
Coming as it did hard on the heels of Greenwich and the
well-publicised fears at the top of the party that the 'loony left'
– particularly the gay and lesbian elements – were irretrievably
damaging its chances at the polls, it gave further fuel to the
feeling that Labour was not just going to lose the election but
was in for its third devastating defeat in a row. Reports began
to leak out that all was not well in the Kinnock camp. Just as a
year before it had been Mrs Thatcher who was said to have
taken to the bunker, now Kinnock's staff were said to have
sealed him off from reality.

By comparison, the evidence of her transformation in the
eyes of the party and many in the country was remarkable. In
November 1986 she had given an interview to the *Financial
Times* in which she had talked of leading the Tories through one
or two more terms – the time it would take to 'eliminate socialism
as a second force in British politics'. At the time, as with so many
of her beliefs, it had seemed too distant a horizon to be seriously
contemplated. It was not the sort of thing politicians are meant
to say. They are meant to want to hang on to power at the next
election, not have extraordinary visions of the future. But now,
suddenly, to the Tories this also did not seem too extravagant a
claim: the horizon was nearer than they thought. It seemed to
them she had an almost uncanny ability – an extra gear not
available to other politicians, which she had demonstrated in
Moscow – which enabled her to bring distant goals nearer, or
at least to persuade people that they were nearer.

Many people close to her mentioned this ability to me during
the preparation of this book: several described it as 'uncanny'.
At the risk of being accused of hagiography, let me quote one of
her most senior Cabinet Ministers: 'She is the most incredible
human being I know. Difficult – absolutely. She drives you mad
at times. But I have never come across anybody who has caused

me to admire them as much as she does. She is outstanding.
There is no other word for it. I don't say that she is not occasionally wrong – but often when she appears wrong to me, events
have a habit of proving her right. It's uncanny how lucky she is, if
that is what you call it.'

It appeared also from the polls that she had managed to
persuade the electorate out of the fashionable view, held through
the years of consensus politics, that there was somehow a distant
shore – a heaven on earth – to which one party or the other
could be trusted to bring the populace safely. Her bald statements
that there were no easy solutions had lowered people's expectations. We were, under her steady leadership, involved in something more akin to Star Trek than a Calais–Dover crossing. It
was this subtle switch of emphasis which enabled her – after
nearly eight years in office – to end her speech to the Institute of
Directors at the end of February with the words: 'This is a
government which has work *yet* to do. And it is my hope and
dream that we may complete the task to which we have set our
hand.'

Was this an ambition that the public shared, sympathised with
– or even understood? We would need to study the polls in the
coming weeks to answer that and to find out what had been the
effect of the Moscow trip. Not that she places very great faith
in the polls – on the surface. She acknowledges that they are
only snapshots of opinion taken at a particular time – not a
pointer to future behaviour. She knows that they are subject to
variation and that – as she is fond of saying – 'There is only one
opinion poll that counts and that is the vote itself.' Yet she is the
only leader in the Western world regularly to measure her image
on a weekly assessment and circulate it round her Cabinet. She,
like all political leaders, values the polls as pointers and the
private tracking studies that Gallup do for the Tories are a
constant and invaluable guide to how both she and the party are
doing.

It must therefore have been a slight disappointment to her
and to many in the party that after the Budget, the unemployment figures, the razzmatazz of Moscow and the collapse of
Labour, the party did not do much better in the polls. True, in
all but a few the Tories established themselves over 40 per cent,

but only just over – not the 45-plus they had secretly been hoping for.

There are, of course, variations between opinion polls. Most of them are carried out in conjunction with commercial market research on specific products or services, and it is believed to make a difference where in the order of questions the political ones come: those with them at the beginning are known as 'cold start polls', those placing them at the end as 'warm start'. The same terms, and slight differences in results, are found in relation to the order in which the political questions are asked. In other words, is voting intention put at the beginning or the end? Marplan, which is carried out mid-week, is reckoned to have a slight Conservative bias. (Not for any political reason, but because many more of the people at home and out and about on the streets are Conservative housewives. Although this is weighted against in the the findings, it is felt in the profession that it still gives a percentage point or two of bias.) Gallup, which is conducted over weekends, is felt to go the other way and consistently to downgrade the Tories by a point or two to the benefit of the Alliance. Telephone polls – advantageous because they can be completed quickly – have fallen under a good deal of suspicion, principally because they are, after all, only polls of people who own telephones.

All the parties commission their own private polls. The Tories use two companies at election time – Gallup to do their weekly national tracking studies and Harris, from March onwards in 1987, to do a parallel fortnightly tracking study in their 72 target seats. From the beginning the Harris results were more promising in the target seats than the extrapolation of the national polls indicated.

Newspapers and television stations pay anything up to £6000 for a poll – a total of £5 million a year – but, particularly as elections approach, they can be seen as a better and better investment; every poll gets mentions in most of the other papers and in the television and radio newscasts, gaining the company that sponsors it hundreds of thousands of pounds worth of free publicity. However, there was some concern in the spring of 1987 that all this polling – 52 were published in the month of the election campaign in 1983 – could, at a time when the electorate was clearly volatile, actually have an effect on the result itself. Research at the 1983 election showed that between 2 and 4 per cent of people changed their votes as a result of the polls, with a slight tendency to move away from the top and bottom parties towards the middle. This time the pollsters themselves believed as many as 10 per cent of voters could change their minds as a result of what they read the polls were saying.

The political parties, particularly the Alliance, have not been slow to exploit this factor and, as we saw in Greenwich, they were able to start their bandwagon rolling, simply by saying it was rolling. In mid-April one SDP MP was hawking around the offices of Fleet Street the results of a totally bogus report which was, he said, a private Tory poll. It purported to show the Alliance catching up on the Tories, and that was why they were trying to keep it quiet. No paper published it and it was seen in CCO as a desperate attempt to keep the Alliance in second place by pretending that it actually was. By this time, however, it was clear the party was on its way back to third spot after the successes of Greenwich and Truro.

Another area where so-called 'dirty tricks' were anticipated was direct mail. During March and early April, Norman Tebbit had spent a great deal of time with lawyers, trying to get from them a firm opinion as to where the party stood legally with its plans. He was aware that the other parties were planning to invest considerable time and money in direct mailing initially – Labour, at least, without apparently seeking legal advice on what they were doing.

Having spent large sums of money preparing a massive direct mail campaign of their own, the Tories did not want to abandon the project. The law on the subject is highly complex and direct mailing was not invented when it was written. However, broadly, it says that all election expenditure is divided into national and local headings. Local advertising for individual constituencies – or groups of them – has to be paid for out of the local constituency budget, which averaged around £4500 in 1983. National expenditure must be just that: if it is in newspapers or on hoardings they must be national papers and on a spread of hoardings all over the country – not concentrated in marginal constituencies as the Tories understood Labour were planning. Nor may national advertising refer to any local areas, candidates or issues, with the exception of Scotland, where reference to Scottish issues may be made.

Not only is it, the Tories discovered, illegal to send local doctors in, say, Reading, a local message referring to Reading candidates or the Reading area, unless that message is agreed in writing beforehand by the candidate and charged on his election expenses, but also it is illegal to send doctors nationally a national message, even if it makes no reference at all to any local issue or candidate, without charging it locally to each individual constituency, for the law says that because not everyone has access to the message it is not, technically, a national message. With so much at stake and the law having so many grey areas, Tebbit and Dobbs therefore asked for an urgent and full legal briefing on what they wanted to do, and the other parties seemed hell-bent on doing. It was to take many meetings and hours of wrangling in March and April before a clear picture began to emerge and then it was, to say the least, disappointing, for it appeared that all attempts at direct mailing on a national basis would be illegal unless charged locally. Thus, reluctantly, the Tories had to abandon their plans; they heard a few days later that the Alliance had done the same.

In examining and raising the issue, Norman Tebbit also drew the attention of the other parties to possible breaches of the law in the concentration of poster sites in marginal constituencies and the use of them by interested parties for political purposes. The local government union NALGO was known to be planning posters for the general election and the legality of this was questioned too.

The verdict on direct mail did not affect the Tories' 72 target seats, where local constituency parties had planned extensive use of it. In most other respects, too, progress in these seats had kept up to the objectives set for them in the winter. Most of them had sitting members as candidates, but a handful of 'new boys' had gone through the obstacle course that is the route to a Tory seat in the House, and a few were still going through it.

With a total of 40 sitting members retiring and about 110 new candidates in other constituencies in England and Wales, the selection procedure had been working overtime since the summer of 1986, under Tom Arnold MP, the party vice-chairman in charge of candidates. Just to be considered as a candidate is a process involving two separate 'boards', one of which assesses applicants over an entire weekend. Acceptance by them puts the hopeful on to the approved candidates list which is published by CCO and consists, at any one time, of no more than 750 names. You cannot be considered unless you are on this list, or you apply merely to be considered on a once and once only basis for your local seat.

No candidate stands much of a chance of securing a winnable seat until he or she has fought through the rough-and-tumble of one or two hopeless cases and then a doubtful marginal or a by-election. At all stages the candidate is assessed and reports on him or her go into a personal file at CCO. It is these files, and the guidance of Tom Arnold, which is used in helping local constituency associations make up their minds about which to choose of the 20 or 30 applicants they might get.

By the spring of 1987, most of the candidates were selected – there were 150 new ones in England and Wales, of whom 70 had fought before – and their training had begun. The Tories do more than the other parties to prepare their candidates for the campaign. The vast majority of them would have been to week-end schools and to at least two special conferences by the time polling day came. Most of them would have been trained in how to handle local media, some in television techniques – how to cope with aggressive questioning, how to appear before the cameras and so on. At the special conferences they would have been briefed on government thinking by Cabinet ministers and have had a chance to ask their own questions – particularly the ones they would be having thrown at them on the doorstep.

Towards the end of April the Prime Minister and most of the Cabinet went to Birmingham for the last of these conferences, which turned into a pre-pre-election rally of the faithful. In an unscripted hour-long speech she told the candidates to go out and sell the government's message to the country. 'We *are* the next move forward. People tell us there is a lot more to be done – but we are not running out steam. We are just picking up steam.' There was to be one more such gathering – the candidates' conference for the launch of the manifesto – after the date

was announced. But everyone seemed to think, in Birmingham
on 25 April, that the date had already picked itself.

Had it? The answer is both 'yes' and 'no'. The riddle itself is a
clue to the complexities of Mrs Thatcher's thinking when it
comes to this all-important subject. The one major head start
which a prime minister has over his or her rivals in an election
campaign is in the choice of the date itself. It is crucial and
depends on many, many factors. Go too soon and the country
feels you have cut and run – or you can be accused of having
bad news up your sleeve that you are trying to conceal until after
the election. Leave it too late, as James Callaghan did in 1979,
and you are boxed in, allowing your opponents to run a six-
month rather than a six-week campaign against you.

Mrs Thatcher is by nature a very cautious person, who likes
to keep all her options open. Therefore, when the process of
picking the actual date for the election began for her at her
meeting with Norman Tebbit in early February, the first objective
was to establish exactly what her options were. The 20-page
paper which the chairman went through with her sought to do
precisely this. In no sense did it try to pick the day at this
stage, it merely looked at the summer and autumn of 1987
and examined which would be the best dates to choose from,
whichever season she picked for the election. It did not go into
1988, because it presumed that if she did not pick the summer
of 1986 then another similar paper would be required in the
run-up to the autumn.

Norman Tebbit and the Prime Minister went through each of
the nine possible dates selected for the election: 7 May; 4, 11
and 18 June; 9 July; 10 September; 1 and 8 October; and 5
November. Of these only six were considered serious – the others
were representational. For example, if she did not go in June
there was little point in having a long campaign and going in
July; if she waited until the autumn she might as well rule out
September, since more Tories than Labour people tend to go on
holiday in that month, and November was almost certainly too
risky from a weather point of view.

It seemed that 7 May was a possibility, if the party was ready
and far enough ahead in the polls by 8 April, when she would

THE OCTOBER MEN AND THE JUNE WOMAN 103

have to call it. It would be a short, sharp campaign which would take the others by surprise, but it would mean going without the results of the local elections due on 7 May as a guide. And it would be less than four years since the last election – a crucial factor in the Prime Minister's mind. Each possible date had, listed under it, first the advantages: in this case the element of surprise, the proximity to Mrs Thatcher's Moscow visit and the fact that any controversial statistics were likely to come out at the beginning of the campaign. The disadvantages were then listed: the pre-empting of the local elections and the loss of Bills currently going through Parliament. The build-up period was outlined: including Moscow, the Sizewell Report, the fifth anniversary of the Falklands war and the change in the Social Security rates. The main events during the campaign which might have some bearing on it included the Retail Price Index, the Producer Prices Index and the unemployment figures.

Though it was never seriously considered by Mrs Thatcher – even at the February meeting – 7 May was nevertheless 'chosen' as election day by David Owen at the end of March. In his desperation to keep the Alliance bandwagon rolling after Greenwich and Truro, he started confidently predicting that she was about to go to the Palace and ask for the Dissolution of Parliament. Over the weekend of April 4–5 he built his campaign to a crescendo: newspapers were bombarded with 'tips' that Central Office had been put on a war footing, that Saatchi's artwork had been prepared in secret in Belgium and flown to England in a private plane, all leave had been cancelled, emergency meetings were being called and so on . . . But it was all bogus. If you really wanted to know if there was going to be an election, somebody should have told him, you should check if the painters and decorators had yet been called in to Smith Square. They had not. (They arrived on 27 April. Another sure sign: the curtains were sent to the cleaners that day, too.) Nevertheless, Owen managed to get a considerable ferment going in the ever news-hungry media and Mrs Thatcher had to take the precautionary step, on 8 April, of telling the House that the choice of the election date was hers, and hers alone. 'The date,' she said, 'will not be decided in Fleet Street, but in Downing Street.'

The serious dates, therefore, were the three in June and the two in October. The least likely of the summer ones was 4 June, on the grounds that it did not give enough time, 18 June the second least likely on the grounds that it gave too much time. Presuming that Mrs Thatcher would wait until after the local election results on 7 May – there was little point in not waiting since they would, if analysed properly, give the best indication of how the country felt (30 million people were eligible to vote in wards in 477 of the 650 constituencies) – then it was technically possible to go on 4 June; but to do so would mean jettisoning important legislation because of the speed at which Parliament would have to be dissolved. The Criminal Justice Bill might have to go anyway, but the government was not prepared to lose either the Scottish Rates Bill or the Finance Bill.

If Mrs Thatcher spent the weekend of 9–10 May analysing the local election results, her own polls done specially for that weekend, the regional polls, the charts prepared by Dobbs and talking to her advisers, then she would be ready to make up her mind on the night of 10–11 May – she likes to sleep on these decisions. She would therefore tell the Cabinet on the 11th and go to the Queen. The race would then be on: 11 June would be just over four weeks – long enough in the view of most Tories; 18 June would be too long – and the ferment for a decision, any decision, on 11 May would make it impossible to delay. The only strike against 11 June was that there would be an economic summit in Venice early in election week itself; but it was pointed out that Mrs Thatcher's trip to Williamsburg immediately before the 1983 election had not exactly harmed her image as a world leader.

In favour of 11 June, the paper showed that she would start the campaign with the unemployment figures – almost certainly showing a further dramatic drop towards three million – on Thursday 14 May. The next day she was due to make her wind-up speech to the Scottish Conservative Conference in Perth, which could be used as a well publicised rallying call to the troops. And the same day, events later showed, the Chancellor's tax cuts would arrive for the first time in the nation's wage packets, further swelling those already benefiting from the drop in mortgage rates – a thumping good start to the campaign, it was felt.

It must be stressed that, at the time, similarly powerful arguments were put for and against the dates in October. This was not an attempt to force her into a June election, but merely to guide her towards the best dates, whichever season she chose. Nevertheless she reacted surprisingly warmly to the document and studied it carefully – making a joke at one stage about having her own calendar of useful dates, which included one or two surprises up her sleeve that CCO clearly did not know about.

This was the first indication that her attitude to the choice of date was going to be considerably different this time. In 1983 her instinct from the beginning had been to wait until the autumn – although not until 1984. When Tim Bell had suggested once in casual conversation that she go the full term she had looked at him as though he was mad. Therefore in the early months of 1983 she had reluctantly authorised the preparations that had to be set in motion, but it was very much a 'just-in-case' series of measures. It had been difficult to get her to focus on discussing the possibility of an election at all until April, when her election team, led by Cecil Parkinson, had gone to her with their final plans. Within a few days it was obvious that she had changed her mind and was now much more open about the idea of June; but she still insisted that no final decision would be made until the weekend after the local elections, which fell that year on 4 May.

This time, however, her receptiveness itself at the February meeting with Norman Tebbit was a sign that things might be different. Over the succeeding weeks, she increasingly made it clear that she was psychologically much more prepared to consider June, while always saying she would not finally make up her mind until after 7 May. This, in turn, further fuelled the speculation that it was to be June after all.

In 1983, well into the spring, there had been edicts issued that it would be autumn, to dampen down speculation; now the only fluctuations in the date came with the fluctuations in the Tories' fortunes. After Greenwich and the Alliance surge it was felt that June was receding because it would take a long summer to hammer the Alliance back into third place, where it was felt safest to have them: it was truly remarkable to hear senior Tories anxious to get Labour well established back in second place before an election was called, on the grounds of better the enemy they knew than the one they did not. October was thus suddenly resurrected again. The tax cuts would by then be regularly felt in every pocket in the land. (It was fervently hoped that they would not have all been spent on Japanese goods and ruined our balance of payments.) The long summer, with its built-in advantage to the government, would have worked its magic on the polls and it would be totally safe to go.

A measure of her openness of mind this time came in late March when she took the unprecedented step of winding up a Cabinet meeting with a discussion about possible dates, surprising her colleagues by asking each of them in turn what they felt. Only one was definitely for June. The majority of the rest, thus put on the spot, could see advantages to both but felt perhaps that on balance October was the best time. No one disagreed that they should wait until after 7 May before committing themselves. But after Moscow and the slow resurgence of the Labour Party in April, June became first the favourite again – then the racing certainty. One by one the October men – Young, Lawson, Whitelaw and John Moore – began to swing to June, with the constant proviso that the state of the polls over that crucial May weekend should be the final arbiter.

Lord Young's co-option on to the election team must have done much to calm not only Mrs Thatcher's anxieties in the early weeks of April, but also those of senior members of the party whose reasons for opting for October had been founded principally in fears that the machine might not be ready for June. Indeed the gossip at a party given by Jeffrey Archer on 31 March in his penthouse suite overlooking the Thames and the Houses of Parliament was of little else than how good Lord Young's appointment was and what a state CCO was in. The speed with which he could get to grips with the areas over which she had asked him to exercise some control would obviously also dictate the date of the election; but he found, by and large, that the gossips were wrong. Central Office was not a happy place and it was not ready; but all it needed was lubrication here and there and the breaking of a few logjams to get things moving – the exerting of the sort of managerial pressure which was second nature to him. He was confident it would not take long to sort out.

The crucial factor now was whether the Prime Minister would agree with that verdict. At three secret meetings – on 16, 21 and 24 April – she did agree, came off the fence, and, while still saying she would not finally commit herself until 11 May, became – for the first time positively – a June woman.

6 | The Smile on Norman's Face

Just after 8.30 p.m. on Wednesday 15 April 1987, Mrs Thatcher and Norman Tebbit began one of those wide-ranging discussions of a very personal nature between two people who have been close, still share the same ideals, but who find themselves increasingly at loggerheads; a conversation which had the qualities of both a heart-to-heart and a clearing of the air. There was never any doubt that they both wanted the same thing – a third Conservative victory at the polls; but there was also none that the gulf between them over the manner in which that victory might be achieved had never been greater.

Until one or other writes memoirs we are unlikely to know what prompted the half-hour conversation, or what exactly was its content. It can, however, be established that it followed immediately after the Prime Minister's first meeting with representatives of Saatchi & Saatchi since the disastrous presentation at Chequers almost exactly a year before; that the three-hour meeting, which had started at 5.30 in her first-floor study at Downing Street, had been 'not a happy one'; that Tebbit was persuaded by Stephen Sherbourne to stay on after Maurice Saatchi and his team had left; and that, as a result of their subsequent chat, both were much more relaxed and happy about the prospects for the election campaign.

It is also clear that they struck a deal that day, and within a week or so the outline terms of that deal began to become known: after the election Tebbit would be given a senior post within the Tory party, one on which he had always set his heart and which would reflect the Prime Minister's, and her party's, gratitude for the way in which he had led their drive to historic victory. The quid pro quo – perhaps unstated, but nevertheless understood by both – was that he would allow Lord Young to play a larger if still subordinate role in the running of the election. No longer would Young be concerned only with co-ordinating her tour, with launching the manifesto and having an input into the Party Political Broadcasts; he would now step into a pivotal organisational role during the campaign itself, with an office in Smith Square and direct access to the Prime Minister. Tebbit, as Party Chairman, would of course remain the titular head of the campaign, and indeed David Young would, as punctiliously as ever, continue to defer to him. But while the Prime Minister was out on the road, so too, for much of the time, would be Norman Tebbit, touring the constituencies and rousing the troops. And on those occasions, back in Central Office (in Emma Nicholson's 'boudoir' behind the special office the Prime Minister was having prepared for the campaign), David Young would, on his own and through Peter Morrison, guide the CCO machinery of the campaign itself. Whereas the effect of their 17 March meeting had been to put Lord Young in charge of her (as opposed to the party's) campaign, now the balance was tipping very much harder in his direction and his managerial skills were now those chosen to get the best out of many of the plans put together by Norman Tebbit and his chief-of-staff.

Within days speculation started about what it was that had 'put the smile on Norman's face' and why he suddenly seemed so relaxed in the Prime Minister's company, where he had often seemed moody and difficult before. He had carried what his critics saw as his obsessive secrecy and suspicion of imagined enemies into Downing Street with him, sometimes showing great hostility to suggestions made there – dismissing them on the grounds that they were being done already or were not necessary. Now, suddenly, he was 'his old, genial, easy-going self again', as one colleague put it. 'And we all wondered why.' There was one very good personal reason for his happiness. His wife at last had a full-time nurse whom she liked and trusted and her new contentment had spread to him. But that was only part of the reason. Stories began appearing sporadically in newspapers from 26 April on, predicting, first, that he had been promised the Leadership of the House in the new Parliament and later that he

might be made Home Secretary. He himself confirmed privately
at a dinner party given by Nicholas Lloyd, the editor of the *Daily
Express*, that he had been offered something – but would not
say what.

Within days also it became clear that, while Lord Young
continued to defer to him and was careful to put his suggestions
and plans to him, through Peter Morrison or Michael Dobbs,
he was nevertheless playing an ever more central role in the
arrangements. Privately also, the Prime Minister confirmed some
of her dissatisfactions with Tebbit and her joy that, at last, she
had managed to get someone of the calibre of Young into the
centre of the operation.

However, all this was not achieved without a great deal of
delicate manoeuvring, so as not to wound further the Party
Chairman's already bruised ego. It was deemed necessary, for
example, for Mrs Thatcher, Lord Young and Peter Morrison to
enter into a secret agreement to 'fix' all the decisions taken at
the meeting the following day, 16 April, rather than run the risk
of upsetting Norman Tebbit by openly handing over the direction
of so much of the work to Young. Thus, by prior agreement,
every time during the meeting, that Mrs Thatcher said: 'Peter
will you deal with this', or 'Peter will you deal with that', it was
really a message to him to work with Lord Young on whatever
the project was. The arrangement continued for several weeks,
until Tebbit clearly felt relaxed and safe enough in David Young's
presence to work more easily and openly with him; by which
time most of the immediate snags and hold-ups had been cleared
by a combination of Morrison's laid-back charm, masking, as it
did, a fairly ruthless efficiency, and Lord Young's efficiency,
masking as it did a gentle charm.

There were still to be several areas where secrecy had to be
maintained between the three men – notably over the increasing
involvement of Tim Bell in the campaign – and some bizarrely
comic incidents occurred between them in their efforts to keep
things quiet, which were worthy of the best traditions of
Whitehall farce.

The move to involve Lord Young more closely also took some
of the pressure off Stephen Sherbourne, whose workload had
increased steadily with the Prime Minister's dissatisfaction with

CCO and the strain on whom had been doubled by the consequent rise in the amount of soothing of ruffled feathers that had become necessary. When he was picked as one of six targets for IRA letter bombs at the end of April, he was said to have wryly attributed his calm reaction to discovering the bomb to the fact that it was by no means the biggest danger he had faced that week.

Lord Young had, in fact, been surprised by the high grade of the preparations made at CCO – indeed he felt they had not done enough to blow their own trumpets – but he was equally amazed by the way the logjam of decisions had been allowed to build up. It was clear also that his role would be as much to soothe the Prime Minister's anxieties as to correct the sources of them. He had worked with all three of the key personnel at CCO before (Tebbit, Morrison and Dobbs) and worked hard, particularly in the difficult first few weeks, to re-establish a good relationship with them. He got on especially well with Morrison, whom he found excellent at motivating the staff within Smith Square, especially those who had not been totally loyal to the Chairman and his chief-of-staff.

Indeed, with almost perfect timing, morale at Central Office began to improve during the latter half of April and, as decision day came nearer, the feeling in Downing Street – that there was no thought of defeat – spread across Westminster to Smith Square. Although the pace of work quickened in most offices, there was, correspondingly, much more laughter than for many months. There was great amusement in the press department, for example, at the constant trail of media people coming through the front door to ask the date of the election – and passing, on the way in, the planning notices attached to the lamp-posts outside declaring the intention to erect two temporary Portakabins in front of the building in June (for the extra security checks that would be needed on all visitors).

The smile that was to stay on Norman Tebbit's face for weeks, well into the start of the campaign, had not been there when he had gone into the meeting that had preceded his talk with Mrs Thatcher, nor indeed during it. Once again it was one of those difficult encounters where each of the three parties to it – the Prime Minister, her party chairman and the men from Saatchi – had arrived with a different impression of what it was to be about. Saatchi had been told that it was a general chat to go over their outline plans for the campaign – bearing in mind that no one from the advertising agency had been to see her since the disastrous encounter a year before. Norman Tebbit may well have been told this too; but he had also been alerted to the possibility that she might well raise the matter of the involvement of Tim Bell in the campaign. Norman Tebbit, Michael Dobbs and Saatchi all felt his inclusion was not only unnecessary but would also be disruptive to the new team, and they had stated so, both frequently and forcibly. Bell himself was anxious to contribute to the Prime Minister's third campaign and increasingly frustrated at the efforts being made to block him.

At one stage the Prime Minister had been so convinced that it was he who had severed all relationships with the Saatchis, even to the extent of not working on the CCO account as agreed, that she told Lord Young that she would love to have him working on the advertising but that he could not. Lord Young rang Bell, who promptly sent him a copy of his contract with Saatchi. But the pressure to keep him out had by then become such a personal issue, not only for the Party Chairman but for the Saatchis as well, that it was felt best not to force the issue, but to use more roundabout means of involving him all the same. It was some of Bell's ideas which were to prove among the most helpful and successful of the campaign.

Therefore she did not in fact raise the issue of Bell. That, however, did not prevent her discontent from emerging; her frustration at not being able to involve one of her oldest and most trusted allies almost certainly fuelled it and, for the next three hours, she was, to say the least, irritable with the group assembled in front of her, demanding to see advertising, which they had not brought with them. The description of the meeting as 'not a happy one' is probably something of an understatement.

Why was it not possible for her simply to tell Norman Tebbit and Maurice Saatchi that she wanted Tim Bell to be involved and that was that? She is, after all, supposed to be the harsh, autocratic, bossy woman who keeps half the most powerful men in the country quaking in their boots. Here, again, we run up against the disparity between the image of the lady, as portrayed by those who either do not know her or who do not understand her, and the reality of what she is and how she works. Most people would find it ridiculous that she could not get her own way over something so apparently trivial. But, according to one person close to her, the question she almost certainly asked herself was: 'Was it worth the row it would cause?' It also reveals, he believes, that she is much more of a team player than people suspect. She will not lay down the law and force everyone to toe the line, if the consequence of that would be to undermine the team. 'She probably thought that there must be another way round this, without the hassle,' he said. 'In the short time of an election campaign, tempers get frayed to the very limit and you run the risk, if you force someone on to the team, of the whole effort falling apart. And that she could not take.' Once again it illustrates, on a general level, the huge insecurities that many of our leading politicians of all parties have.

A fortnight later at a Small Businessmen's lunch Mrs Thatcher made her affection for Tim Bell, who was one of the other speakers, quite clear by drawing him aside and talking to him at great length. As always she asked him what she should do – in this case what she should say in her speech – and as always he was prepared for the question and told her to talk positively about confidence – for small business, for the whole economy, for Britain in the world. That was the point which featured prominently in the newspapers the following day. It was to be by no means the last time she was to see him in the run-up to the campaign and during it.

Faced with her querulousness, Saatchi batted as well as they could for the three hours of the Downing Street meeting – pointing out, not unreasonably, that it was difficult to have many positive advertisements to show her until the manifesto was ready. However, they promised to return with material nine days later and an appointment was made. Not all was negative; one item did emerge from the meeting which was quickly seen as a potential major vote-winner. From a discussion about the legal problems of direct mail came the suggestion that, instead of targeting mail to special groups, thereby running the risk of breaking the law, they might saturate the entire country with one massive mailshot. Why not have a special Tory newspaper delivered to every household in the country on the last weekend of the campaign? Both Norman Tebbit and the Saatchi team were dispatched to cost such a plan and work out a feasibility study for it. Eventually it was to be established that a four-page paper could be produced and delivered to 16 million homes at a net cost of about £400,000, and the project was given the go-ahead. Its main headline would reflect the theme of the last week of the campaign: 'Don't throw eight years' work away with one stroke of the pen.'

For all that her discussion with Norman Tebbit after the meeting arose out of the simmering difficulties between them, were those difficulties any worse than ones Cecil Parkinson had faced at the same time four years earlier? In style, almost certainly 'Yes' – but in content 'No'. Mrs Thatcher had apparently suffered many of the same anxieties then as she was clearly suffering now. A few days after the Saatchi meeting Michael Spicer, now Aviation Minister but Deputy Chairman in 1983, had a 'sympathy' lunch with Peter Morrison, the present incumbent. Had Morrison and the rest of the team at CCO yet been told to get her room ready for *permanent* occupation – because they were all so incompetent she would have to do it all herself?, Spicer asked. 'No,' said Morrison. 'Has she threatened to sack you all and put her own men in there, because you couldn't organise your way out of a paper bag?' asked Spicer. 'No,' said Morrison. 'Has she told you you are all a bunch of complete idiots with no idea at all about how to organise her tour?' Again, 'No.' 'Actually, Michael, it's not as bad as that at all,' Morrison added. 'It will be,' said Spicer. 'Just hang on. It will be!'

The joke, when retold at Central Office, did much to reassure senior people there, who were beginning to worry that what they were going through was somehow unique to this election campaign. The Prime Minister's anxieties were exactly the same – but now the reasons had changed. She needed a team with the ability to put her mind at rest, to be positive and, when things got tough, to be quick-thinking and optimistic. This was clearly something she felt she had had from Cecil Parkinson, would have from Lord Young – but had not hitherto been getting from Norman Tebbit.

Or, for that matter, from Michael Dobbs. Surprisingly, considering that he was a deputy chairman of Saatchi & Saatchi,

Compton Ltd, had been handling the account at CCO for more than a year and been giving first approval to most of their work since he had run the account with Tim Bell in 1983, and especially since he was now Norman Tebbit's right-hand man, he had not been invited to the Downing Street meeting. Nor was his name on the list of those who were to attend the crucial election decision meeting, also at Number 10, the next day. It was an extraordinary situation, and word of it spread like wildfire within Central Office. It was not news that came as a total surprise to one or two of the inmates, who now saw the public exclusion of Dobbs as the culmination of weeks of effort to undermine him. They had not stinted in their efforts to spread their disquiet about Norman Tebbit's chief-of-staff throughout the upper echelons of the party and, through any route they could, into Downing Street itself. Now their efforts had paid off, they had found a not unreceptive audience in the Prime Minister and Dobbs was effectively removed from the centre of operations.

There were many sides to the story. Dobbs undoubtedly had upset people within CCO. He admitted it himself; that was, after all, sometimes his job. If the chairman wanted stricter management of departmental budgets and instructed him to ensure that this was done, then it was his duty to carry the orders out. In one case, one of the people who complained the most vociferously about Dobbs had only a few days earlier had an argument with him which had ended up with Tebbit siding with his aide and proving the man wrong. The man, who believed himself too experienced to be humiliated in this way, lost no time in spreading the word about how impossible it was to work with Dobbs. Obviously if you wish to sow the seeds of uncertainty in Downing Street, you did not attack the chairman, who was the Prime Minister's appointment. It was easier to undermine Dobbs – especially if you had reason to suspect that the Prime Minister did not particularly want him there in the first place.

Dobbs could see that, by allying himself so closely with Tebbit, he had made himself more vulnerable to this sort of attack. He could also see that, especially since his presentation at Chequers a year earlier, he could not exactly have stuck in Mrs Thatcher's mind as one of the world's most dynamic optimists and that, therefore, when complaints were made about him, they found a ready ear. She had, after all, at election times especially, a predisposition to believe that all was not well in Smith Square – a belief that was bolstered by the fact that she had never worked there and therefore had little idea of the huge management problems inherent in the place. Dobbs could also see how important it was for her to feel reassured by those around her at election times – and that only by making her feel comfortable with those around her and with what they were suggesting to her, would any real progress be made. He recognised that he simply did not inspire confidence in her; nevertheless he felt deeply hurt that so much of his hard groundwork should now be taken out of his hands at the very moment of bringing it to fruition. For example, nine of the eleven papers which were to form the core of the most important meeting to be held before the election itself – the one at which the Prime Minister would decide whether or not June really was an option – had been either researched or written by him, and were now to be presented by others.

It was stated by people with no axe to grind that Dobbs had become hopelessly entangled in his master's passion for secrecy and belief in intrigue – to such an extent that the two of them would spend hours behind closed doors, rarely communicating their thoughts or decisions to anyone else in the building, while plans that urgently needed to be implemented were held up. For a few days he put his whole position in CCO in abeyance. He thought of resigning to apply for the seat at Ludlow, which had suddenly become vacant following the British Telecom share applications disclosures. He even went to visit the constituency, under the guise of looking for the graves of ancestors who had lived in the area. He talked the problem over with friends and his case was even taken up privately with the Prime Minister, where it met with a frosty response. In the end he wrote to her to assure her of his continued efforts and loyalty (even that had been doubted in some of the whispers) and told Norman Tebbit he would soldier on. A number of people congratulated him on the mature way he had handled what was a very bitter blow to his pride, if not his actual future. To have flounced out now, with a matter of weeks to go to the election, would have left Norman Tebbit personally isolated and the CCO machinery, as a whole, without a vital component.

From the Prime Minister's point of view the exclusion of
Michael Dobbs was a simple and necessary expedient – part of
the process of gathering round her the machine which, in her
view, functioned the most efficiently and was most responsive
to her needs. Although it would have been logical to have Dobbs
at meetings as Norman Tebbit's chief-of-staff, it was not at all
necessary now she had Lord Young and Peter Morrison to get
things moving. Indeed, if the precedent of 1983 was anything to
go by only 'chiefs' attended the crucial April meeting; number
twos were not invited. She replied to Dobbs's letter in most
generous terms.

The meeting at Number 10 on 16 April, Maundy Thursday,
was therefore convened with the Prime Minister, Stephen Sherbourne, David Young, Norman Tebbit, Peter Morrison and
Robin Harris, the director of the research department, in attendance. All except Lord Young had been at the January meeting.

The meeting began at 10.30 a.m. and continued through lunch
until just after 4 p.m. Parliament was in recess, so it was not
necessary to be as secretive as in 1983, when the equivalent
meeting had taken place at Chequers. No word of it leaked out,
despite the importance of the decisions taken there that day.
Each of the eleven papers was gone through in great detail,
and Mrs Thatcher's attitude throughout was, I gather, while
questioning, now friendly. The first two papers dealt with the
political strategy for the next three months, whether there was
an election or not. They were basically an update of the first
chapter of the Christmas Blue Book – looking at how the Tories
were presenting themselves and how the other parties seemed to
be faring. The papers paid particular attention to the Alliance and
covered Michael Dobbs's preliminary work on the 'Doomsday
Scenario', for use in the last week of the campaign in the event
of an Alliance breakthrough. Out of the discussions came the
idea of carrying out fresh research on the Alliance, to see how
people viewed it and how they would respond to the various
forms of attack the Tories might launch on it.

For example, the papers outlined three possible attacks on
Alliance policies. Any one of them could be used – but not all
three. It was possible for the Tories to say the Alliance had no
policies, or to say that they had policies, but that they were

divided on them, or even to say that they had policies, but they were all left-wing policies. It was felt necessary to find out to which of these approaches the voters would best respond, in other words, to establish exactly what were the Alliance strengths and weaknesses.

Papers three and four were the first to demonstrate the involvement of Lord Young since his recruitment to the team a month earlier. They concerned the arrangements for the design and launch of the manifesto. It was decided that, instead of launching the document, which was after all central to the whole campaign, at an ordinary press conference, the opportunities for ballyhoo and razzmatazz would be much greater if it were to be tied in with the traditional Candidates' Conference, the meeting hosted by the backbench 1922 Committee, at which all the candidates are given a last rousing pep talk and sent off to storm the constituencies. It was suggested that part of this normally closed meeting should now be opened up to the media, launching the manifesto in an atmosphere of some excitement. Serious discussion of the document could then be handled at a special press conference next day.

The initial layouts and artwork for the manifesto itself were looked at and approved. Those, including Lord Young, the Prime Minister and Peter Morrison, who knew that they had been prepared not at Saatchi, but at the offices of Lowe, Howard-Spink & Bell, refrained from mentioning the fact.

Paper five covered the technical preparations for the daily morning press conferences and an outline schedule of the themes to be presented at them. It was followed by two technical papers, one on the advertising programme – the renting of sites for the posters and of space in newspapers – the other on the preparations for the election broadcasts. This included the possibility, raised for the first time, of making a ten-minute promotional video of the Prime Minister. This would be the first time that the full range of American political advertising techniques had been used to promote a British politician, and it was believed it would have a huge impact; it would be particularly effective when shown immediately before her platform appearances. The debate on this led into a discussion of a paper on all aspects of the Prime Minister's and her senior ministers' TV strategy.

The last three papers covered the artwork pack to be sent to all candidates to help them with their own publicity material, a timetable of what would happen in the days immediately following the local council elections on 7 May, when the computer analysis would be ready, when the special polls would be completed and so on – and a paper giving a rough breakdown of events from D−31 to polling day ('D-Day'), whenever that might be. The positive acceptance of this document by the Prime Minister gave those at the meeting the impression that, barring accidents, her mind was now firmly set on June. Indeed, before the meeting ended she told them that, although she would not make up her mind finally until after 7 May, she was now very firmly a June woman and, of the three possible dates, 11 June seemed the one.

If the Maundy Thursday meeting had involved the process of getting the Prime Minister's mind thoroughly attuned to June, then the equally secret discussions which took place the following Tuesday at Chequers were the ones from which the final set of instructions was passed down the line to have the machine fuelled and ready to run. Again the meeting lasted all day, but on this occasion some people were invited to come for the morning session and some for the afternoon.

Over the Easter weekend – as at Christmas – Mrs Thatcher had been busy reading. The pile of documents which had accumulated in Stephen Sherbourne's office in Downing Street had now been boiled down to the first draft of the manifesto, which had gone into her box for the weekend, as had the first draft of the new proposed tour assembled under Lord Young's guidance. In the morning session of the meeting, with the A-Team plus Lord Young, she dealt with the manifesto. It was, she found, a veritable tome: long, unreadable, obscure, and lacking in firm commitments. It had none of the guts or grit she wanted, and very little to show the electorate that she meant business for the next five years.

It seemed that a certain amount of 'trimming' had gone on – backing off from originally firm objectives down to generalised ambitions. Just as her vision of what she wanted to do had been clear in 'The Right Approach', more than 10 years before, she now wanted the manifesto to be absolutely unequivocal about where she intended to take the country, such a forthright document that it would make the other parties look feeble and lacking in ideas. The national press had already been laced in recent weeks with a number of accurate-looking leaks about how robust the manifesto would be – particularly in the areas of education, health, employment, housing and the inner cities. It was her intention that, having achieved the total turnaround and recovery of the economy in the last eight years, the Tories should now offer the country a truly radical programme of change.

She did not want there to be any ambiguity, drawing accusations that there was another 'hidden' Tory manifesto waiting in the wings. Ministers were therefore ordered to go back over everything they had in the pipeline and check that it was all covered by the document. There were several specific areas, including housing, which she felt were not as positive as she wished. But her principal criticism was of the style of the document. Its authors – Brian Griffiths, Robin Harris, John Mac-Gregor, the Chief Secretary to the Treasury, and John O'Sullivan, on loan from *The Times*, were told to go away and do it again. During the meeting Lord Young spotted what he thought was one of the weaknesses of the document – that it juxtaposed too clumsily the government's record over the last eight years with its ambitions now – and he began to think of possible solutions to the problem.

There were to be four more meetings – most of them involving the writers and the A-Team strategy group – and a lot more argument and banging of the table before the document began to take its final shape. Perhaps it was fortunate for those at Central Office that this most crucial aspect of the Tory campaign, about which Mrs Thatcher was now clearly most concerned, was the only one which had been nurtured and come to fruition entirely within Downing Street. The people in Smith Square found themselves smiling wryly as the number of re-writes notched up to four and then five and as they heard a steady flow of stories about Mrs Thatcher's dissatisfaction and inability to get the sort of document she had in mind.

In the preparation of speeches and major documents she is a perfectionist – and hence a compulsive tinkerer. She still retains a slight nervousness at public speaking, and is at her best when she is relaxed enough to tear up her prepared script and deliver her message off-the-cuff, but, faced with a major occasion, she will weigh every word and try to hear herself saying it. Speechwriters will often be kept at work until dawn, going through draft after draft trying to get the perfect sound and tone – sometimes ending up with whole passages back the way they started. Men like the playwright Sir Ronald Millar, one of her regular speechwriters, are used to this slow process, and are secure enough in their roles to walk out for a break sometimes, knowing that when they return matters will not have progressed significantly. There was one occasion in 1979 when the team, including Gordon Reece and Tim Bell (and Denis Thatcher, who had nobly stayed up pouring the drinks), had been working with her at her Chelsea home for eight hours, through the night, before they finally got it 'right' at about four in the morning. She shooed them all out into Flood Street for a walk to clear their heads while she made coffee for them all. The group had reached the top of the street and turned into King's Road, when Mr Thatcher stopped and said: 'I don't know how you chaps put up with it. First you do it this way. Then you do it that way. Then you go back to the first way. I can't see why Margaret doesn't just stand up and say: "Jim Callaghan, —— him!"'

Her lack of confidence shows in the production of major documents, too. She knows she does not possess a major talent as a writer, but that does not stop her worrying away at a problem, often through many drafts, until she feels it is exactly right. She, Tebbit and Brian Griffiths were still tinkering with the wording of the manifesto as guests were arriving at Chequers for dinner on the Saturday night before the big decision day on 10 May.

The other meeting – at Chequers on the afternoon of Tuesday 21 April – covered the last principal area of the Prime Minister's anxiety: the 'Thatcher tour'. She was brought up to date on the plans for the bus – the Yorkshire coachbuilders had finished the extra armour-plating for it and had started to instal the radio telephones, FAX machines, telexes and the other equipment required to keep her fully in touch with London as she toured. Coincidentally, while making inquiries around the major coach-building firms, CCO staff discovered that the Alliance had ordered two foreign coaches – made by DAF the Dutch/Swedish firm – and were having them sprayed canary yellow for their campaign. They looked forward to making a minor issue of this.

Under Lord Young's guidance the balance of the tour had now swung back from visiting marginals that it was felt she ought to visit, to visiting places where she could gain some benefit from the visit. A theme for the tour had emerged – indeed a theme for the whole campaign: Regeneration. The plan for the 'Thatcher tour' was that it would visit places and meet people who were symbols of the new growth and strength of Britain. It was hoped that they would demonstrate, by their existence, the fact that the government's policies were working through – thus ensuring that the contrast in both detail and in philosophy between Tory and Labour would be underlined. The Tories wanted to project themselves as forward-looking, the party with ideas for the future, the party which had come through the storm and now knew where it was going. On the other hand, they believed, the Labour Party would be seen as the outdated party, bereft of new ideas, tied to the old ways and the old run-down concept of Britain. They hoped it would be Regeneration versus Degeneration.

Roger Boaden, who had managed her tours in the previous two elections – as well as all of Edward Heath's – and who was another trusted face with whom she felt confident, had driven down to Chequers for this afternoon session. He put to her a series of plans on this theme and, with a few exceptions, had most of them accepted. It was also decided to hold one more rally than in the 1983 campaign, making seven major speeches in all. She would start, if it were to be 11 June, with her address to the Scottish Conservative Conference at Perth on 15 May, followed a week later by her adoption meeting in Finchley, then five regional rallies on the tour – Wales, Scotland, the North-West, Midlands and Yorkshire. Still not settled at the end of the meeting was the character of the final weekend's rally, which had been a youth gathering at Wembley in 1983. Now the proposal was for a 'Family' Rally on the last Sunday – but there were problems with the concept. Nobody could decide what form it should take, and it was still open to question whether it would be held at all.

As with the manifesto there were still problems with the tour, but they were by no means as great as those that afflicted the production of the great document. The tour difficulties were very much a matter of details and of reconciling the huge number of conflicting interests involved: the need to be seen about and among the people, with the needs of security; the need to be seen on television among friendly crowds, with the need to boost the marginals where possible; the need for variety and balance – hard-hat visits, white-coat visits, animal visits, and children visits; to be seen in offices and factories, among heavy machinery and high-tech computers, in modern shopping centres and old market places. And all the time there had to be room for the cameramen and photographers, for whom the tour was very much laid on, so that they could operate without mowing down great swathes of the populace. The locations of the visits must be 'feed points' for the TV men to get their films to London and wire machines for the photographers to get their pictures back, and the timing had to be such that those pictures would get to London ready for the early evening news bulletins and the first editions of the morning papers. The tour must be balanced regionally and urban/rurally. It had to be where there would be cheering crowds and not hecklers and where the cheers would echo well rather than be blown away on the wind.

The most difficult of all these considerations, as the start of the tour came nearer, was security. The IRA bombing offensive in Northern Ireland was accelerating and, it was felt, the major political figures would inevitably be targets during the campaign. Security precautions were therefore doubled, if not trebled – to the point where some people began to wonder if some aspects of the scheme were going to be possible at all.

For all that Roger Boaden – and Harvey Thomas – had done all this before, the security situation made formulation of the programme a nightmare and it took two more meetings, at Downing Street on Friday 1 May and Tuesday 5 May, before the last details were finally agreed. Plans were then locked away and, for obvious security reasons, details of them given only on the strictest need-to-know basis. It was at the first of these meetings that Lord Young proved, spectacularly, that, for all he was currently the Prime Minister's blue-eyed boy, he too was capable of putting his foot in it in a fairly major way. He had studied the 1983 tour in some detail and discussed it at great length with Roger Boaden (including the worst day of Boaden's life when he, the tour staff and half her security men lost the Prime Minister) and had come to the conclusion that the most successful day of that tour had been the last one, which had culminated in the Prime Minister standing in front of a vast aircraft hangar door – 60 by 30 feet – painted in one huge Union Jack. 'What a great idea it would be Prime Minister,' he now suggested, 'to repeat that lucky last day for you all over again in 1987.' 'Don't you realise it's owned by Westland?' she snapped.

The pace of all the preparations accelerated as April came to a close. It was now widely assumed that only a disaster in the opinion polls or in the local government elections would delay a June election, and the feeling that all the plans and arrangements were 'just in case' dissipated quickly. The sense that this was the real thing took over in CCO – particularly when the hammering and sawing started as the carpenters got to work on Mrs Thatcher's special high-security campaign office.

Lord Young's expanded role also brought relief in the last crucial area, in which the Prime Minister's anxieties were only too obvious – that of communications. Once he became used to the idea of Young as election 'Underlord', Norman Tebbit began to see a measure of the old 'three-hand team' (Thatcher, Parkinson and Tebbit) in the line-up of Thatcher, Tebbit and Young. The Secretary of State for Employment took on more and more of the 'smiling role' in the media, explaining the government's policies in a somewhat gentler tone than the public had come to expect from the Party Chairman. In one performance on BBC-1's 'This Week Next Week' on the day of the Hands Across Britain protest against unemployment, he floored the opposition Labour spokesmen with a series of tricks – including waving his hands and laughing when one of them was making a point, so that the director would choose those moments for his 'cutaway' shots and the audience would miss the point his opponent was trying to make. (It was a trick he had learned from Denis Healey.) His *pièce de résistance*, however, came at the end when, after a slow, almost hesitant performance in the last half of the hour-long programme, he suddenly came to life in the last five minutes, making several major points and interrupting the interviewer to gain as much time as possible. This baffled even colleagues, until he pointed out that the programme was followed by the *Eastenders* omnibus edition and that in those last five minutes more than five million people, many of whom were not interested in politics but would nevertheless vote, would have turned on their sets and would have seen him. They would hardly have known Labour or the Alliance was on the programme.

With the Prime Minister's encouragement he also took on a portion of the old Gordon Reece role – crucial in the hurly-burly of an election campaign – making sure Fleet Street editors were fully briefed about what was going on and what was Mrs Thatcher's thinking on the issues of the day. This activity is a very difficult two-way street to negotiate, for it involves being informative and chatty – even slightly indiscreet – in the knowledge that some of what is said will appear the following day, and at the same time trying to convey a message and help the editors shape their thinking on a topic. It also involves listening to them and their anxieties – they are after all another real source of information about what is happening in the country and how people are feeling – assessing what they say and relaying it to the Prime Minister and the election team. Many, many times, in both 1979 and 1983, potential disasters were averted in this way by frank exchanges over an evening drink in the editors' offices of Fleet Street. It was not just for their papers' support of the Tories that both David English of the *Daily Mail* and Larry Lamb of the *Sun* and later the *Daily Express* were knighted: their advice delivered both in this way and face-to-face with Mrs Thatcher proved invaluable throughout both campaigns.

It was Lord Young who also solved one of the principal problems with the manifesto which had arisen at the Chequers meeting on 21 April: that it was too cumbersome and wordy. Each chapter in the first draft seemed to be a muddle of the government's record over the last eight years and its new proposals. He suggested that the party produce, in effect, two manifestos: the first to be called 'Our First Eight Years' and the second 'The Next Moves Forward', both presented in one folder. The idea was quickly approved: the achievements booklet and the folder (both again designed at Lowe, Howard-Spink & Bell) were at the printers within a week and 15,000 copies of them printed before Mrs Thatcher went to Chequers on the evening of Friday 8 May to make up her mind whether or not to hold an election in June.

Not only was Lord Young spending more time at CCO as that decision day came nearer, but the building also began to fill up with many of the other people drafted in for the duration. Christine Wall arrived from Number 10 after Easter and started work on her draft schedules of the Prime Minister's major TV performances and of the crew lists for the tour. Sally Oppenheim began her liaison work with Downing Street and getting the article writers briefed.

The title chosen for the manifesto, 'The Next Moves Forward', though difficult to say easily, had come out among the best of all the slogans and themes Saatchi tested in small groups towards the end of April. It was still as popular as it had been at the time of the party conference six months earlier and it was seen to project the right aura of direction and leadership. 'Sharing in Success' – carrying the overtones of the success of the various privatisations, the wider ownership of housing, the recent tax and mortgage rate cuts – was also tested and found to be powerful. And, while not a main theme, the slogan 'It's Great (or Good) to be Great Again' was again found to be very popular; it was used for the first time by William Whitelaw, in a party political broadcast on 22 April. 'Power to the People' was also emerging as a very strong seconder theme to the manifesto.

Saatchi's long-awaited presentation of work to Mrs Thatcher happened at last early in the evening of Friday 24 April. The team went first to Smith Square to run over the material with Norman Tebbit. Then they left in convoy for Downing Street. Michael Dobbs had already seen all the work – indeed he had been involved in the discussions with Maurice Saatchi and John Sharkey as to how it should be presented to the Prime Minister – but once again he did not attend the meeting. The team arrived with Tebbit and a huge chest of their work – rather like a freezer cabinet. Included in it were some advertisements they knew to be duds, to be presented early on in the hope that their rejection would set the mood for the Prime Minister to accept the good material. It was not to be so. She found the work by and large tedious and much of what she did pass, she agreed to only reluctantly.

Nevertheless, during that session and another exactly a week later some of the key advertising for the campaign was approved. The slogan for the first and last weeks (and for the main headline of the newspaper) was to be: 'Don't undo eight years' work in three seconds.' Other advertisements on education, housing and law and order themes were approved – one on education showing a child's hundred lines saying: 'If I vote Labour I will not get a say in my child's education.'

The most dramatic advertisements passed in those sessions were the ones for the 'Doomsday Scenario'. One had three hands, Labour, Liberal and SDP, all on a pen trying to write something. The most dramatic was a picture of the Revd Ian Paisley and a simple slogan on the lines of: 'Do you want this man to govern Britain? Don't vote for a hung Parliament.' As they were passed, each one was put in the 'freezer' for security: Saatchi treat the problem of 'leaks' of their work very seriously – the advertising industry is notorious for its inability to keep secrets. As in 1983 they moved to a 'safe house' in Soho, which even so was burgled, so now on 5 May they moved out of the agency's Charlotte Street offices and into its corporate headquarters in Lower Regent Street. The new premises also had studio space, which meant that all the work on Party Election Broadcasts (PEBs) and on the Prime Minister's video could be done under one roof.

Dobbs's exclusion from meetings with Mrs Thatcher did not mean that he ceased to be involved in the preparation of material for her. He was still involved in the advertising, as indeed he was in the continuous flow of papers that went from Norman Tebbit into her boxes. Two of these which went in for the weekend before she was due to decide brought her up to date on the latest state of the polls – national, marginal and on issues, published and private. In summary, they told Mrs Thatcher that, with a week to go before she had to decide, the clear indications were that she was in a very strong position. The national polls were known; most of them showed the Tories above 40 per cent and, if anything, rising, with Labour around 30 and rising and the Alliance in the mid–high twenties but falling. The secret Harris tracking study of their own target seats indicated that on present form not only would the Tories hold the vast majority of them, but, coupled with other marginal polls available, there was a clear indication that the party could do as well as it did in 1983. One analysis even gave the Tories more than the magic 400 seats on the basis of its data.

On the issues: unemployment was improving, as was education, but health was still weak (the nurses' pay award had only just been announced), as were housing and pensions. This last issue had emerged almost certainly from the poor handling of pension increases and the débâcle the government had made in 1986 of the special cold weather allowances for old people. In the age breakdowns of some of the larger polls there was an alarming swing away from the Tories, who had always done rather well in the over-65 category. But the situation overall was one to give optimism and, when it came to the following weekend, it was this continuity of good news which was to do much to make the decision a swift and relatively painless one.

The countdown to 10 May accelerated. The media excitement intensified dramatically in the last week, with the local elections on 7 May widely ballyhooed as the principal pointer to a June or an October election. Mrs Thatcher had made no secret of her intention of using the results as the basis of her decision and most of the papers painted vivid portraits of her, surrounded by her strategy group – the A-Team – at Chequers after lunch on Sunday, sitting down surrounded by mountains of paper and graphs and polls and reports for a lengthy session to argue it out and make up their minds. As it transpired it was not quite like that. It was a much simpler process than anyone had anticipated.

Publicly Tory spokesmen admitted that they expected to lose some seats in the local elections. Pressed further they said they would be disappointed if the losses rose above 500. Privately they thought they might lose 300 and they would have been happy with a loss of only 200. When they made a net gain of 78 they could not believe their luck. To them it was an equal disappointment both for the Alliance, who had expected to do very well, and for Labour who had expected to hold on and gain a little ground in certain key towns. To the embarrassment of some senior Tories and the delight of others, Norman Tebbit sat in the television studio and played with his direct computer link with the Tories' mainframe back at CCO while the results came in. Some found it an irrelevance and his attitude distracting and superior, others thought it demonstrated how technically advanced the Tory party machine was and how confident it was about its ability to fight the elections. As if reading their minds, the Party Chairman described himself the following day as being neither 'cocky nor complacent' about the prospects now; perhaps that statement was atonement for the mild reprimand he had received earlier in the week for saying in the House that when the election came his party would 'walk it'.

There is one attitude guaranteed to upset the Prime Minister above all others at election time – complacency. That evening, Friday 8 May, as she climbed into her car for the hour's drive to Chequers, where over the weekend she would make the decision, she knew that her party machine was at last all but ready to go into action. She knew that when the statisticians at Central Office had finished their massive analysis of the local election results in the early hours of Sunday morning they were all but certain to show her party in a commanding lead. She knew that when she talked to her A-Team of ministers on Sunday afternoon and solicited their views they were all but certain to be unanimous in their support for June. She knew that all the other secret advice she would take over the next forty-eight hours would point the same way. But she was *not* complacent. She had still to *win* the election.

7 | Enter Bell,
Past the Dustbins

At exactly 6.30 p.m. on Saturday 9 May a metallic-grey chauffeur-driven Mercedes pulled past the gaggle of waiting reporters, photographers and TV crews and into the short road leading to the security gatehouse at Chequers. It was clearly not a government car, nor were its occupants – a man and a woman – immediately identifiable, so its presence at the Prime Minister's country residence for the next six hours was never commented on in the national media. The vehicle received brisk clearance at the gatehouse and proceeded round the right-hand sweep of the drive to the main house 200 yards away, where, as it drew up, the door opened and the couple were shown quickly through the small entrance lobby and into the downstairs study.

Half an hour later the Prime Minister came bustling in to meet them, apologising for having kept them 'hidden' while she concluded the meeting she had been having for most of the afternoon – putting the finishing touches to the manifesto with Professor Brian Griffiths and Norman Tebbit. But, she joked, they had gone now, so Tim Bell and his fiancée Virginia Hornbrook could come out. The implication was that, while there was no reason why they should not be there, it would be better for the time being not to advertise the fact that Bell had spent the evening with the Prime Minister – especially in view of the antagonism that mention of his very name aroused in some quarters of the party.

The ostensible reason for the visit was a private family dinner for Denis Thatcher, whose 72nd birthday it was the next day; because of the pressing nature of the business to be conducted all through Sunday, it had been decided to celebrate it the evening before. His favourite food – salmon steak with chips and peas, followed by steamed sultana pudding – was being prepared in the kitchens, their daughter Carol had arrived earlier for the weekend and Mrs Thatcher was in a very good mood. As it happened that was just as well, for Denis had gone to the Rugby Sevens at Twickenham and, as was almost expected of him after 35 years of marriage, arrived home neither on time nor in need of much topping up. She treated both, as would almost any other wife in a successful and longlasting marriage, with good-humoured tolerance.

However the occasion itself, the privacy of it and the greater time thus given for Mrs Thatcher and Tim Bell to talk were a godsend to her, for there was much to discuss. For the best part of the evening – apart from a somewhat delayed dinner – the two talked through almost every aspect of her communications strategy for the coming election campaign. As they chatted she took copious notes of items to think about and to ask to be done in the next few days. They discussed her presentation of herself, and the tone of voice she wanted to adopt. Bell suggested that she should start to drop the 'we' of the government, because it was redolent of the Royal 'we', and switch instead to the 'I' of the Prime Minister. They agreed that her instinct was right not to try to be 'cuddly' during the campaign, as some siren voices would have her be, and that even though she might be attacked for being uncaring, she should remain above the fray – although never remote from it. They discussed which major set-piece television interviews she should take part in, and when, which ministers were best on television in which circumstances, the preparation of her newspaper articles, and the themes for her major speeches and election broadcasts.

They talked about how they thought the campaign would go: the first week to launch the manifesto, which would summarise the government's record and predict future success, the second week would punch home all the positive messages in the manifesto, the third week would probably be the rough one, in which it would be necessary to examine the polls carefully for signs of an Alliance revival (in case the Doomsday Scenario was needed), and then there would be the last frantic dash to polling day.

They also discussed her proposed visit to the world economic summit in Venice. Bell was among those who had persuaded her to go to Williamsburg in 1983 and believed just as firmly now that she should go to Venice for the effect it would have of portraying her as a world leader. There was, of course, the risk that it might be harmful to be out of the country for even one day in the middle of an election campaign, especially if it was going badly for the Tories; but they agreed the converse was worse: to cancel now, or later, would seem like panic. Surprisingly, in view of the comprehensive nature of the discussion, they did not at any stage talk about the date – that was not a matter the Prime Minister would discuss with Tim Bell except in the most general of terms, nor would he expect it to be on the agenda.

Throughout the long evening she was more relaxed about the prospects of an election than Bell could ever remember her being in 1983. She was happier with the state of readiness claimed by Central Office – after all the trials of the previous two months, which had irritated her considerably. She made it clear, as indeed she had to others, that she missed Cecil Parkinson's smooth organisational ability and reassuring presence, but that she was nevertheless pleased with the way Lord Young had stepped in and begun to get things moving in the areas allocated to him. It was unfair, but nevertheless probably better for all concerned, that she must continue to indulge in the minor subterfuges necessary to meet whoever she wanted to and get what she wanted done, rather than run the risk of a major row which would be in nobody's best interests. After all, there was no doubt in anyone's mind that they all wanted to win the next election. It remained to be seen as the campaign went on whether this policy of deception in order to keep people happy would, in itself, cause more problems than it solved. While it might bring fresh insight to the Prime Minister's thinking, and while it might supply a whole range of new ideas, might it not also result in faction fights and unseemly and wasteful squabbling?

One other topic raised by Tim Bell during the evening illustrates the potential for disagreement there was in the Tory camp at this time and the lack of clear lines of communication. In organising the presentation of the manifesto, the suggestion had been made to Lord Young that a video should be made of the principal ministers talking about their parts of it; the film would be given to the media and to all the candidates to show at their meetings. Preparatory work had gone ahead for it during the previous week. An outline script had been written by one of the creators of *Yes, Prime Minister*, Antony Jay (whose company Video Arts was, ironically, heavily involved with the Alliance through John Cleese, one of the other partners), and all it needed was the nod to go ahead from Mrs Thatcher, who had originally been against the idea. Lord Young had tried to see her to talk about it, but had had appointments cancelled because of crises at the last moment and had asked Tim Bell, since he was being employed with Jay to make the video, if he would go through the scheme with her. This he did, and she responded enthusiastically. The following day, when all the ministers of the A-Team were having coffee after lunch at Chequers, Young discreetly asked the Prime Minister, 'Did Tim by any chance talk to you last night about the video?' 'Tim!' she whispered to Young, turning round to see if anyone was listening. 'Come over here – shhh about Tim. No one here must know about his visit.' Then she told him she thought the idea was marvellous.

The video was shot the following Wednesday in Lord McAlpine's house where the January meeting had taken place. The ministers arrived and said their pieces unscripted under the supervision of Antony Jay and Tim Bell. The aim was to get them to talk spontaneously and with some feeling about what they felt they had achieved and what they now wanted to do. When Norman Tebbit was due, Bell diplomatically returned to his office until that part of the recording was finished. Nobody talked about the fact that a major piece of promotional work for the party was being undertaken separately from Saatchi & Saatchi. Although it must have been obvious that Bell was involved, it simply was not talked about – just as it had been taboo on the previous Sunday.

The atmosphere at Chequers on that much-talked-of day was by all accounts almost surreal. William Whitelaw, Norman Tebbit, Nigel Lawson, Douglas Hurd, Sir Geoffrey Howe, John Wakeham and Lord Young – the 'Seven Dwarfs', as the *Observer* christened them – were bidden to be at the Buckinghamshire mansion for 12.30 p.m. There is a charm in the fact that even trusted senior colleagues have a common anxiety about being on time for their Prime Minister – an anxiety which manifested itself this day in the small queue of cars which formed in the lay-by up the road waiting for the last few minutes to tick away before it was time to enter the drive. Young and Hurd – along with Kenneth Baker, who was not to be at the meeting – had spent the night at the Whitelaws' home nearby. Whitelaw and Young were the first to arrive in the vicinity – far too early, so they went for a drive round the nearby country lanes, emerging back on to the road in time to take the lead of the convoy as it left the lay-by to drive up to the house.

Norman Tebbit, wearing a garish purple and green shirt 'in protest at having to work on a Sunday', he joked, was already there with the Prime Minister, and coffee was served while for nearly an hour the group discussed the best dates – should she decide to hold an election. The fourth and the eighteenth of June were examined and swiftly discarded. If there was to be an election then 11 June was the obvious date. The air of unreality was sustained throughout most of the rest of the day by the constant refrain at the end of people's sentences: 'this is, of course, if we decide to have an election.' Indeed, it almost became a joke, for everyone there knew it to be an odds-on certainty. Nigel Wickes sat in on the short morning session to advise on the governmental arrangements that would have to be made – should there be an election.

Lunch at 1.30 p.m. was lighthearted, and *the* subject was studiously avoided throughout. Then, after coffee in the main hall, the Prime Minister led them upstairs to the meeting-room, where at just after three o'clock Norman Tebbit opened a 29-page document and began to run through its contents. Though slim, the paper was the product of 50 hours' hard work by Central Office statisticians and computer staff. Fuelled by takeaway pizzas, endless coffee and occasional champagne, they had striven to extract every possible relevant fact from the local election results and from their own and the national polls, to analyse it and have those findings ready for this meeting. The final document had been finished only at two o'clock that morning, and delivered to Tebbit by Michael Dobbs at breakfast time.

First it covered the recent opinion polls: the average of the last month's national surveys applied nationally would, if there were an election that day, give a parliamentary split of 352 seats to the Tories, 251 to Labour, 25 to the Alliance and 22 others, giving a majority to the Tories of 54. The special Harris poll done for the Tories in the last two days, however, gave the Tories 44 per cent, Labour 32 and Alliance 21, which, if translated into parliamentary seats, would mean a majority of 126. It then looked at regional polls – first the average of the last month's Harris tracking studies in the marginals, then the special one carried out in the last two days – and they showed a consolidation of the Labour vote since 1983 at the expense of the Alliance. Extrapolated from these polls, the Tories could expect a majority of between 120 and 130. The local election results, bearing in mind that there had been no polling in London or Scotland, pointed to a majority of 94 if voting intentions remained the same. And the analysis of the reports of the party's area agents – a naturally cautious and pessimistic group – predicted a majority of 72 on the basis of current feeling.

The paper then gave a computer analysis of the 'worse case scenario'. The worst case, which included all the seats that could be lost in the present climate and with the polls as they were that weekend, gave the Tories a majority of 26. Norman Tebbit's exposition also took a brief look at his chief-of-staff's charts to show how variations in the vote would affect each region, concluding that the polls would have to change substantially before drastic dangers threatened the party. He spoke for about half an hour. There was a short discussion afterwards with a few questions on the document, which were answered by Dr Keith Britto, the party's statistician, who was called into the room. Then, after a break for tea, the meeting closed with Mrs Thatcher smiling and saying, not for the first time: 'Thank you very much – I shall sleep on it.'

Although they all 'knew', they did not finally know until the calls went out from Downing Street just before nine the next morning summoning the Cabinet to a meeting at eleven. It was brief and to the point. Yes, it was 11 June. It was not going to be easy, she told them. 'We shall have to fight every inch of the way. We do not assume. We work.' A few immediate plans were made; there was a short discussion on the technicalities of

Dissolution – and within the hour the members were back on the doorstep of Number 10, smiling slightly sheepishly because they were sworn to secrecy until 2 p.m. and therefore could not answer the shouted questions from the dozens of reporters and photographers penned in across the street to await the news and the ritual comings and goings.

Mrs Thatcher went to the Palace formally to advise the Queen to dissolve Parliament; the date was fixed for the following Monday. That night on television she spoke of her passionate belief in freedom and in seeing an end to socialism and her wish to stay on as Prime Minister – for as long as that would take. 'There is a long way to go,' she said. 'When you have a lot of ideas for the future, as we have, you want to feel you have a number of years in which to implement them. I would hope that this is not my last election – this is only the third time of asking. Yes, I hope to go on and on.' As she spoke the lights in Central Office were burning late – this time in earnest. The plans for the election, so long kept under lock and key, had been brought out at 2 p.m. and the first of the thousands of phone calls had been made to finalise the arrangements, the booking of trains and planes, halls to speak in and factories to visit.

One of the first of these calls was to Saatchi & Saatchi, summoning them to a meeting that evening with Norman Tebbit so that he could, at last, brief them on the likely contents of the manifesto and give them their first chance to get to grips with the 'positive' advertising work they would be expected to produce in a matter of days. Because Tebbit was delayed at that meeting, hasty arrangements were made to substitute Lord Young for him on Channel Four News and later in the 'Newsnight' studios. The somewhat chaotic last-minute switch worked very well on this occasion, further proof that the Young/Tebbit soft/heavy combination was potentially a great success, but it was a haphazard arrangement. At the Chequers meeting on Sunday, the Prime Minister had finally decided to establish, under John Wakeham, a formalised system of allocating ministers to appear on the dozens of radio and television programmes which proliferate at election times, and it took a few days for this policy to begin to operate.

A much longer Cabinet meeting was held next morning, Tuesday 12 May. This time the gathering was in more serious mood and swiftly got down to business, for there was much to do. The plans for dealing with the remaining legislation were already well in hand – the Finance Bill and the Scottish Rates Bill were to be saved, but the Criminal Justice Bill had to be jettisoned. Finalising the second part of the manifesto – The Next Moves Forward – took up the lion's share of the time. The version worked on by Mrs Thatcher, Norman Tebbit and Brian Griffiths on Saturday afternoon was now put before the members for discussion. Mrs Thatcher made it clear that this was very much how she wanted the final version to be, and implicitly they were invited to 'speak now or forever hold your peace'. All of them were familiar with most of the contents of the document, and most were happy to confine themselves to comments on its style, which was now seen to be 'punchy and meaty', and its design, which won praise for its anonymous creators. There were two problems, however: the first was one of clarity in a section covering housing, part of Environment Secretary Nicholas Ridley's contribution. The second problem was over one of the industrial relations proposals, which Lord Young felt had not been given enough time for consultation. The Cabinet overruled his objection and the proposal stayed in the manifesto.

Time was now of the essence, if the document was to be produced and printed ready for the proposed launch the following Tuesday. Their deliberations lasted more than three hours: they did not break until just before one o'clock, causing many of them to scurry off late to lunch appointments. All the final corrections were collated, the writing team working with Lord Young and Howell James that afternoon, and the final go-ahead was given to the printers on Wednesday night.

The announcement of the election, while it had been widely predicted by almost all politicians, party workers and the media, and while it cannot exactly have been a spur-of-the-moment decision by Mrs Thatcher, nevertheless gave her a huge burst of adrenalin and she went into overdrive in planning for the next 31 crucial days. At times like this her pace is frankly exhausting to all those around her – in a sense many of her closest aides pick themselves by their ability to survive the pace. From the Cabinet meeting she went straight into the preparation of Parliamentary Questions, to the House, and back for a meeting to discuss the final plans for the tour – including a hasty reappraisal of the security arrangements in view of the heightened threat after the successful ambush of the IRA at the weekend, in which eight terrorists had been killed. The meeting also cleared up the final arrangements for the last three days of the tour before election day. All the tour 'staff' were now ready and briefed on their tasks. Apart from the four security men who would travel everywhere with her, augmented by dozens of others at every point on the trip, the travelling party would consist each day of the Prime Minister and Denis Thatcher, Stephen Sherbourne and either Michael Alison, her PPS, or Sir David Wolfson, two secretaries, two media 'handlers' (Christine Wall and Bill Haresnape), two or three tour organisers (Roger Boaden, Harvey Thomas and Sheila Howe), a computer expert and John Whittingdale, who had already fed into his memory almost every fact he might be expected to know in the next four weeks and compiled in several vast files all those that he might be expected to have at his fingertips.

Christine Wall's plan for the all-important television coverage was to have one major set-piece interview in each of the three weeks of actual campaigning. The rest of the week after the announcement was to be taken up with clearing away parliamentary business and making final plans, the next week with launching the manifesto, receiving the bus and one day's travelling at the end, then, from Bank Holiday Monday on, the serious business would begin. For all of that week, the week after and the first three days of the following week – up to the eve of polling day – Mrs Thatcher would hit the road with a vengeance, visiting every region of the country in a series of darting raids out of London immediately after her daily press conference at 9.30 a.m. It was in these last three weeks that she would make her major television appearances, and she would also give local TV and radio interviews as she went around each of the regions. The plan was based on the Prime Minister's belief that three weeks was quite long enough to ask the British public to concentrate on the election: she did not want to bore them, either by being on national television too much over that period or by stretching her campaign out over too long a period.

When it became clear, during the week, that this was to be

the Prime Minister's strategy, there were a number of people in the party who expressed grave reservations about it. To some it smacked of the sort of approach Bernard Ingham might adopt in keeping Mrs Thatcher away from the media until the time was deemed right for a magisterial statement to be made. They feared that it might be construed as arrogance, as distancing herself from the electorate, at a time when the public liked to see their politicians questioned closely and brought to book. Others felt that, while the policy might be right, it left too long an interval between calling the election and the first of her major appearances. In fact, they thought, it would give the other parties almost a fortnight's clear run before she started in earnest, and the party could not afford to let them have two days – let alone two weeks. The whole arrangement, according to critics, showed the lack of a Gordon Reece figure at the heart of the campaign – a person of sufficient weight to *tell* the Prime Minister what she should do, instead of pandering to her and trying to cocoon her from the electorate. It is significant that, despite a personal letter from Sue Lawley apologising for the way Mrs Thatcher had been 'ambushed' about the Falklands on 'Nationwide' in the 1983 election, her request for a chance to make up for the mistake on the equivalent and very popular programme 'On the Spot' in 1987 was refused out of hand. A major figure in charge of her communications would not have let that happen, it was thought.

John Wakeham's task of co-ordinating the TV and radio appearances of all the other ministers was more difficult. A delicate minuet is always danced with the producer of a programme inviting a minister or spokesman for the other parties, because the producer's interests are not always those of the politicians – in fact they are very rarely those of the politicians. He wants 'good radio' or 'good television': in other words he wants controversy, a row or incident which will make the listener or viewer sit up and take notice and maybe even get the programme mentioned in news broadcasts or in the papers. To achieve this some producers deliberately plan 'ambushes' of the politician: they invite him to come on their show and promise a broad discussion on all his favourite topics; only at the last minute is the subject matter changed or a mystery guest revealed who can, it is hoped, embarrass the man. Others, particularly on discussion programmes, deliberately prime one or more of their guests with the questions they are going to be asked in order to make the respected government figure, of whatever party, seem less clever than he is, if not a total fool. This is rarely a matter of political bias, more the desire simply to 'get a row going', and is common to all media people.

Most senior politicians are aware of the tricks that can be played to throw them off balance, and therefore highly complicated negotiations take place between their staff and the producers before any appearance can be agreed. Who is going to be on the programme with them? Are they of equal status? Are they superior to them in argument? Are they 'bruisers', while our man is gentle and analytical in his approach? Is there a studio audience who will be invited to join in? How has it been picked? Will anyone else from outside be asked to join in? What is the subject matter? Do they have any surprise research or nasty statements from people that might be thrown at our man during the programme? All these questions are gone over and negotiated heavily long before the programme goes out.

If John Wakeham needed an instruction manual, all he had to do was to read Brian Walden's article in the *Sunday Times* ten days earlier, laying out the golden rules for politicians appearing on television at election time. 'Use only those who are good on television,' he wrote. 'What could be more obvious? Yet the advice is seldom taken. Putting big-wigs in just because they are big-wigs is unprofessional. Politicians forget that the public knows next to nothing about a man's place in the party hierarchy.' It was a lesson Wakeham himself ignored, to his high cost just a week later.

Why was the activation of his appointment left until the last moment? This was, perhaps, the first sign that the much-vaunted arrangements made by Central Office might not be as good as they had been claimed to be. In this first week after the announcement, a week in which everybody − especially the media − expected the Tory machine, widely touted as being by far the best of the three parties, to slip effortlessly into top gear and cruise away down the road to victory, there were distinct signs such as this that all was not well. There were several worrying occasions when the left hand did not seem to know what the right hand was doing.

Lord Young's inclusion in the CCO team had certainly put some impetus behind the preparations in those areas where he had been asked to help, but he was not in charge. He was meticulously careful always to refer major decisions and requests to Norman Tebbit, but he too was beginning to find the management structure at Smith Square frustrating. In the early days of his involvement, for example, he had suggested to the Prime Minister that it might be a good idea to set up a smokescreen about the date of the election by booking several major halls for September. She had been enthusiastic, as had Tebbit, and it was agreed in writing to go ahead. But nothing was ever done about it, which made Young begin to realise, for the first time, how great the problems of inertia and lack of communication and co-ordination might become in an election campaign.

There were undoubtedly plenty of good ideas about: the Barnum side of Lord Young's personality was rampant and he dreamed up new schemes almost daily to add attraction to the tour. Some were unworkable from the start, but others were investigated thoroughly. He conceived one idea of hiring an airship, painting the Tory logo on the side and flying it over every town the Prime Minister was on her way to visit with 'Maggie's Coming' in flashing lights as the message underneath. In CCO itself Michael Dobbs had the idea of countering the Brahms of the Labour Party and the Purcell of the Alliance with a specially written theme tune for the Thatcher campaign. He persuaded Andrew Lloyd Webber to compose it; it was recorded by session musicians in a West End studio on Friday 15 May and ready for the Prime Minister to listen to when she returned from Chequers on the Sunday night. The idea was to make it the sound-track of the video which was being prepared for use as the warm-up to her major speeches.

At the same time as these preparations were reaching their climax another, infinitely more subtle, less flamboyant, but nevertheless just as vital campaign was being waged from CCO – the campaign to raise the money to pay for it all. Along the first-floor corridor, at the opposite front corner from Norman Tebbit's office is the lair of Lord McAlpine, the party treasurer.

It is his job to nudge, hint, whisper, cajole, beg, and twist the arms of sufficient people each year to supply the funds to run the party. At the end of March he stated his purpose was to raise £20 million, but neither was this an accurate figure, nor was it, as widely reported, all for the election. In 1983 the Tories spent just under four million pounds on the central campaign itself. This was broken down roughly as follows: £2.6 million on advertising (£850,000 on poster sites and £1,725,000 on press advertising), £360,000 on producing the Election Broadcasts, £96,000 on opinion polls, £212,000 on publications, £52,000 on the leader's tour and £262,000 on extra staff and administrative costs. They also spent £440,000 on necessary preparations before the campaign. In addition that year it cost nearly five million just to keep CCO going. These figures do not include the two million raised locally and spent locally by candidates during the campaign.

In contrast to the Tories' four million on the national election campaign, the Labour party spent two-and-a-half million and the Alliance about two million. Inflation alone over the last four years could be expected to put all these costs up by at least 20 per cent, in addition to which the Tories were anticipating much greater expenditure because the fight was expected to be more of a three-cornered contest in 1987. Thus Lord McAlpine's calculations had to allow for up to six million each on the campaign itself and the annual running costs of CCO – a total of about twelve million pounds. His problem, however, was that he had to raise it all at once. When he started at the beginning of April, writing dozens of letters each day to businessmen and regular contacts, he knew that the date would be either June or October. There is little use in trying to raise money after an election (presuming, that is, that the party had been victorious), so it all has to be done beforehand: hence his inflated figure of £20 million, to scare the donors into action. In fact his target was £15 million, to give him a comfortable margin above the twelve he needed.

His techniques of fundraising have been honed somewhat in the 12 years since he was given the job by Mrs Thatcher just after she became leader. In those early days he cheerfully admits he was somewhat naïve in the arm-twisting involved. One morning he received a letter from the chairman of one of London's most famous, but most staid, gentlemen's outfitters, containing £5 for the Tory coffers. Enraged at the man's meanness, McAlpine rushed round to the shop, marched into the chairman's office and gave him a half-hour lecture on the dangers of Socialism, the threat to business and the need for generosity in the cause of Conservatism at times like this. At the end the man nodded his head in agreement and said: 'You are right, Alastair. I should have given you more.' He then took out his wallet and handed over another fiver.

Now he finds he seldom has to pressure people: they know who he is and what he wants. 'I have a certain amount of pity,' he says, 'for the businessman who thinks he can survive just as well under Socialism. I discuss the realities of life with them. I rarely have to ask for money – they know I'm a reasonable, amiable sort of chap and they know they can usually get a glass of champagne and a cigar out of me.' About 10 per cent of contributions to Tory party funds comes from the City; most of the rest comes not from established major industries but from people who are running their own businesses, people, he says, who have put their whole lives into what they are doing and are reluctant to see it thrown away. They are mostly fairly new, middle-sized companies and the contributions from them range from £1,000 to £50,000. McAlpine's, the family firm, gives £35,000 a year to the party. At the lower end of the contributions scale there are a large number of small businessmen and farmers. The announcement of 11 June was probably unwelcome only in his office, for it meant that, with his two fellow treasurers and staff of 18, he now had to complete a year's fundraising work in a few weeks, a task which they set about frantically.

The rest of the first week, despite the media's insistence that battle was joined, was very much a phoney war. The ritual moves were made by the opposition to try to press the Prime Minister into a televised debate. There were attempts by most television stations to start debates on the major issues immediately – a week before the manifestos appeared – and seemingly endless programmes so full of speculation and clips of old film that it was little wonder many of the populace professed to be bored by the whole event long before it even started. It was, to a great extent, television's bid to dictate the agenda of the election itself. As David Dimbleby said, not without irony, in one of these early programmes: 'It was my father . . . who invented elections.' As never before, politicians would try to use the medium to put their message across; while the medium would clearly try to dictate where, when and how the politicians were going to do it.

The last days of Parliament were used shamelessly by all three sides for pre-election showboating. Much was made in the media of the prospects of a hung parliament and Mrs Thatcher stated, not for the first time, that she would have 'no dealings in smoke-filled rooms' with another party if hers was the largest one but lacking a majority after the election. She made it clear that the Tories would present their programme and defy the minorities to bring them down.

All three parties had minor embarrassments still causing concern. The Alliance could not seem to silence Neville Sandelson and his proposition that all their supporters vote Tory, Labour got into difficulties with Linda Bellos and the controversy over black sections (a row which Neil Kinnock swiftly defused, although for how long remained to be seen) and the Tories still had waiting to come to court the case of Keith Best, the ex-MP for Ynys Mon, who, it was alleged, had made multiple applications for BT – as well as the much more serious case against the Billericay MP Harvey Proctor. (He resigned his seat at the weekend and pleaded guilty to charges of gross indecency the following week.)

The Labour Party accused the Tories of having a 'hidden' manifesto and tried out a few of its lines of attack. The use of the out-of-context or slightly bogus quote is one that all politicians indulge in; the art is to deny it cleverly, by turning it on your opponents, or to ignore it altogether. Labour used the technique during the week on both the Prime Minister and Lord Young, accusing Mrs Thatcher of arrogance in believing she would rule for ever and David Young of saying he never lost any sleep over the unemployed. Neither rose to the bait. The media, particularly television, tried hard to make unemployment the issue of the campaign, which was not as harmful to the Tories as many would have anticipated. It enabled them to re-emphasise that, by whatever criteria the figures were counted, the numbers were falling and had been falling every month for nine months – ten by the end of the week, when a further fall of nearly 20,000 was announced for May bringing the government figures to 3,020,100.

In all three parties dry runs of the daily press conferences were being held. At the Labour Party headquarters in Walworth Road, just south of the river, the trio of party secretary Larry Whitty, communications expert Peter Mandelson and campaign chief Bryan Gould had welded themselves into a formidable force despite the disaster at Greenwich. It was clear that under Neil Kinnock they had been given a free hand, for the first time in Labour history, to plan the campaign on a professional basis and not according to socialist dogma. Gone was the slightly ashamed attitude towards media presentation, as though it were somehow against their principles – now the party machine was ready to take on the might of Saatchi & Saatchi and the fabled Tory imagemakers and play them at their own game.

In the first week it was already clear that Labour intended to concentrate on two sides of the same coin. Their attack would concentrate primarily on the Tories, presenting them, and particularly their leader, as mean and uncaring. At the same time they would present Labour, and particularly its leader, as the very models of compassion and care. Word which had come some months before that Neil Kinnock would be kept well away from the national press seemed to be borne out by the plans to hold a large number of regional press conferences each week – thus, according to the Tories, avoiding the big guns of television and the political editors of the papers in London. As Tim Bell had pointed out in 1979, so Gould now practised in 1987: the first aim was to rubbish the party in power. Thus it was already clear that it would be a major struggle between the Labour Party's bid to discredit the government and its eight years' record and the Tories' attempts to defend the record and attack the lack of policies in the Labour manifesto. As Gould said, anticipating the campaign: 'The election is there to be won. If the Tories' position begins to slip, and I confidently expect it will, they will come under greater and greater pressure. Our agenda is the one we think people will want to discuss, and that will give us a head start. Last time both Labour and the Alliance altered their tactics; this time the Tories are at greater risk than we are.'

The Alliance 'Siamese twins', David Owen and David Steel, began their campaign straight away, anxious to draw first blood in the opinion polls. Throughout the week they were seen giving press conferences in cities all over Britain – on one occasion not even knowing, at first, in which city they were. It was already clear the Alliance planned to spend far less on its advertising than either Labour or the Tories and that the two leaders planned to stick close to each other throughout the campaign – in order to run less risk of contradicting each other, the Tory strategists believed. In the first few days their initial target was not immediately apparent. Were they going to go for Labour first – the obvious thing to do – to establish themselves early on in second place, then turn the heat on the Tories? Or would they believe they were going to rise above Labour anyway and concentrate, from the start, on the Tories? John Pardoe, the former MP for North Cornwall, who was head of the Alliance campaign – working with Des Wilson – said at the beginning of the week that his technique would be quite simple: to aim a knockout blow at Neil Kinnock and the Labour Party early on, then go for the voters who were only backing Mrs Thatcher because they were frightened of a left-wing government. 'If we can remove that fear of Labour in the first week, then God help the Conservatives,' he said. By the weekend – even though it was still in the period of the 'phoney war' – it was already becoming clear that the Alliance intentions, if indeed these were what they were, were not being matched in reality and that they were concentrating just as much, if not more, on the Tories.

On Friday 15 May, Mrs Thatcher flew to Scotland to give the closing address to the Scottish Conservatives in Perth and, as she had in 1983, she used the occasion as a curtain-raiser on the campaign itself. 'There is only one party in this election which knows what it wants to do and has the courage to tell the people about its plans for the future,' she said. 'Indeed it seems the Conservative Party alone is interested in the future. The other parties shy away from policies. They talk only about the paraphernalia of politics – black sections, tactical voting and hung parliaments. Don't be surprised by this. They are inhibited from talking about policies – the Liberals and the SDP because they wish they had more, and Labour because they wish they had fewer.

'So from the Labour Party expect "The Iceberg Manifesto" – one-tenth of its socialism visible, nine-tenths beneath the surface. And from the Liberals and the SDP expect "The Blurred Manifesto" – easy reading for those with double vision. But from our party there will be no flimsy manifesto, no hidden manifesto. Our Conservative manifesto will present a *full* programme for a *full* parliament in the *full* light of day.'

It was a performance of typical fire and conviction. She did not have the slightest doubt she could win, or that, given the hard work necessary, she would win. As she had told Sir David English two days before: 'It's not going to be a pushover. We are going to fight every inch of the way . . . The next four weeks will be rough, tough, exciting and full of surprises.'

Could any of those surprises puncture her confidence? Could anything prevent a third Tory term? A Marplan poll of key marginals, carried out earlier in the week for *The Times*, showed that the party was on course for another victory: if the voting intentions stayed the same until 11 June the size of that win would be the same as in 1983. Nearly all the polls that week had placed the Tories comfortably above 40 per cent, Labour hovering around 30 and the Alliance around 25. It was clear that enough of the electorate believed that the nation was better off, that they themselves were better off and that the Tories were the party to ensure that this state of affairs continued. So what could go wrong?

There were five broad areas of potential peril for the Tories. Failure in any one of them – or a combination of them – could bring them down. They could lose on the issues. They knew they were vulnerable on pensions, health, education and unemployment, and that the under-twenty-fives and over-fifty-fives were their weakest groups. They would have good policies in their manifesto, they were confident that those policies were better than those of the opposition parties and that they could fire them with bigger guns. The number of ministers capable of scoring well in media debate was far greater than any of the other parties could put up. Therefore the Tories felt they were unlikely to be beaten on the full range of issues. But that did not rule out the possibility of the other parties managing to isolate one issue, to latch on to it and for the Tories not to be able to dislodge them from it. This was possible, but unlikely.

They could lose because of a lack of issues. It already seemed clear to the Tories that both Labour and Alliance were anxious to hide policies, where indeed they had them. In the case of Neil Kinnock, the Labour Party would be trying to 'sell' him as a Presidential figure. The feeling was that the Labour strategists had recognised that they could not go into an election with the full-blown socialist manifesto dictated by the decisions of their Party Conference — that way would lie another disaster on the scale of 1983. Instead they would strip the manifesto of every-thing contentious and build up Kinnock with a massive person-ality campaign, hoping to obscure the fact that they had few policies and sweep the electorate away on an American-style bandwagon. If both Labour and Alliance took to the high ground in this way, they would be able to snipe at the Tory policies from the rocks above, putting the party on the defensive, causing it to issue clarifying statement after clarifying statement and bogging it down in detail. It could be that, faced with these tactics, the Tory big guns might not be able to dislodge the enemy from the rocks above and bring them out into the open where it could be shown they had no policies. In other words, if the Tories could not get the contrast between what they had and what the others had to offer into the debate, then again they could lose. Also possible, but unlikely.

They could lose by paying too much attention to either the Alliance or Labour and letting the other one through by default. This was, of course, presuming that the bandwagon effect could be made to work in a general election and that, having made it work, the party that did so could keep it rolling inexorably on. As already described, the Tories had planned carefully for just such an eventuality occurring with the Alliance. Had they paid enough attention to the possibility of its happening with Labour? Norman Tebbit and Michael Dobbs were certainly very confident that they could beat Labour on every count. Were they perhaps over-confident? Had they underestimated the nation's affection for the underdog, the power of playing 'Mr Niceguy' against 'TBW' and the greater natural interest of the media in the rising star than in the one who has been around for eight years? Possible, and not as unlikely as they believed.

They could lose by failures in Central Office – or between CCO and Number 10. Each of the other parties had a clearly defined, visible management structure – even the Alliance had merged the organisations of both parties for the election. Not only did CCO itself have inherent weaknesses, but there were potential problems with the personnel of the campaign, too. Its critics claimed there were too many chiefs and not enough Indians; too many glory seekers anxious to score the winning goal and not enough to do the hard, selfless slog necessary for victory; too many people in charge of parts of the campaign and no one in overall charge; too many people working in isolation from one another and no one to draw all the threads together; too many people ready to shed the blame rather than take it – turn away rather than get involved – if anything went wrong. The knowledge that they were a dozen or so points ahead in the polls had, however much they tried to fight against it, bred a deep complacency. The fact that in 1970, Harold Wilson had lost 12 points in the first 12 days of his campaign was not the slightest cause for concern among certain of the senior party officials. But the complacency was not just in CCO, it was in the party and perhaps among the voters too. A shock to the system, a swift rise of one of the other parties, might bring the voters to their senses, might buck the party workers up, might put some zip into Smith Square – but it might equally well lead to catastrophic squabbling and collapse. Possible again, and to some quite likely.

Or they could lose because of Mrs Thatcher. It could be that there were still, despite what the polls showed, more people who, come the day, disliked her and would not vote for her, than there were people who disliked her but nevertheless admired her. It was possible that her recovery in the polls, and in the nation's regard, from the low of 1986, was still too flimsy; that she had not sufficiently re-established herself with a firm base of respect among the voters. It was obvious from the opening day of the campaign that the opposition parties were going to try to play this factor to the hilt: they believed that by making her THE ISSUE, they could bring her down. Labour, particularly, aimed to promote Neil Kinnock in contrast to her. He was caring, he was compassionate, he believed in people: she was all the opposites. Her every statement was examined by the Labour team for signs of the harshness and arrogance they believed they could convince the voters was her nature. The suffering of the poor and the unemployed was quickly transmuted into the price to be paid in Thatcher's Britain for making the few rich. When she had talked of going on and on – possibly into a fourth term – she had qualified it by stating clearly that whether she could would be up to the voters. The qualification was swiftly forgotten and her arrogance was proclaimed throughout the media. Could she yet be the principal factor in her own defeat? Possible, but again unlikely.

What then was her private attitude as she prepared at Chequers that weekend for the campaign? According to one of those closest to her it was: 'First, she is genuinely convinced that what she has to offer the British people is right and it is what they want – that she has a mission to change Britain and pull it back from Socialism. She does not waver from that, however bad the polls or however much the criticism. There is no sense of defeatism about her. That is her belief and conviction. Second, however, is the belief that she has in no way any divine right to rule. She knows she has to go before the electorate every four or five years and they can throw her out just like that. There is no sense in her, as there was in Ted Heath, that the electorate would not dare to be so ungrateful as to throw him out. She knows she has to earn that vote and it can never be taken for granted. Therefore the third element is that, whatever the polls are showing, nothing can be taken for granted and she will fight this election as hard as she has ever fought any one and will not relax for one second until it is over. She is in no way arrogant about power – she knows she has to earn it. She really believes that if you start to take it for granted then that is the beginning of the slippery slope.'

There was one other factor which four people centrally involved in the campaign mentioned, without prompting, as being one which could cause the Tories to lose. Acknowledging that without her towering presence as leader the party would at first be left rudderless, they all prefaced it by lowering their voices and whispering, 'God forbid . . .' That she be killed by terrorists.

8 | Summon the Exiles

In the Tory camp the first week of the election proper belonged to Norman Tebbit. He opened it in Hammersmith on the morning of Saturday 16 May by standing with a British bulldog in front of a poster showing the same animal dwarfing a German alsatian and a French poodle. As he bent down to touch the 18-month-old 'Duke', he joked to the assembled TV cameras and reporters: 'You can tell an election is on when the Tory chairman starts patting dogs.' He was at the centre of most of the activities launched by the Tory party during the week. And inevitably he took the blame at the end of it, when things had not gone as well as most of his colleagues would have liked.

It was the week the election went in search of an issue; and the issue very nearly became the failure of the Tories' own much-vaunted campaign machine itself. Within the space of a few days it was seen as leaderless, rudderless, haphazard and, in the words of one cabinet minister – 'quite clearly the worst of the three party operations'. It and the Tories – even Mrs Thatcher herself – had been trumped on almost every hand they had played. By midnight the following Friday night, the Prime Minister was so anxious about what was happening that she picked up the phone in Downing Street and summoned an emergency meeting of what she came to call 'Central Office in exile' for the following day.

It had always been Mrs Thatcher's intention to start the campaign slowly. She told reporters when she went on the Thursday to take delivery of her 'Battlebus' in London's Dockland that she thought three weeks was quite long enough – otherwise 'people would get fed up to the back teeth' with the election. But it was certainly not her intention that her rivals – particularly Neil Kinnock – should be allowed to steal a march on her in the way they did.

Part of the problem was the party's advertising which, according to its critics, lacked cohesion and any sense of style. Where it was pedestrian, the Labour Party's particularly was aggressive and brash. The 'three dogs' poster was obscure, as was the 'three red books' poster which went up with it. Neither had a memorable or an instantly understandable message. The press advertisements were equally disappointing in the first week – one on the Health Service being set in such an unsuitable typeface that it was almost unreadable in a tabloid paper. The only successful advertisement – with the slogan: 'Don't undo eight year's work in three seconds' and a list of the party's achievements – mystified many by its sudden appearance because they thought it was aimed at the last few days of the campaign, not the opening shot of it. Explanations that it would be used again in the last week to 'bring the campaign full circle' were thought to be hollow. When Mrs Thatcher was congratulated on it she remarked that it was a nice slogan: but she had had to go to the trouble of telling Saatchi & Saatchi what her achievements were. There was clearly no meeting of minds, as there had been in the days of Tim Bell.

Much against his will, the role of advertising liaison between Saatchi and Norman Tebbit and Mrs Thatcher had been thrust on Michael Dobbs. For the first time for months he found himself, on Tuesday morning, face to face with Mrs Thatcher and in the invidious position of trying to 'sell' her advertising. The chemistry between them was no better now than it had been when they last met, which did nothing to improve her satisfaction with the Saatchi work. If the poster and press advertisements were not the best possible, then there was greater happiness at the first of the PEBs. The theme was 'Freedom' and it was one of only two the Tories planned to let run for the full ten minutes. It was due to go out that night and it was, by any standards, a powerful, if controversial, statement of freedom as the historical bedrock of our society. It ended with a fluttering Union Jack, the hymn 'I vow to thee my country' and the slogan 'It's Great

To Be Great Again'. It set a tone for the campaign early and suffered only by comparison with Labour's first effort.

But by that comparison it was wiped out. For some months Peter Mandelson, Labour's communications supremo, had been working with Hugh Hudson, the director of *Chariots of Fire*, on the party's PEBs. The first sought in its ten minutes to present Neil Kinnock as a presidential figure of Olympian proportions. It was a brilliant and highly emotional piece of work, in many ways a direct copy of a famous Ronald Reagan advertisement from the 1984 US election campaign, in which the President had talked movingly of the day he met his wife Nancy and what she meant to him, mixed in with soft-focus shots of the two of them walking hand in hand through the countryside. It had nothing to do with politics or the issues, as the Tories were swift to point out. When it was shown on the Thursday night it infuriated many of their party faithful, and it was shrugged off as rubbish by most of the occupants of CCO. But its effect – along with the other notable successes of the week – on Labour supporters, Alliance doubters and a number of waverers, was to be startling. Kinnock's rating as a potential Prime Minister went up by 16 points in the space of seven days. Mrs Thatcher did not see it: nobody thought to show it to her, and in any case she did not have a video machine that worked in the flat in Downing Street.

Thus it was clear early in the campaign that in a crucial area, where the Tories had come to expect success, they had a serious challenge on their hands. Neither Michael Dobbs nor Norman Tebbit was helped in their task by the amount of time they found themselves spending with lawyers probing the ramifications of election law to establish whether they, or any of the other parties, were acting illegally in their plans to reach the public during the campaign. There were a number of disappointments as projects on which they had spent much effort had to be abandoned. Direct mail had already gone, now the planned nationwide newspaper had to go too. The fact that it would have reached every voter in every constituency was not seen in its favour as a national expense, but counted against it on the grounds that the voter had no choice but to come into contact with it, whereas he did have a choice with national newspapers. Therefore it was deemed to be aimed at special voters (all of them) in special seats (all of them also). The chief-of-staff also spent some time with lawyers examining the advertising plans of the other parties – particularly those of Labour, who made no secret of intending to concentrate their poster sites in marginal seats. Saatchi & Saatchi had, in the end, achieved a nationwide spread of sites with very little effort – by taking an early option on the sites being used for the government's Action For Jobs campaign. Their knowledge that all government advertising has to be withdrawn during an election enabled them to steal a march on the other parties, without being in danger of breaking the law.

The early disappointments in the advertisement campaign naturally focused criticism within the party once again on the chairman and his chief-of-staff, criticisms which were to be amplified further after the launch of the parties' manifestos. The documents themselves were well ballyhooed beforehand. The Alliance launched theirs on Monday and the other two principals on Tuesday. The Tory document was by far the meatiest – twenty-six pages of 'Our First Eight Years' and seventy-seven of 'The Next Moves Forward'. It was packed with promises, printed for ease of reading in blue type. The Alliance document had twenty-four pages, but of twice the size, and Labour had only fourteen pages of full text.

The three were best summarised as follows, in the *Economist*'s digest.

Economy   Tory: To beat inflation is the first objective; the aim is stable prices. To make public expenditure fall as share of national earnings. Alliance: Public spending up by £7 billion a year by second year; more for infrastructure, health, education, social security and a jobs programme. Counter-inflation tax on companies giving excessive pay rises. Labour: Spending up by £6 billion in each of first two years (plus £3.6 billion of extra benefits paid for by soaking the rich). More investment, more training, more public sector jobs. Borrowing to rise by £3 billion. Nothing on wages policy.

Jobs and Training   Tory: Guaranteed places on the Youth Training Scheme for all school leavers; no dole money for those who unreasonably refuse. Community programme to become full-time, paying more than social security benefit. A place on a scheme guaranteed to 18–25-year-olds out of work for 6–12 months. Within five years, a place for all those under 50 and jobless for two years on a government job or training scheme. Alliance: In three years, cut unemployment by one million: training, building programme, an employment subsidy and more public sector jobs. Job or training guaranteed for all long-term unemployed. Cut employers' insurance contributions in high unemployment areas. Labour: Unemployment cut by one million in two years: training, investment, lower employers' national insurance contributions, more jobs in health and education. Job or training guarantee for all 16-year-olds and long-term unemployed. A statutory minimum wage.

Benefits and Taxes Tory: Basic rate tax to fall to 25p as soon as prudent. More tax reform – no hint what. Tax incentives for personal pensions and profit-related pay. Mortgage tax relief to stay. Maintain value of state pension. Alliance: Basic rate stays at 27p. Tax, benefits and insurance to be merged and reformed: women to be taxed independently, and standard allowances for all, with married man's allowance frozen. Tackle poverty with higher pensions, child benefit, family income support and benefits for long-term unemployed. Mortgage tax relief only at basic rate. Labour: Basic tax back up to 29p, higher taxes on richest 5 per cent. More for pensioners, children and long-term unemployed. Wealth tax on richest 1 per cent. Mortgage tax relief only at basic rate.

Industry Tory: More privatisation: airports, water and electricity ('subject to proper regulation'). Resist protectionism. Alliance: Industrial investment bonds, paying tax-free interest. Tax allowance for investing in new technologies. Less tax and red tape for small companies. No buying back of privatised firms, but water and electricity to stay public. Tax incentives for workers' ownership and profit-sharing. Labour: Tax penalties to induce capital back from abroad. Investment bank to provide cheap long-term finance for industry. 'Social ownership': Telecom and British Gas shareholders keep shares, which become non-voting. New holding company to buy into high-tech industries.

Labour relations Tory: New rights for union members: to re-elect all union bosses, to vote on strikes, but then to have right not to strike anyway. Ballots to be postal. A union commissioner to enforce law. End post-entry closed shop. New consultative machinery for teachers. Alliance: New laws on employee participation. More incentives for workers' share-ownership. Support union reforms so far; but give positive right to strike and to be recognised. Disputes to be arbitrated before strikes. Encourage no-strike deals. Restore teachers' negotiating rights. Labour: Repeal of all Tory laws. Extend employment protection and restore the wage councils. Secondary picketing legal again. Keep secret ballots for strikes and elections (details incomprehensible). New tribunal to handle union complaints.

Education Tory: A national curriculum. Let schools run their own finances, and opt for funding by central government, not local councils. More city technology colleges, more assisted places in private schools. Schools able to run own finances. Alliance: Reform A-levels, make them less specialised. One year's nursery school for all. Keep current assisted places, but phase out system later. 'Uphold rights' of those who want private schools. Labour: National curriculum. Means-tested maintenance for 16–18-year-olds. End the 11-plus everywhere, the assisted-places scheme and subsidies to private schools. Nursery education for all three- and four-year-olds.

Health Tory: Make NHS more efficient – no figures. Full review of 'community care'. Improve screening for breast and cervical cancer. Alliance: New benefits for 'carers'. Limit prescription rises to inflation rate. Preventive health check-ups, ban on tobacco advertising. A new fund of £250m over three years to equalise standards between regions. Labour: Better family doctor service. Cut (eventually abolish) prescription charges, competitive tendering. Separate public and private medicine. Phase out 'pay beds'. Good pay for nurses *et al.*, not just 'pre-election sweeteners'. Carers' benefits.

Housing Tory: Council tenants to transfer to a housing association or co-operative or other landlord, if they wish. Relax controls on rental market, with new system of shortholds. Stronger laws against harassment and eviction. Alliance: Cancel cuts in housing benefit. Relax restrictions on council-house building. Tax credits, and no stamp duty, for first-time buyers. Let people rent rooms out, up to £60 a week, without paying income tax. Labour: 'Major' housebuilding drive. Council tenants to

keep right to buy; councils must spend proceeds on more houses.
Crime Tory: Revive Criminal Justice Bill dropped for the election. More police, no local control of policing priorities. Build more prisons. New rules on evidence of City fraud. Alliance: Recruit 4000 more policemen. Local police authorities remain, but proportional representation will keep out 'extremists'. Rethink youth custody, limit time spent in prison on remand. Labour: More street-lights, window locks and alarm buttons at police stations. Locally elected police authorities. A statutory commission to stop City fraud.

Home Affairs Tory: Broadcasting deregulation; television stations to take more independent programmes; curbs on broadcast sex and violence. Immigration controls 'firm but fair'; tighter laws. Alliance: Decentralise arts finance. Royal Commission on media violence. Immigration controls 'fair'; rights of appeal against deportation or refusal of citizenship. Citizenship for all born in Britain. Labour: Protect broadcasting independence; prevent foreign control. Immigration policy 'firm and fair', but non-discriminatory, too.

Environment Tory: Privatise water and sewerage but set up new rivers authority to control pollution. More nuclear power. Maintain green belt. Alliance: Stronger penalties for pollution. New environmental protection department, with Cabinet Minister. No more nuclear power stations; 'no case' for Sizewell. Protect green belt. Labour: Extend planning control to farming and forestry. End hunting with hounds. Reduce dependence on nuclear energy, cancel Sizewell. Protect green belt.

Local Government Tory: Replace rates in England with community charge (in law for Scotland already) and national uniform business rate. Make councils contract out many services. New urban development corporations. Alliance: Local income tax to replace rates. Proportional representation. Assemblies for Scotland, Wales and regions, including Greater London. Labour: Annual local elections everywhere. Bring back the GLC. Repeal community charge in Scotland. Inner cities: let councils declare 'public action zones', more grants, programmes, partnerships and land reclamation.

Government Tory: More management reforms in Civil Service; may reshape some ministeries. Alliance: Proportional representation for general elections and Euro-Parliament. Reform Commons procedure, phase out hereditary peerages. Fixed-term parliaments. Labour: Reform secrecy laws. Freedom of Information Act. No mention of Lords.

Defence Tory: Keep nuclear weapons, modernise them with Trident. More efficient armed forces (no mention of more money). 50% strategic missile cut and the elimination of medium-range missiles – in 'balanced and verifiable' deals. Alliance: Nuclear weapons to stay until they can be negotiated away. Cancel Trident, pull back from SDI. Stay in NATO but persuade it not to rely on nuclear weapons so much. Lobby for a European nuclear-free zone 150 kilometres around the East–West line. Labour: Support nuclear disarmament talks, especially to remove cruise 'and other nuclear weapons' in Britain. Then remove them ('after consultation') anyway. Other defence arrangements with the Americans to be unaffected.

Foreign Tory: 'A leading role' in the EEC, and an attempt to control its budget. Open its financial market; cut its air fares. No negotiating Falklands sovereignty, no South African sanctions, no change in status of Northern Irish unless they wish. Alliance: 'Enthusiastic' EEC member. Reform its elections, institutions and agricultural policy. Selective South African sanctions. Less deference to USA. Labour: stay in the EEC, try to end agricultural policy 'abuses and scandals'. Sanctions against South Africa; back Anglo-Irish agreement and Northern Irish self-determination. Double foreign aid.

The three documents were the central objects of the week – indeed of the whole campaign. What was in them, or not in them, was to be plotted over strategically, manoeuvred tactically and finally argued over endlessly by and between each of the parties. They contained the 'ishooos' with which the politicians and the pundits transfixed the nation on television each night. This, we were to be told endlessly, was what the election was all about – but, as it transpired, it was not so much about policies, but about the politicians themselves.

All three parties take their manifestos very seriously: as we have seen, the launching of them and the daily press conferences at which the main issues in them are discussed are regarded as being of supreme importance in the election. They are indeed important, but not because the public has any real knowledge of what is in the manifestos as they go into the polling booths, rather because they provide the backdrop for the whole campaign – the point at which almost every argument starts and many finish. It is the politicians themselves, particularly the leaders of the parties, who are the focus of the election. Even people who are interested in the policies of the respective parties tend to make up their minds not so much about the issues themselves, but by how well, or badly, the politicians handle those issues in the media and how successfully they manipulate the presentation of them to their own advantage.

This was the battle which Neil Kinnock won hands down during the first week. The Tories' manifesto was undoubtedly meatier, punchier and more full of new ideas and radical proposals than the other two. It lived up to its billing. And indeed there were in Downing Street and in CCO great hopes that the party would be able to take the electorate in stately procession through the document day by day – leaving it convinced by 11 June that there was only one party to vote for. The first evidence was that this was not to be so. The initiative was snatched away from the Tories early in the week and it was a disturbingly long time before they regained it. It is possible that Mrs Thatcher had taken her eye off the ball and, in her four years cocooned away by the government machine, had forgotten the need for the sort of co-ordinated presentation that she had accepted so readily from Gordon Reece and Cecil Parkinson – that she thought she could make do with what she had. Perhaps those around her no longer saw the need – if they ever had – for a communications chief she could work with easily and whose judgement and opinions she could trust. Perhaps the lack of one communications expert in charge was the first, and the deepest, flaw to be exposed in the Tory machine; for it began to seem that a number of people in charge meant, in reality, that no one was.

Whatever the explanation, the Tory manifesto launch was a disappointing affair, especially by comparison with Labour's. At the end of the week everybody was blaming just about everybody else for what had happened. The Alliance had launched theirs on the Monday; it had passed off smoothly and creditably, but with very little fire. The public had already had seven full days of 'the two Davids' flitting round the country and the contents of the document had been well telegraphed ahead in the media, so there was very little about the launch to make the event stand out.

When Mrs Thatcher arrived at Central Office shortly before 9.30 on the Tuesday morning she went straight into a briefing from the CCO team. This was to set the pattern of her days during the campaign, when she would normally arrive an hour or so before the press conference time to be given a full rundown on the topics of the day. The meeting in her new first-floor office, which for security reasons overlooked a central well in the building and not the street, was businesslike and brisk, since the entire manifesto, not just one topic, was being covered. She was in a good mood and exuded a buoyant confidence to her fellow ministers who were to share the platform. Finally, with just one minute to go before 10.30 a.m., she picked up her files and led the way downstairs and along the corridor to the conference room.

It would be difficult to say which of the four groups of people represented in that cramped room that morning was the most uncomfortable – the six or seven television crews who sought to film the event, the three dozen photographers, behind whom the Prime Minister literally vanished for the first five minutes she was in the room, the hundred or so writing and broadcasting journalists and commentators, most of whom were forced to stand in conditions of real discomfort – or Mrs Thatcher and her nine senior ministers, who sat hunched together on the platform like a bunch of schoolboys jostling on a bench. There was a feeling that if she had sneezed, the two on the ends (Kenneth Baker and Nicholas Ridley) would have fallen off their chairs. It looked on television that night precisely what it was: hot, cramped and uncomfortable. The Tory team batted as well as it could, but the message was as disjointed as its visual presentation. Every time one minister shifted, two or three others had to move also to accommodate his movement.

An hour earlier Labour had launched their manifesto only 200 yards away in the spaciousness of the Queen Elizabeth II Conference Hall, where the stage had been carefully prepared in the new beige colour of Labour with the red rose motif. To the strains of an electronic version of Brahms, Neil Kinnock and Roy Hattersley strode purposefully together down the central aisle of the hall (looking, as Michael White of the *Guardian* described it, for all the world like a couple at a San Francisco gay wedding), split left and right at the top to go up the steps, and arrived on the platform simultaneously and to the announcement of their names over the PA system. Several journalists there complained of feeling like extras on a film set, which is precisely what they were; for all the bulletins that day and evening could not help but reflect the extraordinary gloss of the occasion. It was suggested that Labour's manifesto was purposely thin; this was not to be a campaign in which they wanted their policies to come under too much scrutiny. Here was the first real proof that the personality build-up of Neil Kinnock, and the contrast of this carefully packaged presentation with that of Margaret Thatcher, was to be central to their strategy.

Once again there was criticism of CCO by those who were concerned about what they had seen on television that night. They felt that the party machine had let Labour steal a march on what should have been their big day of the week. In its defence one or two of those who had been in on the early planning of the campaign pointed out that it was Mrs Thatcher's decision to stick with the cramped facilities at Smith Square, even though five other possible sites had been reconnoitred as early as a year before and offered to her. Nevertheless, it was pointed out, a better job could have been made of allocating the spaces in the room – to make sure, for example, that the top correspondents from newspapers and broadcasting had seats; that, perhaps, the foreign press were put in the overflow room, even that the numbers of TV crews and photographers be limited, since there was little possibility of variation in their end results. The problem appeared to be that, since Mrs Thatcher had insisted they stay in CCO, no one had thought any further about the consequences. There was a feeling of 'Well if that's what she wants, that's what she's going to get.' Those who were horrified by what they saw, among them Lord Young, had little chance to interfere with something which was not directly part of their remit. Once again, the lack of anyone in overall charge of communications was clear. A Gordon Reece or a Cecil Parkinson might even have been strong enough to make her change her mind and certainly strong enough to make sure a better job was made of it if she would not.

To the critics there was also a sluggishness about Central Office, almost an air of sleepwalking, during this first week. They were not slow to point out, for example, that it took two senior Tories who were, by no stretch of the imagination, connected to the centre of the operation, to make the most devastating attacks on the Labour manifesto. Michael Heseltine used the words 'Never has so much been hidden from so many by so few' that night and several papers used it in their headlines the following day; and Peter Walker's was the first serious attack on the document, listing exactly what was missing from it in terms of Labour Party conference resolutions. Norman Tebbit's office had pointed this out, but in a press release (they fall like snow on news editors' desks during elections) which stated baldly: 'I attach a note from Conservative Research Department, which lists some of Labour's policy commitments now missing from the edited manifesto.'

The Candidates' Conference on Wednesday was a greater success. It was a godsend that at least the first session of it was open to the media, for otherwise there might have been no pictures at all of the Prime Minister to use on television that night. The video made for both the launch of the manifesto and the conference was also a success – particularly after the last-minute alteration in it to include Mrs Thatcher. When she had been shown it for the first time on Monday morning, she had liked it enormously, but had asked why she was not in it. There were many stills and clips of film of her in the role of a world statesman, but no direct contribution. 'I am not a glorified Foreign Secretary,' she said. 'I think, since it is the party's manifesto, I should make a contribution to it.' Tim Bell and Howell James once again 'borrowed' Lord McAlpine's house, got a film crew together, had a script prepared, filmed her at 5 p.m., edited the new version and had two hundred copies of it ready for the manifesto launch next day – and more in time to give one each to the 650 candidates.

In the closed afternoon session of the conference each of the principal ministers talked about his section of the manifesto; then, before questions, Mrs Thatcher spoke for an hour, unscripted, about the party's aims and achievements. The purpose was to send out into the country the best briefed and prepared candidates of all the three parties. The briefing and preparations were, of course, crucial in the marginal seats, into 72 of which the party had poured so much energy and resources.

Among those on the platform that day was Tom Arnold, the party's vice-chairman in charge of candidates. Few were as susceptible as he to swings of political fortune. His Hazel Grove seat, on the southern rim of the Manchester conurbation, had a majority of only 2022 and was vulnerable to a 4.1 per cent swing to the Alliance: already, in the media build-up to the election, it was being written off as an almost certain Liberal gain. He knew by then, though few other people had access to the information, that Mrs Thatcher was due to make his constituency her first visit of the campaign, when she started in earnest on Friday. Hazel Grove was one of the party's tactical seats and already over the previous months much effort had gone into direct mailing and sending out local newspapers. He was convinced he could hold the seat, despite Liberal advances in local government and the temptation of the 12–16 per cent Labour support of voting tactically, and he anticipated that Mrs Thatcher's visit would boost his chances considerably. His view of the campaign, locally and nationally over the next few weeks, would be fascinating – particularly since he was one of the few at the time who saw grave dangers in underestimating the Labour Party, particularly if it chose to attack the Tories' handling of health issues.

The view from the other side of the fence – of a Tory hopeful fighting a winnable Labour seat – would be equally interesting. Angela Browning, a 40-year-old management consultant who has all of Edwina Currie's determination but less of her brazenness in promotion of herself, was just such a candidate and was in the audience at the conference. With the Tories so far ahead in the polls, she was happy that Crewe and Nantwich, where she was up against Gwyneth Dunwoody, could be won. But if things were to go wrong with the campaign, she would be among the first to feel it. The seat was the result of the pre-1983 redistribution, which had put Labour Crewe, a railway and Rolls Royce town, in with Tory Nantwich, leaving a flimsy Labour hold on the combination of only 290. Her feeling was that Crewe had not suffered from the recession as had other towns in the Midlands below her or the north-west above and, although the seat was not one of the top layer of Tory target constituencies, she had received some help in building it up during the year since the local party had chosen her. She stood to gain from an Alliance surge at the expense of Labour (under the two-for-one factor) and felt that defence would be Labour's weakest point.

For the second day running the 'item' the Tories had put up as their principal visual offering to television received scant attention. It seemed for the first time that the medium had succeeded in breaking out on its own. It was setting its own agenda, gobbling up new visual offerings by the hour, before moving on to the next topic. The sheer volume of television time devoted to the election – on two channels through early morning and lunchtime, then on all four channels for major parts of the evening – meant that an 'issue' carefully prepared for and launched at a morning conference could be dead after lunchtime, unless something happened to 'give it legs'. It also meant that the need for new material was greater and therefore the coverage seemed – or indeed was – more trivial than before. It took some time for the Tories to begin to realise what was happening, by which time they were locked into the set timetable of Mrs Thatcher's day and there was little they could do to alter it.

Whether by accident or design, Neil Kinnock's decision to opt out of each day's morning press conferences in London not only had the desired effect of keeping him largely away from the political big guns of the media in the capital, but also gave him the priceless advantage of being able to offer four or more different TV 'opportunities' in a day. Programme editors could take his early morning press conference from, say, Newcastle upon Tyne; an hour later they could have his first photo-opportunity of the day, and still be in time for the lunchtime news. They could have another fresh item for the early evening and either a major speech or a further photo-opportunity in the evening. Naturally the sheer variety of it greatly pleased them.

By contrast, particularly in the first week, the Tories simply did not have enough to offer. Apart from set studio guests, it was a barren week visually. The manifesto launch on Tuesday and the open section of the Candidates' Conference were made to seem tired by the evenings. Similarly on Thursday, the handing over to Mrs Thatcher in the London Docklands of the touring 'Battlebus' received very little coverage after lunchtime. The bus (which had been in collision with a BMW at a roundabout in Battersea the night before and had been hastily resprayed on one side) was said to have cost £100,000 to convert to the anti-terrorist standards required by Mrs Thatcher's security advisers. A whole section above the rear axle, where she would sit, had been rebuilt like a special armour-plated box – though the unladen weight painted on the side was still, somewhat incredibly, about the same as any standard coach (11,000 kg).

Nor were things much better on her first full day of the campaign on Friday. Although she had a series of engagements planned for the day after her morning press conference, not even her arrival at the first port of call – Manchester airport, where she ran into crowds of frustrated holidaymakers held up by a French air traffic controllers' strike – came until after the lunchtime news. And, because of late running, the most visual image of the day, her 'white hat' visit to a biscuit factory, missed the early evening news bulletins. Obviously the tour would take time to settle down, but it remained to be seen whether it could ever match for swiftness of foot and visual gimmickry that which was being put on offer on a daily basis by the Kinnock camp.

One of the principal problems which emerged immediately on that Friday was security. Not only did four Special Branch men travel with her to the north-west, but on arrival in the region there were at least four more local officers detailed for what is called 'close protection' work. Others, plus, it was said, men from the SAS, lingered nearby watching every section of the crowds. It was to be the same everywhere. Nearly always a helicopter or a light plane circled overhead, in addition to the obvious presence of sometimes hundreds of uniformed police. Add to this the presence close to her of two, three or sometimes even four three-man TV crews and the chances of her being seen spontaneously meeting joyous crowds of supporters rapidly diminished to near zero. This was before the score of travelling photographers, the equal number of reporters and the dozens of local journalists attached for the day had themselves attempted to find out what was happening in the middle of the scrum which built up round her. It was unsatisfactory from day one, but it was felt necessary, simply because it was the only way she could be seen to be meeting the public and getting around the country. To have stayed in London, as some in the security services wanted, would have been not only to admit defeat by the IRA, but also to allow the other parties to accuse her of hiding from the populace. As it was, they quickly picked up the fact that she was not meeting 'people' and made as much of it as they could. The accusation hurt her considerably, not only because she likes meeting people, but also because – again for security reasons – only the shortest notice could ever be given of her arrival anywhere and therefore the crowds were often smaller than they would otherwise have been and many of her own supporters, who would have given their right arms to see her, did not get the chance.

Indeed there was a moment on that first day at Manchester airport when, unseen by any of the media circus following her, she emerged from the chaos of the terminal building to walk alone with only Denis Thatcher, her immediate entourage and Special Branch guards down a short path to her coach. She stopped and talked for two or three minutes to a group of building workers, aware that there were no cameras around to record it, but, nevertheless, probably relieved just to chat to 'the people' at last. Already it seemed there would be precious few moments like that in the weeks that were to come. And, as if to emphasise how hemmed in she was by both media and security, a team of enterprising reporters from the *News of the World* spent a part of that day trailing her bus at some distance and recording a number of the radio telephone calls made to and from it. Their story on Sunday caused yet further security to be imposed – the installation of scramblers on all the phones on board.

The short attention span and quick changeover of subjects dictated by television also helped to wrong-foot the Tories during the week. They scored some notable triumphs, but were openly puzzled by the failure of 'an issue' to emerge. Indeed, they were equally surprised by the way television this time appeared both to ignore the newspapers and to leave them behind in the rush for new pictures and topics. The Great Education Row of the first week was a case in point. It started when Mrs Thatcher slightly overstated the party's position in questions during the main press conference in London on Friday morning and appeared to contradict the line being taken by Kenneth Baker. First, through no fault of their own (he had accidentally turned his portable phone off), CCO were unable to raise Baker, who was on his way to speak in a constituency. This allowed the issue to be launched in the lunchtime bulletins. Then a statement was put out clarifying the issue and drawing the two positions together, which came in time for the early evening bulletins; and during the evening it was more-or-less 'talked out' in television terms. All the papers carried it the next day and many of them on Sunday too – *The Times* even ran a leader on it the following Tuesday – but the broadcasting media had long turned its attention to something else.

It was a pace much more suited to the hit-and-run tactics of Labour than to the more ponderous plans conceived in Central Office to blast Labour aside with heavy volleys of policy. It was already clear, after the first week, that more battles were going to be won on impressions than on solid arguments. This, coupled with CCO's slowness to respond, left the feeling that the Tories were not only sleepwalking but on the defensive, often caught unawares on issues where they had every reason to attack.

When they did attack they were effective. Norman Tebbit's performance with David Frost the previous Sunday had been masterly. He had spotted that the underlying theme of much of the Labour attack was going to be based on envy. They were going to hammer home the claim that it was all very well having a Tory government if you had a lot of money, but it was a mean and vicious collection of policies for the weak and the poor. When Frost raised the issue, Tebbit turned it on him by talking about TV-AM and how it had made Frost a lot of money, but had also provided jobs and money for a lot of other people, from the canteen lady to the commissionaire. None of them was envious of Frost, Tebbit said, because they knew that without him it would not have happened and none of them would have jobs.

Despite this success, the Tories' television week was marred by two notable 'own goals'. First, John Wakeham (whose job of making sure the party maximised its television opportunities by allocating its best ministerial performers where they could be most effective was seen by some as being dictated, not so much because he was the best man for it, but more because it was best taken out of the hands of CCO) got into terrible trouble on the BBC's morning Election Call programme. A northern housewife, whose complaints seemed as endless as her stated determination to vote Labour, reduced him to stuttering, embarrassed silence. A regular performer would have talked his way past the lady in thirty seconds, but the fifty-five minutes of the programme was longer than the sum total of all his previous television experience. Too late, he saw the folly of agreeing to Sir Robin Day's blandishments to appear on the programme. It was, even he agreed privately later, a very silly thing to have done.

But politics is unforgiving: in no time at all his enemies within the party were gleefully spreading the news of 'Wakeham's cock-up' and word of it, predictably, reached Downing Street where it fell on the increasingly nervous Prime Ministerial ear. So assiduous and effective was the undermining of Wakeham, subsequent to the programme – and so anxious was the Prime Minister becoming by the weekend – that it was said to have damaged the Chief Whip's career permanently. It remained to be seen how far, if at all the Prime Minister would carry out her somewhat overwrought threat: 'That man will never hold high office in my government again', but certainly, in the short term, the control of TV allocation was handed over to the joint custody of Norman Tebbit and Lord Young, although Wakeham continued to attend the early morning briefing meetings in his capacity as Chief Whip and nothing had visibly changed between him and the Prime Minister. Indeed her 'best day' of the following week included a visit to Wakeham's constituency, where she and Denis Thatcher warmly greeted Alison Wakeham, their pregnant 'other daughter'.

The second 'goal' was scored by Norman Tebbit, who allowed himself to become embroiled in a fatuous argument about what he had, or had not, said about unemployment in a radio interview four years earlier. The fact that he won on a technicality against Bryan Gould – he had been misquoted in words, but not entirely in meaning – did not, according to many of those who saw the television pictures of him holding up the offending advertisement with most of the words blanked out, excuse what they believed to be a totally excessive reaction to a tiny pinprick. His enemies were swift to raise doubts about his judgement and ability to take the sort of criticism which, they claimed, should be second nature to a politician. In his defence it was said, with some justification, that he had at least deflected the argument away from the Tories not caring about unemployment to an issue of the veracity of the statistics about it.

Nevertheless, the week which had started so promisingly for him belonged to him in a most unwelcome way by the weekend. Friends and foes alike were beginning to question what had gone wrong. Where was the great Tory fighting machine? The *Daily Express* of Friday said: 'The Labour party must not be underestimated; clever packaging can obviously go a long way to conceal its real face ... The Tories have to learn from some of the mistakes of their "non campaigning" of the past few days.' And it roundly scolded both Tebbit and Wakeham for their performances. The next day's *Daily Mail* took up the theme, describing the Tories' start to the campaign as 'less than sunny' and blaming them for allowing Labour to get a head start. *The Times* said that Labour was doing 'astonishingly well'. Neil Kinnock's successful week was beginning to show in the polls: the *Daily Mail*'s poll of polls – an average of all the major opinion samples taken during the week – showed the Tories at 41 per cent and holding, Labour at 33 per cent and rising and the Alliance at 21 per cent and falling.

The principal problem, it seemed, was that nothing could deflect the Tories from their set strategy, which had been carefully worked out in Central Office and which saw the campaign in four weekly stages. A gentle start in the first week (very much, it must be emphasised, at the Prime Minister's insistence) would include the launching of the manifesto on Tuesday, the Candidates' Conference, Mrs Thatcher taking delivery of the bus and would finish on the Friday with the first day of her tour. Each

of their private polls had for some months now also had a series
of questions on 'issues' and in addition some qualitative research
had also been carried out in groups. From this it had been
established that as they went into the election the Tories' most
vulnerable points were health, education and unemployment –
in that order – with housing and pensions not far behind. The
second week, therefore, would get as many of these 'weak' issues
as possible out of the way at the morning press conferences. In
the third week the party would move on to its stronger points:
law and order, defence, the trade unions and the booming
economy. In the fourth: Britain's standing in the world, a reiter-
ation of the economic argument, 'It's Great to Be Great Again',
and finally 'Don't throw it all away'. In reserve was the Doomsday Scenario, should the Alliance surge become a real threat.

It was a marvellous strategy – on paper, according to its critics,
when they began to realise what it was. It had been kept under
wraps; so much so that quite senior personnel in CCO did not
know at the end of the first week what was to be the order of
press conferences for the second. But, its critics were now quick
to point out, it presumed no serious threat from either of the
other two parties, it took little or no account of the possible
strategies those parties might adopt, it counted on setting its own
agenda of issues – presuming that the other parties and the
media would meekly follow, it did not appear to tie in with the
advertising or any of the possible themes of the Prime Minister's
tour (on the day Neil Kinnock planned to talk about education
he would also be visiting schools) and, it appeared to those
privileged enough to see it, it did not really plan to go on
the attack for yet another week.

When Mrs Thatcher returned from the north-west that night
there was a message to call her daughter Carol, who had returned
two days earlier from a journalistic assignment in Jordan and
had been horrified by what she had seen – or not seen – of the
Tory campaign and by what friends and contacts in and around
the party had told her. Tim Bell, who had spoken to the Prime
Minister the previous Sunday but, like her, had anticipated
neither the sureness of Labour's footwork nor the slowness of
CCO's, had also rung and left a message. The Prime Minister
spoke to her daughter first, then made several other calls – she

always canvasses a wide range of trusted opinion – while the
Downing Street switchboard tried to raise Bell, who had gone
out to dinner at Harry's Bar with Nicholas Lloyd and his wife Eve
Pollard, the editor of *You* magazine. None of those conversations
served to calm her rising fears in the slightest. At last Bell rang
in from his car outside the restaurant and was put straight
through to her. He did not pull his punches; he told her he
thought there were dangers in the situation, but not insuperable
ones. They talked for about ten minutes and agreed to talk again
in the morning. Her final call that night was to Lord Young,
who had himself been increasingly anxious since that morning.
He had lunched with Bell and Howell James and had taken a
number of other worried calls during the afternoon. The phone
rang just before midnight in his London home; it was a terrible
line and he could scarcely hear the Prime Minister – but her
nervousness communicated itself clearly to him and he suggested
that he and Bell should work together during the day on Saturday
and call on her in the evening with their thoughts. Readily and
with some relief, she agreed.

9 | 'Unleash the Assassin'

One of the side-effects of the isolation of a Prime Minister within the protective cocoon provided by the Civil Service at Number 10 is that he or she inevitably ends up hearing very little except the good news. The civil servants have a vested interest in presenting a rosy picture of the world as seen from Whitehall, and the majority of the few visitors from the outside world are more than likely to be overawed by the occasion – it being a rarity in their lives – and anxious to go away with a favourable impression of the encounter; they are hardly likely to upset the Prime Minister by listing a series of faults and failings.

Mrs Thatcher has fought this creeping isolation over the years. She has a number of people whom she regards as semi-business 'friends' whom she telephones or meets from time to time. They provide her with advice on a whole range of subjects – some are businessmen like Hector Laing and Lord King; some are communicators, like Tim Bell and Gordon Reece; some are editors like Sir David English and Nicholas Lloyd. Some, even, are politicians – like Cecil Parkinson and Richard Ryder. She uses them because she knows it is essential to keep another perspective on her life, to get a different set of reactions to those offered as the official line.

Some of these friends are closer to her than others; some only get in touch with her when they feel she is in danger of going seriously off the rails. None, however, is a regular 'crony', speaking to her every few days and up to date with her thinking and what she has been hearing officially. Thus the conversations of even this close circle are more one-sided than most of us have with our really close friends – they lack the shorthand of familiarity. Of them all, Parkinson and Bell are perhaps the closest, but even they did not speak to her more than once every two or three weeks in the run-up to or during the first week of the election campaign, and Tim Bell had not been in regular touch for some time.

At election times the 'official' line comes from Central Office, and it is on the staff there that the Prime Minister depends for much of her information and 'feel' of the situation. If the line from CCO is that all is well, that the fast pace set by Neil Kinnock is a flash in the pan, and that the shift to Labour in the opinion polls is purely temporary, then the natural inclination would be for her – as indeed for any Prime Minister – to disbelieve any Jeremiahs who might say otherwise. For example, it is said that in 1970, when George Brown went to tell Harold Wilson, a week into the campaign, that he was losing ground hand over fist, Wilson was so furious at the suggestion that he sent him away with a flea in his ear and refused to see him for a week – by which time it was all over bar the shouting.

What is more, this Prime Minister never actually sees the newspapers, only a typed digest provided by Bernard Ingham's office; she rarely watches television, or has the chance to, and the video in the flat at Number 10 has not worked since her daughter Carol borrowed it more than a year ago. Therefore it was quite understandable that she was unaware of the criticisms of the Tory party campaign which had appeared in the *Daily Mail* and *Daily Express* – penned by two of these 'friends' – and was oblivious of any electoral danger to her at the end of that first week.

Thus, Carol's call to her on the evening of Friday 22 May with its stark and anxious message, 'You'd better get your act together, or start packing', clearly shocked her into setting up the meeting which took place in the flat above 10 Downing Street the following night. A dreadful day, during which it had hardly stopped raining, the tour of Finchley and other north London constituencies had gone badly, and she had started to fret that she still did not have the makings of her first major speech for Tuesday night, had not helped her mood by the time the small group gathered in the flat at 6.30 p.m. She was as upset, rattled and consequently querulous as Carol could remember her being for a long time. It was going to be a difficult session – and it was going to require special talents to deliver the message and to say what needed to be said. Apart from Mrs Thatcher, her husband and Carol, the group consisted of Stephen Sherbourne, Lord Young and Tim Bell.

Where Carol had bluntly delivered the blow the previous night, she now concentrated, as did they all, on making sure the message was put over in no uncertain terms but in a positive, upbeat way. There was, and is, no point in going to Margaret Thatcher with a series of moans about what is wrong – you must offer solutions. In Carol's view there are very few people who can handle her mother in circumstances as difficult as these, and it was fortunate that one of those, Tim Bell, was present. It was not the first time in Mrs Thatcher's eight years in office that he had been called in by Carol to help pull 'Mum' through a crisis. While she concentrated on pouring the drinks – occasionally joining in with Denis Thatcher in telling her mother to listen to what she was being told – Bell, in this case backed up by Lord Young, went through their analysis of the situation. It may seem surprising that Young played a somewhat secondary role to Bell at the meeting, but it is a measure of the stature of them both that it was naturally assumed before they went to Downing Street that this would be the case – for the issue at stake that night, while it involved the politics of the campaign, was primarily about the communication of those politics, not the politics themselves. Bell would never dream of trying to influence either Young or the Prime Minister in their sphere, but he was recognised by them both as being a master in his own. It was also recognised that, while Young was widely claimed to be 'close' to Mrs Thatcher, this was only in political terms – he was not a 'friend' like Bell. He had, for instance, never visited the upstairs flat at Downing Street before that evening.

A week earlier Bell had spoken to the Prime Minister for three-quarters of an hour on the telephone. Neither had been unduly anxious or worried by the situation as it was then. Mrs Thatcher had gone into the campaign confident of victory, and prepared to work hard for it. She had been told that CCO was ready, and indeed the parts of the campaign that affected her –

her tour and TV appearances – gave every indication of the
level of preparedness she remembered from 1979 and 1983. In
conversation they had agreed that the principal issue of the
campaign might well be whether or not her vision of Britain,
and the policies she had adopted and was advocating to bring
that about, was one that was fair to all. It had already become
clear by then that the Labour Party were going to do their best
to portray both her and her policies as a mean and vicious
amalgam prejudicial to the weakest in society. They agreed that
the best way to counter this would be to be positive about the
Tory policies as outlined in the manifesto and to point out
that only through the success of the economy, only through
encouraging people to succeed, could everybody enjoy a better
life. The corollary of this, urged upon her by Bell, was that
people should not feel guilty about doing well, for it was only
by their success that society could afford to care for the less
fortunate.

Now, however, he was among the first to realise that the
campaign was not going according to plan for the Tories, nor
was it likely to. It was to be a long and uphill struggle to persuade
a Prime Minister who was first of all doubting, then depressed,
that all was not lost. He and Lord Young had spent the afternoon
together (and in regular contact with Stephen Sherbourne) planning what they were to say to her. They had each consulted a
range of people whose instincts and judgement they trusted –
among them Gordon Reece, who had done much to cheer them
up with his analysis of the situation. Reece believed that there
were good signs: the Alliance had ruled themselves out of the
race by attacking the Tories first instead of going for Labour.
The only strategy that made any sense for the Alliance was to
defeat Labour first, in the hope of starting a bandwagon which
would carry them through by the last week to challenge the
Tories. This they had failed to do, and thus, according to Reece
and many commentators, too, the Tories now only had one
target – Labour. His view was that, in the scrap with Labour,
the Tories still had three advantages: their powder was still dry,
the Prime Minister had not been hurt in the initial onslaught and
the Tory support was still solid.

Labour had proved themselves better co-ordinated, better at

handling the press (even though that meant the leader avoiding some of them), better on TV and they had better advertising. It was no good, they all agreed, just to plod on with the steady exposition of Tory policies – good though they were – as though the Labour Party did not exist. It was clear that they were not going to be able to set the agenda in the media, least of all on television, in this way. It was therefore vital to go on to the attack, to start to undo the packaging of Neil Kinnock and expose him and his party for what they were. The informal group which had begun to assemble the proposed new strategy in phone calls and meetings throughout the afternoon – it was to be called 'my communications group in exile' by the Prime Minister – had put together a powerful and detailed case by the time the five-hour meeting began, right down to suggestions about the better use of television time, and which ministers ought to be used more and which less.

Tim Bell's presentation was described to me later as a '*tour de force*', in that he managed to convey to the Prime Minister what was wrong, while at the same time keeping her more or less focused on the prize in store once it had been put right. To understand her frame of mind and the amount of effort required to lift the spirits of one who is arguably the most powerful political figure of the post-war years, it is necessary first to remember that here was a person who believed, with ample justification, that her 'mission' was right, her record of achieving her goals was unparalleled, her judgement of when to seek the third term was right, that the machinery for achieving that third term was in place and ready and that her programme for that third term was more detailed and attractive than any of the other parties could offer. What then could go wrong? It had, according to Carol Thatcher, come as a considerable shock to her mother to realise, for the first time that weekend, that she *could* lose the election.

Thus, when Bell pointed out that Hugh Hudson's Labour PEB had been a very powerful broadcast, her first reaction was to be defensive and overdramatic and to believe that all was lost. When he pointed to the leader articles in the *Express* and the *Mail*, her first overreaction was to accuse them of being unhelpful, to which Bell replied that they were meant to be constructive.

Somewhat petulantly, she said that she failed to see what was constructive about saying that Labour won the first week, to which Bell replied heatedly: 'It is a FACT, Prime Minister, that's what is constructive about it. It's no good surrounding yourself with people who tell you everything's fine – that way you'll miss the boat.' The crisis came when Denis Thatcher urged her repeatedly to listen to a point Lord Young was making: she turned on him. Her reaction showed all her shock coming out and despair momentarily overwhelming her. One of Tim Bell's great strengths with her, which neither Lord Young nor Stephen Sherbourne had, was the history of having fought with her in the two previous elections. It was these shared memories which Bell returned to time and again to rekindle the fire in her. And slowly, out of the constant reassurance that all was not lost and that victory was still there to be won, came the acceptance of, first, the need for a new strategy, then the outline of what it was to be.

There was undoubtedly a sense of self-recrimination in her for having been complacent – even though she had constantly stated the opposite. More importantly, her despair stemmed from a sense of being isolated, of having no one to lean on, a feeling that she had to do everything herself. In terms of speech-writing, for example, she has never found a winning team – and maybe never will – who can put her thoughts down on paper without involving her in hours of late night rewriting. In her personal organisation – everything from the provision of meals in the Downing Street flat to preparing her wardrobe for the following day – things were not running as smoothly as they had in previous elections. She had, in essence, a sense of being put upon. But perhaps, through talking about it that night, she came to realise at last that this was not 1983, that there was no Cecil Parkinson or Gordon Reece in charge, that her personal entourage, too, no longer had many of the old reliable faces such as Alison Wakeham and Caroline Ryder, that she now as never before had to lead. She is, at the best of times, an almost totally self-sufficient person: she would not have survived unless she had been; but, come rough weather, she would be inhuman if she did not need the support of those she loved and/or trusted. If nothing else, the group there that night – whose contribution may well be played down and even decried by others – can at least claim the crucial achievement of having reassured and bolstered her and given her the will to lead, sufficient at least to see her back into the fray the following week.

The strategy was to attack. She would go for Labour's policies, or lack of them; she was to revive the theme she had developed at Perth of Labour's 'Iceberg Manifesto' – one-tenth visible, nine-tenths hidden. A new PEB would be shot for the following Tuesday night and Lord Young would immediately start to try to co-ordinate the press conferences and Ministers' television appearances to fit in with the new plans. Young also reminded the Prime Minister that the Tories had another weapon of great potency, which could be used in concert with her attacks on Labour policy. Was it not time, he suggested, to 'unleash the assassin' – time, in other words, to set Norman Tebbit on to Neil Kinnock?

Although the Prime Minister had shown herself to lack the faith in Norman Tebbit's ability to manage Central Office that she had had in Cecil Parkinson or even Lord Thorneycroft, there was no doubt whatsoever at any stage in the campaign, or in the months leading up to it, that she was a great admirer of his political abilities. Those of his enemies and potential rivals who sought to make capital out of her clear displeasure with CCO when it arose, more often than not forgot the high value she placed on his political judgement. She was as aware as he was of the value of his role as the 'lightning conductor', and was grateful to him for it. Indeed, he was on occasions happy for her to use Downing Street leaks to distance herself from some of his more abrasive attacks, knowing that she in turn was happy with what he was saying. Now she responded enthusiastically to the suggestion that he be, so to speak, unshackled from the con- straints of promoting the positive sides of the Tory campaign and let loose, as only he knew how, on the weaknesses of the opposition and their case.

As in so many of the decisions which she had taken and was to take – the inclusion of Lord Young, the consultations with Tim Bell, the greater use of George Younger – the move was very much that of a general changing the direction and role of her troops to get the best out of them. No one in Downing Street or CCO doubted Tebbit's vast abilities in the task she now set him. Despite speculation that Mrs Thatcher was displeased with him and the first signs of rumblings in the press that all was not well, in her view, with the way the campaign was being administered, there was no falling out between them. While she may in her most frustrated moments have expressed the view that it was a mistake to have put him in charge of CCO, and while she had found it necessary to move Lord Young increasingly into the operation, these things in no way reflected her opinion of Tebbit personally or as a politician. She was a Prime Minister, she was fighting one of the toughest battles of her career and decisions had to be taken to get the job done in the best way she thought possible. She was not doing Tebbit down. She needed him as much as she needed anyone in the party. But she needed his demonstrable strengths, not the areas where she felt he was weaker.

It was clear from all the discussion that Saturday night that, for whatever reasons, the Prime Ministerial and the Party campaigns simply were not meshing as expected. It was early days, but, it was felt, there was little co-ordination in the efforts being made to put the Tory case – the press conference plan did not appear to have been thought through, the PEBs seemed to bear little relationship to the advertising and none of it was made particularly relevant by the tour, which was Lord Young's responsibility. Norman Tebbit's management style, of keeping his cards close to his chest, was seen to be a contributory factor in this. For example, Steve Robin, who was working under John Wakeham allocating Ministers to television programmes, had by that weekend still not received the planned programme for the following week's press conferences, and the media monitoring unit which had been established to keep an eye on all political statements on all four television channels, so that quick responses could be made to attacks or mistakes by the opposition, seemed in danger of overload, with consequent considerable delay in alerting the party to important openings.

Already it was obvious that, by comparison, Labour were going to appear well co-ordinated: when they were to talk about education, Neil Kinnock would be visiting a school that day, when they were talking about pensions, he would be at an old people's home. As often as three times a day all Labour candidates who had computers in their campaign offices – and that included most of those in their 'target' seats – would receive up-to-the-minute briefings on the latest political issues and suggestions as to how to play them. It was accepted too, though perhaps by default, that it had been a mistake to start the campaign so late. Already sides were being taken about the wisdom of this decision, with the defenders of the move, some of them in CCO, saying that a fortnight was easily enough to deal with Labour, now that the Alliance was out of the way. Others saw the only good to have come out of it as being the fright it gave everyone, and they blamed the Prime Minister and Norman Tebbit equally for allowing it to happen. Labour's rise, some claimed, had been predictable. It was not the Falklands factor which had swept Mrs Thatcher to victory in 1983; it was the Foot factor. Labour had collapsed because of Michael Foot's leadership and the party's appalling manifesto, dubbed 'the longest suicide note in history'. Now, with a young, energetic leader and his attractive wife, both carefully packaged, Labour would not be the pushover they had been last time.

Out in the constituencies it was a little early for the effects of Neil Kinnock's good start to have caused any major anxieties. Candidates found the electorate aware of the Hugh Hudson PEB, but as many seemed repelled as were attracted by it. Both Angela Browning and Tom Arnold found the Tory vote holding up well that weekend and very few waverers in evidence. If the first day of the tour had not gone too well from the point of view of the press and television, it had at least had the desired result as far as Tom Arnold was concerned. The PM's visit was having a major impact on the local media, he reported – as indeed it had had on the party workers, who were setting about their jobs with renewed enthusiasm.

It is, as we have seen, traditional in the Tory party, particularly at election times, that when things go wrong the chairman, and those associated with him, bear the brunt of the criticism. Never was this more true than during this first anxious weekend and in the early days of the following week, though it must be said that comparatively little of it was emanating from Downing Street, where the main thrust was to alter the strategy rather than apportion blame. However, there were those who took the opportunity over the next few days for a traditional bout of Tebbit-bashing, while those close to him, although admitting that the Prime Minister was probably right to have a higher view of his political judgement than of his organisational ability, stoutly defended his and CCO's record to date.

The idea of having a positive manifesto and fighting the campaign on it was not Tebbit's idea but hers, it was pointed out. It was she who had said that the party must tell the electorate what it had achieved and be positive about what it yet had to do. It was largely her fault that the manifesto had been rushed through at the last moment and some of the items in it had not been thought through properly, with the consequence that the row over education in the first few days had robbed the Tories of the initiative – later in the second week housing came dangerously near to doing the same. It was not Norman Tebbit's fault that the party had thus been forced on to the defensive at a time when all his instincts were to go on to the attack. It was pointed out that in their early planning Tebbit and Dobbs had wanted a more traditional campaign based on a sound and well-thought-out manifesto – alternating with kicking the opposition parties' shins. Nor was the order of the press conferences their decision alone: it had been agreed by the Prime Minister and therefore she should share the blame for the fact that the programme appeared unco-ordinated.

In the cold light of day these disagreements seem trivial (though they were heatedly stated at the time), but they do reveal what was probably the fundamental problem between CCO and Number 10. For they contain within them a sense of resignation, a washing of hands almost, an attitude that, since decisions were taken out of CCO's hands, then those who took those decisions should bear responsibility for them. There was to be an incident later in the week over the release of the Prime Minister's speech in Solihull, which perfectly illustrates this. The speech she delivered in South Wales on Tuesday had been distributed early in Fleet Street and ballyhooed widely among the editors. Consequently it received major coverage, but its release to Fleet Street before the press travelling with Mrs Thatcher had had a chance to file it to their offices left many of them angry and feeling like extras in someone else's extravaganza. All day they had traipsed around from photo-opportunity to photo-opportunity, sometimes watching from outside while the Prime Minister with the television crews and one or two photographers were allowed into the factories she was visiting and now, just when they had some real work to get their teeth into, they were told it had already gone to their London offices. Naturally there were complaints, and so for the right reasons (i.e. to keep the travelling press happy) the wrong decision was taken: to hold Friday's speech up in London on Thursday night and give it to those reporters who were with Mrs Thatcher in Solihull. This time, because the speech was filed so much later and no one had promoted it with the editors in advance, it received very little mention in the papers.

This unfortunate incident was presented to me, by senior people within CCO, as a typical example of Downing Street intransigence and unwillingness to listen to reason. Elections are full of silly, frustrating decisions and the anger those decisions arouse is often only fleeting, for there is a consciousness that everyone is part of the same team and that life is too short and the task too urgent to get seriously upset. But this criticism, on Norman Tebbit's behalf, was said in a tone which conveyed resignation and a feeling of 'If that's what they want then let them get on with it.' Throughout the build-up to the campaign there was a resentment at any interference from Downing Street in the plans of CCO. This was the nub of the problem, for it pinpointed the crucial question: was CCO Mrs Thatcher's to direct like a Private Office or was it Norman Tebbit's own department? It was pointed out to me more than once that any complaints the Prime Minister might have about the efficiency or otherwise of CCO were a little late in the day, since it was she who had insisted on Jeffrey Archer as Tebbit's Deputy Chairman and had refused to allow Dobbs the same status, and since it was she who had blocked the appointment of a communications chief and accepted the unsatisfactory 'team' approach instead. 'Maybe it does reflect badly on Norman,' one person close to him told me. 'But it also reflects on her. She is, after all, in charge.'

The same attitude prevailed towards the insertion of Lord

Young and John Wakeham into the campaign. They were not unwelcome in themselves, but their arrival was seen as further unnecessary clouding of the lines of management and they were left to get on with their own tasks – almost as though, according to one source, they were part of another campaign. The resentment was not aimed at them, but at the thought that anyone should consider it necessary that they be there. Similar resentment was expressed at the fact that the Prime Minister was quite clearly listening to other people. As it became clear on the Sunday after the meeting in Downing Street and during the succeeding days that she had sought advice elsewhere, and that the suggestions she was making were not entirely her own spontaneous thoughts, the attitude towards the change of strategy, although partly one of relief that at last Tebbit could get his gloves off, was also tinged with resentment. It was seen in CCO as another sign of her 'Byzantine' political dealings and as further confirmation that others were using her in these matters to promote their own position after the election, so that they would be better placed come the fight for the succession.

It is a measure of Lord Young's skill during these difficult days, when, he confided to one close associate, 'it was like walking on eggshells in CCO', that he managed to remain on close terms with Norman Tebbit. And it was a measure of Tebbit's graciousness and fundamental desire for a Tory victory that he too never publicly allowed whatever feeling he might have had to show. Indeed, although he was not exactly happy when he heard talk of Tim Bell's involvement, he was at least grateful to Young for not flaunting it in front of him.

Whatever the differences between Downing Street and CCO, there was one weakness in the Prime Minister's own campaigning style which was touched on during the Saturday night meeting, and it was to take her more than another week to come to terms with it. It arose, ironically, from one of her strengths. She is acknowledged to have become one of the most formidable performers across the Dispatch Box in the House of Commons of the post-war era. In twelve years she has faced two Labour Prime Ministers and two Leaders of the Opposition and, particularly in recent years, has not often been bettered. But it is a combative medium of debate and one to which, over the years she has become totally adapted. Going into the campaign, her style with both journalists and members of the public often came over as aggressive, and sometimes humourless and domineering. It was not until the last week of the campaign that she was to relax sufficiently to really warm her questioners, whether press or public.

The Saturday meeting broke up at about 11 p.m. – Lord Young had left earlier after telling Mrs Thatcher: 'Prime Minister, believe us; if we make these changes we will regain the initiative and we will be back in control of this campaign by next Friday night.' The new agenda now consisted of attack on two fronts: better co-ordination of Ministers' television appearances (John Wakeham was to be moved aside after his blunder) and Norman Tebbit and Lord Young would take over the task. The issue was to be the 'Iceberg Manifesto' and a new PEB was to be made on the theme, pointing out how many extreme left candidates the Labour Party had standing. All efforts were to be directed at making this the central issue of the week, unless something else came up in the meantime. Carol Thatcher later apologised to her mother for being so hard on her, to which she replied that it did not matter, it had had the right results.

The 'something else' came up just before nine o'clock the following morning. In the opinion of many people, the two or three minutes Neil Kinnock spent discussing defence with David Frost on TV–AM at that early hour on Sunday morning, were the two or three minutes in which, if he were to be defeated, he lost the election. Frost, in his deceptively discursive way, brought the questioning round to the subject of possible armed conflict in Europe. Would Kinnock send conventionally armed British forces into battle in Europe against an enemy armed with nuclear ones? he asked. The Labour leader dismissed the idea that the British army fighting in Europe could be defended by nuclear weapons, because the weapons would kill as many British troops as Soviet ones. Frost then asked him if, without nuclear weapons the choice would be to subject British forces to an unfair battle or surrender. Kinnock appeared to agree that the alternatives for the British were between the 'gesture, the threat, or the use of their nuclear weapons – and surrender'.

He then said: 'In those circumstances the choice is posed –

and this is the classical choice – of either exterminating every-thing that you stand for . . . or using the resources that you've got to make any occupation totally untenable. And of course any effort to occupy Western Europe, or certainly to occupy the United Kingdom, would be utterly untenable, and any potential force knows that very well and are not going to be ready to engage in attempting to dominate conditions that they couldn't dominate.'

The *Daily Express* and the *Daily Telegraph* immediately saw the potential in what Neil Kinnock had said. Each led its front page on Monday with the story of Labour's policy of surrender and its leader's idea of guerrilla resistance as a deterrent to the Russians. Significantly, it was well into Sunday evening before the CCO media monitoring unit drew the attention of the powers that be to the gaffe – too late to make a massive blitz of it that day. Nevertheless the Tories, at last, had their issue. It was tailor-made for them: defence was one of their strong points, they could appeal over Neil Kinnock's head to the old style anti-unilateralist Labour voter as well as possibly frightening a number of waverers back into line. By Monday afternoon Nor-man Tebbit – 'the assassin' – was fired with enthusiasm, pre-paring for a major onslaught on the following night, as were Mrs Thatcher's speechwriting team. At last they had something to get their teeth into.

Many of the thoughts expressed on Saturday night were in the opening section of her speech in Newport, South Wales, on Tuesday – the idea of making a profit and being proud of success, the dangers of the trade unions and above all the 'Hidden Manifesto'. But it was when she turned to defence that she really let loose. She described Labour's policy as outlined by Kinnock on Sunday as: 'a policy for defeat, surrender, occupation and finally prolonged guerrilla fighting'.

'The Labour leader,' she said, 'has abandoned all his claims that conventional forces can provide an effective defence against nuclear weapons. He has conceded that, once this country has renounced its independent deterrent, it has no alternative but to surrender to the nuclear threat. He has left himself no policy but to yield to invasion and to trust in the forlorn hope that a guerrilla struggle would eventually persuade the army of occupation to withdraw. I do not understand how anyone who aspires to Government can treat the defence of our country so lightly.'

It was a double-barrelled blast; at the same time, Norman Tebbit was delivering his broadside in his own constituency at Chingford. He described Neil Kinnock as a runaway. 'He runs away from the questioning of the voters. He is a runaway from the trade union bosses. He is a runaway into the arms of his own extremists. He is a runaway from any bully, however big or small, who would threaten this nation. Britain has no ambition to live under the red flag of socialism or the white flag of surrender.'

Other ministers joined in – as did President Reagan, who described Labour's policies as 'grievous errors' – and television was forced to acknowledge defence as an issue, if not *the* issue, of the campaign. More by luck than judgement, the best Saatchi advertisement of the campaign so far was due to run during the week – and it was on defence. It showed a soldier with his hands up and the slogan: 'Labour's Policy On Arms'. Morale in CCO lifted perceptibly as, seventeen days after the calling of the election, the party had the campaign agenda under control for the first time.

Once again preferring to use subterfuge rather than cause unnecessary upset, the Prime Minister had, when she wound up the meeting on Saturday night, arranged to discuss all the items with Norman Tebbit before notifying Lord Young that the way was clear for him to talk to the Party Chairman about them. The call came early on Sunday afternoon and the message was that everything had been agreed apart from the re-ordering of the press conference schedule: it was apparently too late to change that. Later that afternoon Young went to CCO where he and Tebbit ran through the list of items and he agreed straight away to get on with supervising the problem of the television appearances. However it swiftly emerged that the Prime Minister had not yet spoken to John Wakeham. It is possible that she was having second thoughts about the whole business of his removal from this aspect of the campaign, for, despite a reminder from CCO to Downing Street that evening, nothing was done. On Monday, when it was raised with her again, she was clearly reluctant; in the end she fudged it by calling Wakeham in and saying that both Young and Tebbit were going to be involved with him.

Her reluctance now to spill political blood, however, did not mean that she had failed to be thoroughly alarmed by what the group had told her on Saturday night. It was clear henceforth that she intended to take her own regular soundings from other sources as well as having fixed meetings with her group of 'exiles'. During the weekend she spoke to several friends and, on Sunday night she talked at length with Cecil Parkinson, who had also become alarmed at what was happening and had left a message for her. She got him out of a dinner party given for ex-President Nixon and questioned him closely about what he thought was wrong. While reluctant as a former chairman to criticise the present incumbent, he had answered her honestly and suggested a number of obvious improvements, including making sure that speakers who were being filmed for BBC–2's 'On the Hustings' programme had a party insignia and slogan behind them. Twice in the previous week he had been filmed in halls where no preparations at all had been made. He was mystified by some of the things she told him about the Tory campaign, as he had been horrified by some of the things he had heard himself, but, like Bell and Reece ever an optimist, he saw only good coming out of the initial setback. 'It has scared our voters and concentrated our minds,' he told the Prime Minister. He also warned her about the pensioners' vote – there were 10 million of them – and suggested that she devote some space in her speeches to them.

His fiercest criticism was reserved for the appearance of the Tory first team of ministers. 'Our whole reputation is based on the fact that we are competent,' he told her. 'But we don't look competent. Nigel Lawson's hair is far too long – as is Kenneth Clark's. And what is Nicholas Ridley doing wearing an old cardigan? Suddenly Labour are the ones in the smart suits and we look like the scruffy party of protest.' The message obviously hit home, because next morning, when she was speaking to Norman Tebbit and Lord Young, she repeated what Parkinson had said almost word for word. Then she said to them: 'Will you tell them to smarten up?' Almost in unison the pair of them said: 'No, Prime Minister. *You* tell them.' Somebody did: within twenty-four hours Lawson's locks had been well and truly shorn and the Ridley cardigan had vanished.

Mrs Thatcher had also discussed with Parkinson the size of the morning briefing meetings she had had with him in 1983. As she remembered it there had only been seven or eight people present each day, whereas on Friday there had been more than twenty people in the room. He understood the point she was making. He knew how uncomfortable she feels in large meetings and how reluctant she is, in such circumstances, to speak her mind. It was on his advice that she asked Lord Young on Monday to add to his list of tasks the reduction of the numbers to eight. It may not seem an important or significant matter, but the pain and anguish that the reduction caused at first, and the way that within a week the numbers had crept back up again, was to many a measure of the lack of central direction within CCO.

Nevertheless the whole organisation of the party's communications did improve dramatically during the week, partly as a result of these measures, partly as a result of higher morale and partly as a result of having an issue to get their teeth into. The press conferences went better and the PEB on Wednesday night, using John Moore for the commentary, was widely praised.

There were, however, still alarming signs of CCO's slowness to react and stiffness of thinking. The Prime Minister had always been fond of the slogan 'Power to the People', which she felt perfectly encapsulated her feelings about the manifesto and was a great deal more inspiring than the pedestrian 'Next Moves Forward'. For some reason CCO and Saatchi had been reluctant to have it tested or to become involved in using it. Now, as a result of her talks at the weekend, it was decided to put 'Power to the People' up on the main conference platform along with 'Next Moves . . .' The decision may have been taken – but execution was another thing. It never happened. Similarly at that Monday morning meeting Alastair McAlpine had suggested that they put a huge church-appeal-fund-type of thermometer right up the side of Central Office so that all the journalists and the TV crews could see the amount of the public's money Labour was planning to spend. As each wild promise came in, they would paint another red strip of however many billions it was up the thermometer. A week later a planning meeting was held to discuss the project and, with just seven days to go to the polls, the idea was quietly dropped – because 'none of the suggestions for the design were exciting enough', I was told.

Problems also emerged with the Prime Minister's tour during its first full week, some of them to do with the organisation of it and some to do with its operation. Once again the situation was distinguished by a shifting of the blame for what had gone wrong, rather than by anyone seizing the opportunity to put it right. The end result was that the show remained on the road – jogging along in its slightly unsatisfactory way – but at no stage did it appear to match the Kinnock show for either cohesiveness, relevance, or photogenic quality. It was, in the end, as though the tour of 1983 had been diligently copied through tracing paper: all the outline was there but the colour and flair had been taken out of it. There were seemingly endless visits to factories and only two to schools and one to an old people's home. For security reasons the opportunities for walkabouts were severely curtailed, as were the hustings meetings in village squares which had been so exciting four years earlier. Now, because no one could be told until a short time in advance that the Prime Minister was coming, attendances were much smaller and, in any case, the venues were less conducive to the feel of an election meeting – sometimes they were in open fields. One of the delights, photographically, of the tour four years earlier had been the variety of vehicles on to which Mrs Thatcher had climbed to address the public: now she was confined time after time to a very boring mobile speaking platform, albeit done out in Tory colours.

The feeling began to grow during the week that the world of the photo-opportunity had moved on somewhat since Gordon Reece had 'invented' it for British political use in 1979 by posing the future Prime Minister cuddling a young calf (which subsequently expired and since then has passed into the myth-ology of the tour as the 'dead calf shot'). It was simply not enough to be seen in the white hat shot, or the hard hat shot or the car factory or computer factory shot – there had to be some message, some reason for being there. This feeling grew partly because, by comparison, the Kinnock tour appeared to have a logic to it and a distinct message to convey each day. It could, of course, have been the case that the Prime Minister's tour did have a theme — the regeneration of Britain — but if it did, it was a message that appeared to be lost on most of its participants and most political observers.

Those in CCO who resented Lord Young's 'intrusion' into the campaign were swift to point out that, in its first full week, the tour managed to visit an East Midlands school on a Bank Holiday and Wales during Wakes Week, when most of the factories were closed, and then hold three events in one constituency in the West Country. It had taken only two days to antagonise the travelling press and build up a resentment which was fuelled the following day when, on a visit to a Guide Dogs training centre, a briefing of the reporters was finally arranged only for them to be told high-handedly that it was 'off the record'; when most of them walked out, the official line was swiftly changed.

These criticisms ignored the fact that the tour was nevertheless achieving its primary desired effect — albeit less successfully than the Kinnock version — of showing the Prime Minister out and about in the country canvassing the national vote. They also ignored the problem, inherent in the composition of the tour itself, that most newspapers and other media sent staff from their political offices on the trip; they inevitably found themselves mere spectators at a series of essentially trivial events. These tours are planned to be 'non-political' in their terms and are in any case primarily aimed at television: this naturally tends to build up resentment.

But this time the intrusion of 'politics' into the tour was a more frequent occurrence. The innovation of the cellular phone brought political questioning directly from London on to the campaign trail itself and posed problems for the organisers, particularly the hard-working press bus leader Sheila Howe, who, instead of shepherding a fairly docile flock from photo-opportunity to photo-opportunity, frequently found herself being ambushed by her 'sheep', all anxious to get close to the Prime Minister and question her on the latest twist in the issue of the moment. The CCO press officer presence on the bus was stepped up towards the end of the week, but the matter was still not satisfactorily resolved – nor was it helped by what many reporters found to be the increasingly distant presence on the tour of the one person who was supposed to be in charge of helping them, Christine Wall.

Meanwhile the mood on the blue Battlebus fluctuated from day to day and was primarily dictated, as is customary by now on these tours, by the state of readiness of the next major Prime Ministerial speech. Her campaign day starts at 6.30 each morning, when she gets up and makes breakfast for herself and Denis Thatcher – cooked for him, coffee and toast for her – before settling down to an hour's work on her 'boxes', followed by half an hour on government business with Nigel Wicks. At 8.20 she leaves for CCO and, once there, goes straight into a briefing meeting where the papers, the polls and the likely issues of the day are discussed, followed by her daily press conference and more meetings to discuss policy before setting out by 11 a.m. to join the day's tour. She travels and meets people all day, visiting anything up to half a dozen locations and making one or two ten-minute hustings speeches, often not returning to Downing Street until eight or nine at night. If she has a rally speech in the evening she will stop her tour at about 5.30 p.m. and go to a hotel to change and freshen up before the big event. She arrives at the hall about 15 minutes before she is due to speak and never gives her audience less than 40 minutes-worth. Then it is back on to the plane, or into a car, and back to London, sometimes not reaching Downing Street until after 11 p.m. One of the women on the tour always carries an 'emergency' bag with heated rollers, make-up, needle and thread in it; and she never travels without one or two changes of clothing. Most of the clothes she wears now come from Aquascutum, though she still uses the 'little lady' in Battersea whose name is kept secret and who has been dressmaking for her since before she became Prime Minister.

Into this crowded schedule, which also has to include all her media appearances, article-writing meetings and other election business, has to be fitted the hours and hours of preparation that go into her key speeches, and usually the only time available is at night. Twice during this first week she did not go to bed until the early hours – on Monday night at 2 a.m. and on Wednesday night not until 3.30 a.m. On the following days, not so much because she was tired but more because she is never satisfied, she was inevitably irritable until the ordeal of speech-making was over.

The impact of these major speeches is enormous. From the moment the lights go down and the dry-ice fog billows out into the audience (as though it were a pop concert rather than a political rally) the audience is stunned into receptivity. The impression of pop is continued with a five-minute laser show which flashes messages like 'Three Times Maggie' and 'Five More Years' into the audience to a thundering piece of modern music. (In the first show the message said 'Ten More Years' – a chant which was taken up first by her 'roadies' then by the entire audience after her speech, must to the embarrassment of her and her advisers, who were still trying to play down the 'on and on' remark.) From the lasers the music switches immediately to Andrew Lloyd Webber and the Dallas-heroic campaign theme tune and the video clips of her meeting world leaders and making speeches plays on two massive screens, leaving the audience applauding wildly before she has even appeared.

The speech itself is constructed carefully in sections, each one designed to bring the audience along another stage towards the climax. The warm-up is followed by the congratulations, the exposition of the record, the centrepiece of her main message for the evening which ends in what the *Independent*'s political correspondent Colin Hughes called 'the final assault on the enemy'. In his analysis of a typical Thatcher rally speech – the one in Solihull on Thursday night – he described its ending and its devastating effect on the audience. 'All the fine preparation, mild self-deprecation, proud recounting of her record, now mean that she can unleash the most viciously vivid language, while still seeming a picture of reasonableness . . . Now she can wither Labour with wave after wave of contemptuous rhetoric – the "termites" of the left. After forty minutes of carefully laying bricks, the demolition job is devastating, complete and leaves her audience fired with enthusiasm. And that is what speech-making on the Thatcher campaign tour is all about: whipping the Tory faithful into winning votes.'

It was indeed a stunning performance – one of her best of the tour – and once again it focused with devastating effect on defence. As she was delivering it, news was coming in of the *Guardian*'s Marplan Poll to be published in the following day's paper: it showed the Tories back with a nine-point lead at 44 per cent to Labour's 35 per cent and the Alliance 20 per cent. Two days later the Tories' own private poll by Harris was to show a further fall in the Labour vote – 44–33–21. It was clear that the slide had been halted and Labour had been forced on to the back foot. While Lord Young was happy with the way things were going, he was nevertheless surprised that, after the ferociousness of the onslaught on Labour, the movement in the polls had not been more dramatic. He and the 'exiles' had met for dinner on Tuesday night and again for lunch on Thursday to plan the next stage of the campaign. In addition they were in touch with each other by phone each day. Gordon Reece was now firmly included in their number – Guinness or no Guinness – and the Prime Minister expressed her happiness, in one of her early morning calls to Young, that the old team was once again working for her.

At the lunch, in Mark's Club, they drew four principal conclusions from the week so far. First, that defence had had a good run, but was not likely to last as a major item dominating the agenda after Sunday. Second, that it was necessary to keep Labour on the defensive, therefore a new 'issue' was required. Third, that it was necessary to dominate the morning press conference coverage more effectively, therefore a sharper approach to it was needed. And fourth, rather negatively, that Labour were obviously going to try to dominate the last full week of the campaign with the caring issues, particularly health, so the Tories should avoid the issues as much as possible and try to disrupt the debate with their own agenda. The plan was to meet again at teatime on Friday at Lord McAlpine's house to put together their final proposals before Bell and Young went to see her when she arrived back from her tour.

That night, Thursday, as Mrs Thatcher was delivering her speech, two things happened: the first gave the Tories the new issue the 'exiles' were looking for, and the second gave them a warning shot – if they needed one – of exactly how rough and personalised Labour planned to make their exposition of the health issue. In a 'This Week' interview, Neil Kinnock not only told Jonathan Dimbleby that Polaris would be recalled the day Labour came to power – thus keeping the defence debate nicely fuelled for the Tories – but also confirmed that secondary picketing, outlawed in the Tories' trade union legislation, would return under a Labour government. Howell James did a rush transcript of this section of the interview and dashed to the Thames TV studios in time to give it to Lord Young before he went on a late night election programme, where he used it to great effect. Nevertheless, in the light of Friday, it was felt by everyone that there was ample mileage left in it – for it enabled the Tories to raise again the whole spectre of union chaos under Labour. This was the issue to concentrate on. The issue to avoid came up in the Labour PEB immediately after Kinnock's appearance. It was on health and it showed, to powerful effect, a man who had the same problem with his hand as Mrs Thatcher had had the previous summer and which she had had treated privately. He was still waiting for his operation.

When Mrs Thatcher heard of it, and of Labour's plans to spend the last week attacking her personally for not caring, she was very upset. Much of the time of the 'exiles' and those in CCO would be spent in the next few days trying to stop her responding equally personally to it. As one of those closest to her said later: 'At the end of that week I thought I had lived through the worst ten days you could possibly imagine. I thought it could not get worse – but it did.'

10| Health Becomes a Hazard

It did not, however, get worse immediately; and when it did, it was for different reasons. The first surge of anxiety had been at Labour's fast and effective start to the campaign. Now that the Tories had started to fight back on defence and the trade unions, there was a period of growing confidence. It was only when it began to seem that all this hard work was to no avail, and that, far from stretching their lead, they might even be losing ground, that the second, and far more severe, bout of anxiety set in throughout the upper echelons of the party. In the intervening period – particularly at the end of the 'defence' week – there was a general feeling that the party had reasserted its control over the campaign.

Labour was still not off the hook on the principal issue: on Thursday 28 May, 24-year-old Horace Warmington, whose brother was an NCO in Germany, cast serious doubt on Labour's defence policy during the BBC's Election Call programme. John Smith, Labour's trade spokesman, found himself joining John Wakeham as yet another major politician brought to a stuttering standstill by an ordinary member of the public. Speaking on behalf of his brother, Mr Warmington gently drew from Mr Smith the tacit admission that Labour's policies in Europe would not protect British soldiers in the event of hostilities, but would sacrifice them in vain. The onslaught of senior Tories on Neil Kinnock also continued, with Michael Heseltine (who, along with fellow former Cabinet members Cecil Parkinson and Leon Brittan, was adding great weight to the party's case throughout the country) telling his audiences that they should not question the Labour leader's patriotism, but his judgement.

The feeling that things were going better was reinforced by the most successful day of the tour so far – in East Anglia on Friday. For the first time things seemed to be well co-ordinated; the Prime Minister made one or two good whistle-stop speeches, greeted Alison and John Wakeham warmly and was the recipient of one piece of good luck. Both BBC and ITN television crews were allowed on to her Battlebus between two of the stops in the afternoon to film her working while on the move. During the filming John Whittingdale took a telephone call from Roger Boaden's secretary in London to let the party know that the British diplomat Edward Chaplin had been freed in Iran. As it happened they already knew this – Mrs Thatcher had been told in a call from Downing Street some time earlier; but, never one to miss a trick, she quickly reached over, took the phone from Whittingdale and said in a very loud voice: 'Oh, that's marvellous! What good news!' The cameras turned on her, aware that something was happening; she then told them what it was, before turning back to the increasingly mystified girl in London and thanking her very much. The item, showing Mrs Thatcher being both Prime Minister and campaigning party leader, led the news bulletins all evening.

However, she was very tired by the time she got back to Downing Street at about 7.30 that evening. The physical, mental and emotional strain was beginning to tell on her. She went straight into a meeting with Charles Powell, to be briefed on the Iran situation, and did not get upstairs to the flat until after eight. Lord Young and Tim Bell had arrived in the meantime, and went upstairs shortly after with Stephen Sherbourne. Carol and Denis Thatcher were already there. For nearly an hour the six of them sat over drinks while she unwound. Among family and friends she felt she could unburden herself more, perhaps, than she would with any other group; and for a while she complained bitterly about the problems of the campaign and how she felt she had to do far too much herself. The others sat and listened, allowing all her frustrations to come out.

Part of the problem was the lack of consideration some of those around her were giving to her age. Few people, except those in the room, seemed to be taking account of the fact that she was sixty-one years old and had been running on the adrenalin of high office for eight years. She was still fit, still alert and still had more stamina than many of those about her. But, quite naturally, she tended to tire more easily and, under the extreme demands of the campaign, was in need of though not always getting more sleep. Most unusually that morning, for example, she had still been asleep when a close colleague had rung Downing Street at ten past seven. There was clearly a limit to what she could do, and for some days it had become obvious that too many people had access to her diary and were literally overloading her with meetings, interviews and the other para- phernalia of election times. She might have been able to cope with more at the age of fifty-three, when she was fighting for the first time, but the pressure was near danger-point now – es- pecially with the added strains of meeting her 'exiles' on a fairly regular basis and having to use roundabout methods of ensuring that their proposed plans were put into practice. Stephen Sher- bourne, who soon left the gathering, had read the riot act earlier in the day about the diary; but this, in turn, had caused problems and tensions as promises of the Prime Minister's time had to be broken.

Just after nine they sat down to a dinner of smoked salmon, veal and baked potatoes, and began the constructive work on the aims for the following week. Mrs Thatcher agreed that the strategy so far had ensured – as Lord Young and Tim Bell had predicted – that the Tory vote would hold steady. Bell then took her through the proposals finalised that afternoon in Lord McAlpine's house. The attack strategy for the next week should concentrate on the 'fear' issues – fear of strikes and secondary picketing after Labour's proposed repeal of the industrial re- lations laws, fear for personal safety with Labour's attitude towards law and order and the police, fear of inflation with Labour's proposals to increase public spending, fear of increased taxation as it became clear Labour's plans included taxing many more people than the very rich. The corollary to each of these fears was, of course, the Tory claim to have saved the country from them over the last eight years and the party's ability to go on doing so.

It was agreed that the press conferences, TV appearances, the PEB and senior ministers' speeches should be co-ordinated to these themes to keep up the momentum against Labour. Ministers who were 'starring' at the press conferences should spend a couple of hours on the day before they were due to appear going through a rigorous question-and-answer session, to rehearse everything they might be asked and their response to it. The aim was to avoid any further mix-ups, such as had happened early on with the education press conference. Once again, there was great praise for Norman Tebbit's role against Neil Kinnock during the week and it was decided he should continue to spearhead the attack, which would last until at least the following Thursday, when the group would meet again to review the situation and decide if, and when, to go on to the positive in the run-up to polling day.

It was also decided that the CCO television monitoring should be improved so that a faster service of 'hot' topics could be supplied. Labour admissions and contradictions were beginning to come in more quickly now that the party was under greater pressure and, it was felt, greater advantage could be taken of the situation. It was suggested that before each of her morning press conferences the Prime Minister might make a series of short statements pointing up the latest Labour 'gaffes'. For example, out of the Jonathan Dimbleby 'This Week' programme the night before had come three admissions by the Labour leader – first on secondary picketing, second on the scrapping of secret ballots and third that the ceiling on National Insurance contributions might have to be lifted. If these points had been spotted more quickly and fast statements drafted, the Prime Minister could have made great use of them that morning at her press conference.

They talked through dinner and for a short while afterwards, but Mrs Thatcher was clearly tired and was under orders from Carol, who had cossetted her mother and made a fuss of her all evening, to go to bed early and restore her energy. It had been a more relaxed and successful evening than that of the week before. One of her close associates told me subsequently: 'I think she lost confidence in herself when the campaign did not start well – and I think that was the time she felt she had been deprived of the advice of the people she valued most – such as Tim and Gordon. It was not so much things going wrong at CCO that had made her anxious – she felt that David Young could cope with that – it was the constant undercurrent in her mind that she did not have a chairman like Cecil and there were none of her old friends left. One by one they had been side-lined, but now she had evolved a system of getting their advice (through Lord Young) she felt much more relaxed. Even though she was still tired, she was more confident.'

The following evening she was due to see Norman Tebbit (the two evening meetings had originally been arranged in the reverse order, but were switched at the last moment for obvious reasons) and, by the time the Party Chairman arrived, she had a fully prepared briefing note to refresh her memory on the items to discuss with him and to help her talk them through. The note had been written on Saturday morning at Alastair McAlpine's house, where the 'exiles' had gathered to go over their plans, and it was delivered to Downing Street by Howell James in the afternoon. The meeting was apparently a great success. The chairman found her relaxed and happy and found many of her suggestions fitted in well with what he had in mind.

Nevertheless his attitude towards what he was hearing was ambivalent, according to one of those close to him. He was aware that David Young talked to the Prime Minister – indeed he was glad he did, because of the pressure that took off himself – but he resented what he saw as the increasing number of outsiders, whom he heard were in competition for the Prime Minister's ear. 'The greatest threat to the campaign comes from this sort of intrigue,' I was told. 'Some of it is a genuine desire to help, but most of it comes from individuals vying for position afterwards.' Once more the longstanding professional and personal relationship between Tebbit and Young saw them through what was a difficult and potentially fraught situation for them both; nor was it helped by a fresh outcrop of criticism of the campaign in the media. *The Times*, a week later, was to describe this period as one in which the Tory campaign was too rigid: it was 'too hung up on the original game plan drawn up when they were expecting the Alliance to come through into second place as the real threat. Although Mr Tebbit has been brilliant at the Tory press conferences, deftly steering the Prime Minister and press, the Tories got off to a slow start, which allowed Labour to seize the initiative.'

The original 'game plan' was, in fact, the one discussed with
the Prime Minister on Maundy Thursday and, bearing in mind
the common faith of all those present in the strength of the
manifesto on its own, had, according to one person who was at
the meeting, consisted of little more than a series of dates pencilled in for press conferences, ministry by ministry. 'The only
strategy the new strategies were replacing was no strategy really,'
I was told. 'It was not Norman's fault in particular. It was
everyone's fault. We had allowed it to happen. None of us had
realised that the arrangements were just being left as they were
– they were not really being slotted into some master plan at
CCO.'

The weekend's polls, public and private, did very little to
reassure any of the Tory team. Gallup had them only 7.5 points
ahead at 41.5 to 34 per cent, and their own private Harris poll
put them only half a point better off at 42:34. The 12-point gap
between Tory and Labour had shrunk by four points since the
start of the campaign and, while the vote seemed to be holding,
the attacks on Kinnock had not yet translated into a appreciable
shift in the opinion polls. The private marginal tracking studies
showed the party still ahead of Labour in the Tory/Labour seats
– but well behind 1983; and the presentation of the manifesto,
on which so many hopes had been pinned, was seen to be only
marginally better than that of the other parties. There were some
crumbs of comfort – more than 50 per cent of people seemed to
think that Neil Kinnock was dodging the issues and more than
70 per cent thought that the Labour manifesto covered up a lot
of issues: the message of the 'Iceberg Manifesto' was clearly
getting through.

Although Mrs Thatcher had recovered her equilibrium, many
of her team were still nervous – so much so that the persuasive
talents of Gordon Reece to cheer people up were used more than
once on Sunday. Out of London, party workers felt the campaign
was at last on the rails and going somewhere. In Crewe and
Nantwich, where Angela Browning was fighting, two visits during the week had immeasurably helped party morale: David
Mitchell, the junior Transport Minister, had arrived to try to
offset the damage done by the laying off of 1000 British Rail
engineering workers only a few days earlier, and a lightning visit

from Norman Tebbit had given her whole campaign a boost. The issues being raised with her – and which she believed the party should attack on – were health and pensions. In Hazel Grove, Tom Arnold felt that his Liberal and Labour opponents were no longer making the running on the issues and that the initiative had been wrested back from them. Fortuitously, however, the one theme which came through time and again in both constituencies was the fear of Neil Kinnock's ever getting near to Downing Street – the very fear that the Tory party was now about to place in the spotlight.

The third week got off to a good start with a classic illustration of how well the new strategy could be made to work. Lord Young and Howell James had, on their own initiative, had a simple graphic of a wilting red rose prepared (at the offices of Lowe Howard-Spink & Bell) and used it as the logo on all their storyboards for the Monday morning press conference. Instead of talking about unemployment defensively, Young had decided to go on the attack under the title of 'Labour's Jobs Destruction Package'. While the Tory government was steadily bringing unemployment down, he said, Labour's plans would actually mean the loss of a million jobs – 600,000 through the introduction of a national minimum wage, 60,000 through the cancellation of Polaris and Trident, 150,000 through the abandonment of nuclear power, 120,000 through the imposition of South African sanctions, 50,000 through restrictions on private education and health. In addition, he claimed, many more jobs would be lost through the imposition of a training levy, loss of investment confidence and repeal of the trade union laws. The wilting red rose and the content of the press conference were covered in every news bulletin throughout the day and evening – the first time the Tories had managed to dominate the media from the start of the day with an issue raised at one of their own press conferences. The next day the *Daily Express* carried a front page story claiming that not only would Labour's plans destroy a million jobs, but that their plans to create a million jobs would not cost £5 billion, as forecast by Labour, but nearer £20 billion. Thus, it pointed out, we would be throwing £20 billion away to achieve nothing. The assault so effectively removed unemployment from the agenda that the Tories learned next day that the

Labour party had, at the last moment, dropped its plans to devote the next PEB to unemployment and 'in response to popular demand from its supporters' decided to re-run Hugh Hudson's film about Neil Kinnock instead. It was the first major sign of unsure footing the Labour strategy team had shown – after all the purpose of elections is to win votes, not to pander to your own supporters by showing them what David Steel described contemptuously as 'old movies'.

The rest of the press conferences in the week were all now planned to hammer the fear/safety theme – Nigel Lawson's on Tuesday was on Labour's threat to the economy, and its corollary: how safe the economy was in Tory hands. The PEB on Tuesday night, hastily assembled to fit in with the new strategy, also carried the theme along. For the first half it used the concept of Labour's conjuring tricks, none of which worked, and then switched to Lord Young talking about the threat from Labour. It was not a satisfactory mixture – 'more like crème brulée with a jacket potato,' one senior Tory told me.

The Prime Minister's speech in Scotland that night was one of many on the same theme made by leading Tories all over Britain during the week. Once again the charge was being led by her and Norman Tebbit. She hammered home the message. First she warmed the audience with the list of the government's achievements. Then, with a series of stark warnings, she hammered home the threat to all they had achieved. She drew particular attention to the threat from the trade unions: 'Today, under a mask of moderation,' she said, 'the Labour Party is in the grip of its hard left. They won't let go. And within days of the election of a Labour government, the unions would be back in the driver's seat and their leaders would, once again, be the nation's masters. We must not let it happen . . . Back would come the enforced closed-shop; shop stewards would once again have the power to decide if a man should be allowed to work or not. Back would come secondary picketing; unions would decide which factories could work normally and which would be closed down – whether they were involved in the strike or not. And when workers and managers tried to keep their factories going – back would come the violence.'

Over the weekend word had begun to leak out of the Labour

camp that Neil Kinnock and his inner council were amazed at the good start they had been allowed to have, were hardly surprised by the strength of the Tory counterattack, and had decided that the only way to recapture the initiative, or at least prevent the Tories continuing to hold it, was to attack Mrs Thatcher personally and through her the lack of caring common, in their minds, to all Tories. This meant that they would begin to concentrate their press conferences, advertising, PEBs, tour themes and speeches around the caring issues – health, education, pensions and unemployment. However, surprisingly, the word was also that Kinnock, Gould and Mandelson had already recognised that there was no possibility that the party could win the election and that the aim must therefore be to settle for a second place which clearly re-established Labour's position as a solid challenger to the Tories. While, quite naturally, continuing to declare that he would be moving into Downing Street on 12 June, Kinnock had, the Tories believed, set his sights not on outright victory at the polls, but on a hung Parliament.

The Alliance, too, were beginning to face up to the fact that their much-vaunted late bandwagon, which was meant to sweep them past Labour into second place, had lost a wheel somewhere down the trail. The first signs were also showing that the public wanted clearly identifiable individual leaders and clearly identifiable policies, and that they did not feel they were getting either from the Owen–Steel combination. It was also being reported that their relationship was not as close as the telegenic orchestration of it portrayed. David Steel was said to want to ignore Labour and to go for the Tories; David Owen was said to have at last realised the folly of this policy being adopted before the Alliance had overtaken Labour. And both were understood to have regretted devoting so much time at the beginning of the campaign to the need for constitutional reform. Proportional representation was one of those issues which many people would support out of a sense of fairness, but few would make it their prime reason for voting for the Alliance at a general election.

The personal attacks on Mrs Thatcher, when they came, were deeply hurtful, but she was ready for them. She and Denis Thatcher had discussed them before the weekend; he was more worried about the effect they might have on her than she was.

Fortunately there was a sort of undergraduate, rag-week spite about them. 'They were,' one senior Tory said, 'the sort of thing you might imagine Neil and Glenys cooking up at Cardiff University to shout at their next ban-the-bomb march.' The Labour PEB on health, in which the man waiting for a hand operation was shown, had signalled the opening shots of the campaign, which was both generalised on the fact that the Tories did not care (backed by the statement that all the Cabinet Ministers sent their children to private schools and that they did not use the NHS) and aimed specifically at individuals, particularly Mrs Thatcher. The Sunday papers were leaked stories of the impending concerted assault on her and in fact Neil Kinnock, Gerald Kaufman and several others all attacked that day. Tony Blair, a Labour Treasury spokesman, went furthest by describing her as having 'an unchecked and unbalanced mind', while Kinnock talked of her 'arrogance and obsessions'. By Sunday night the media interest in the attack was such that the Labour leader went on television to point out that there was, of course, nothing personal in it.

On Tuesday night, in her Edinburgh speech, Mrs Thatcher was contemptuous of the insults: 'First, they tried to hide their socialism. What floated to the surface was Labour's Iceberg Manifesto. Then they tried to re-package socialism. They wrapped it in cellophane and roses. Sweet smelling for a day, but oh, so transparent. And this week they are resorting to personal abuse. This is an excellent sign. Personal abuse is no substitute for policy. It signals panic. In any case let me assure you it will not affect me in the slightest.' It would have been foolish for her to have admitted otherwise; nevertheless she was affected by the barrage, particularly by the charge that she did not care. The very fact that she does care about people – and came close to letting it get the better of her – was one of the contributory factors in the Tories' last major bout of jitters of the campaign. For the accusation stung her so deeply that, over a period of nearly a week, she developed quite a bee in her bonnet about it.

The nub of the problem is that, for all that she is the only Prime Minister in recent times who has taken Britain successfully through a war, for all that she has taken some of the toughest decisions about the economy that any leader of this country has ever had to take, and for all that, in the miners' strike, she faced down one of the most daunting challenges ever mounted against our democratic society – for all that, in other words, she is uncommonly tough – her motive, according to those who know her, has always been a deep concern for the ordinary people of this country. She not only genuinely has a vision of how life can be better for *all* the people – though the message that before you can care you first must be able to cope does not easily lend itself to slogans – but she is also personally very caring, as a legion of examples testify. (On the tour plane she twice found time for little acts of thoughtfulness: once she went to sit in the rear section next to a BBC cameraman who had fallen off a ladder during the day and injured his arm, and on another occasion she wrote a brief note to the wife of a reporter who, because he was on the tour, was missing their wedding anniversary for the first time in 27 years.) Privately and publicly, a large part of her life demonstrates concern for both individuals and the nation. Anyone who knows her well will testify that that is why she is in politics – not for the 'being' but for the 'doing'.

It almost certainly came as a considerable shock to her to realise as the campaign developed that there were a great many people who not only did not recognise those characteristics in her, but actually thought the very opposite – that she was a mean, uncaring tyrant. It was one thing to read the results of polls, such as a Gallup survey at this time which showed the key areas of weakness in the government to be that it only looked after the rich, that it was uncaring, that it was arrogant and that she was its leader, it was quite another to meet that hostility face to face and to have it expressed daily through some of the less than friendly questioning of journalists.

As so often, however, her strength became for a while her weakness and then evolved into a strength again. Her care for people, which is one of her strengths, became her weakness. Because she knew the accusations were false, she thought she ought to correct them; and in the desire to put the record straight, to be honest about what she thought, she became vulnerable. She had started to become anxious about the accusations on the Tuesday and Wednesday of the week before. By the time the campaign began to build up, with the Labour PEB on health and its example of the man with the same hand problem as hers, she was becoming quite agitated about it. The advice from both Norman Tebbit and Lord Young was to ignore the subject. Answer questions on it by all means, they had counselled; point out what the unions had done to hospital patients in the 'winter of discontent'; if necessary, make it the subject of a section of her speeches showing the abysmal record of spending on health of the last Labour government; but basically, steer clear of it as a major topic.

That night, however, she talked to several 'friends' on the phone and the following morning arrived at CCO fired with the idea that she was not appearing on television enough (it was the CCO strategy, agreed by almost every person involved, to use her sparingly before the final week) and that the next PEB, in which she would appear, should be about how the Tories cared for people. It took all the persuasive powers of both Tebbit and Young to talk her out of the idea that morning – then Young and Bell that night and Tebbit again the following night. Their arguments were basically threefold: first, health was one of the Tories' weak spots and it would be unwise to raise it at a time when they had the momentum of attack. Second, by raising the subject themselves, the Tories would be playing into the hands of Labour, giving them a heaven-sent opportunity to regain the initiative and start to set the agenda themselves. And third, if, as seemed likely, the attack on the Tories as uncaring was to become focused on her, then it would swiftly rebound in the eyes of the British public, who dislike bitter attacks on television – even by politicians – and the men delivering the message would be made to look mean and cheap.

None of this, of course, did anything to comfort Mrs Thatcher personally or to prepare her for the major onslaught when it came the following week. As one of those close to her said that weekend: 'We all wondered if it might rock her. We knew how sensitive she was on the subject. I was left wondering, how do you prepare yourself for attacks like that?' Behind all the calming talk she received during those few days was one other, unstated, argument – that the image of a person and a government who were uncaring had been acquired over a number of years. It was the product of the persistent neglect of positive communications at the centre of things in Downing Street and it could not be put right in five days, particularly not in the heat of an election battle.

That weekend she reluctantly agreed on the strategic inadvisability of making health a central issue, but, as she frequently does when a problem is exercising her mind, she did not let the matter go; and Denis Thatcher, perhaps knowing her better than anyone, continued to say that he too did not think she should ignore it. Nature also intervened in a most extraordinary way to remind her, if she needed it, exactly how important health is to us all. Early in the week she developed an abscess on a tooth. The pain left her understandably irritable and the use of antibiotics and painkillers made her marginally less able to focus her mind on things. Many of the journalists on the tour, not knowing what her problem was, remarked that she seemed tired and distracted. But it was a measure of her determination that she drove herself on through the week, never complaining of the pain or backing out of her commitments. The campaign was becoming yet another example of her ability to persevere until her goals were achieved. She was going to need all those powers by the end of the following week.

The Labour Party's attacks on her, and through her on the caring issues, were a constant counterpoint to the Tories' attacks on the dangers of Labour through that week. It was the crucial, penultimate, week of the campaign and the one in which each side expected to do its big hitting. It was Thatcher versus Kinnock and Tories versus Labour, and whoever and whichever was able to get through to the next week intact and visibly the stronger would be the victor. On position, on strength, the Tories looked the likely winners; but there was still a long way to go, and health and caring were twice more to lurch Mrs Thatcher and her party close to the precipice before it was all over.

It was neither a particularly happy tour party that returned from Scotland and the north-east on the Wednesday night, nor a particularly happy CCO that greeted them. The tour was still not right – even after an emergency meeting at Downing Street on Sunday night to review it with a view to trimming away anything unnecessary. Day after day the Kinnock tour was

beating the Thatcher tour – in the eyes of television and newspaper editors – for timing, visual impact and relevance. The
Kinnock shots were in earlier, were better and seemed to have
some bearing on what was going on that day. On some days
this, coupled with continuing problems with the speeches ('Who
could imagine the leading lady still up at 3.30 a.m. writing her
lines for the play next day?' asked one exasperated aide), made
the atmosphere on the Battlebus very tense.

Not all the coverage given by television was as unbiased as
the mere measurement of time given to each of the parties would
suggest. It is certainly true that much of the film shown of the
Kinnock campaign was shot in warm, emotional surroundings,
with lots of slapping on the back and hand-clasping, whereas
much of Mrs Thatcher's used coverage was shot from a distance,
even though she had two camera crews tied to her almost as
though by an umbilical cord. A certain amount of 'irrelevant'
footage was used. For example, in the brief coverage shown of
her press conference in Glasgow, the second half of one of her
answers to a question was shown followed by a ten-second shot
of her turning away to drink a glass of water. A fascinating study
could be done, not of the quantity of footage shown throughout
the campaign, but of the quality. It was reported that Peter
Mandelson regularly complained to programme editors about
the lack of fairness in the presentation of his party's case throughout the campaign. None of those complaints ever made headline
news, but the only protest made by Norman Tebbit in the run-up
to polling day attracted wide attention. In the early hours of
Monday morning he telephoned Duke Hussey, the BBC's chairman, to protest about the treatment of Cecil Parkinson, who had
been 'bumped off' the 'Today' programme because David Owen
did not want to appear with him. Although the story was very
much a non-story, because the matter was amicably settled
before Mr Hussey could intervene, it achieved considerable
prominence in the heavier press.

The BBC was, however, involved in one other project which,
in the end, both Labour and Tory politicians were to condemn.
It has been the habit of Vincent Hanna, a reporter on 'Newsnight', to institute his own polls at times of by-elections. The
role of these polls in predicting swings, particularly to the Al-

liance, thus – his enemies would say – assisting in the creation of a bandwagon, has always been controversial, to say the least. He argues that if his polling techniques reveal swings first, then that is the sign of good polling; if they subsequently turn into bandwagons that is not his responsibility. However it was not his motives, rather his techniques, which aroused suspicion among politicians and the panjandrums of the polling business. They suspected the accuracy of his findings on three grounds: first, that he used polytechnic students to carry out his polling, second, that he used a fixed group of respondents (these have never been reckoned to be as accurate as sampling the general populace, since any fixed group is bound to consist of people who have an above average interest in the subject on which they are being polled), third, that he would never reveal how he 'weighted' his results. All pollsters weight their findings to take account of inaccuracies in their polling procedures, but Hanna would never say how and on what grounds he conducted his.

In this election Hanna had taken his somewhat controversial by-election techniques and used them on a national basis, with the result that on 2 June a Newsnight/Vincent Hanna poll showed the Tories at 40.2 per cent, Labour 37.7 per cent and Alliance at 21.9. Although there was widespread cynicism in all parties about the validity of these findings, the presence of the poll was bound to have an effect on Tory morale. It was the first crack in the armour they had built up so carefully in the previous ten days, a crack in their confidence which was to split much wider open two days later, when 'Wobble Thursday' dawned.

On the day-by-day chart of the election campaign in Lord McAlpine's office there is a squiggly line drawn through the last Thursday before polling day. It was he who christened it 'Wobble Thursday' because, in every election campaign, roughly the same sort of thing happens on that day. In 1979 it was the day that a nervous Mrs Thatcher was told of Lord Thorneycroft's plans to recruit Edward Heath into the campaign. In 1983 it was the day she became separated from the tour and came back to London in a very angry mood. Confidently, and with a certain amount of trepidation, McAlpine had predicted that there would be a similar upset this time. Tension mounts at this particular stage in the campaign; it is rather like aircraft taking off – there comes a point on the runway and a speed of the plane at which it is no longer possible to turn back: it must take off. By analogy, as the end of the last full week of the campaign approaches, the runway is running out in terms of days left to polling day and speed is represented by the results of the polls. A party is either far enough ahead to be confident of take-off, or it is going to crash, and on 'Wobble Thursday' the realisation dawns that it is very nearly too late to do anything about it either way.

The Hanna poll on Tuesday night did not help. Rumours of it, spread beforehand, made everyone at CCO uneasy that day. On Wednesday the rumours were about an altogether more substantial poll: that week's Gallup to be published in the following day's *Daily Telegraph*. Throughout the campaign the Gallup results had been at variance with the mainstream of the polls. The company had altered its question order and one or two other details of technique just before the election, but it did not seem to have worked out satisfactorily. Panic selling had taken place in the City over the 'Newsnight' poll the afternoon before, and now the same happened again as rumours of the Gallup circulated on Wednesday afternoon. It was a time for steady nerves – and they were found in CCO that day. Norman Tebbit refused to comment on the rumours and appeared calm in the face of a relentless and hostile barrage from Sue Lawley in 'On the Spot'. Then, that night, he launched his second attack of the day on Labour's domination by the hard left and the trade unions. The poll, when it came, showed the Tories at 40.5 per cent, the lowest any reputable pollster had given them so far, Labour on 36 per cent and the Alliance on 21.5. In quality of campaign Neil Kinnock was 16 points ahead of Mrs Thatcher at 39 to her 23.

Although there was near-panic among many senior people in CCO, Norman Tebbit and Michael Dobbs had good reason to hold steady. Both polls were suspect, they believed. Both were contrary to all the feedback the party was getting from the constituencies, where it was felt there was definitely no slide. And both were contrary to the TV–AM/Harris rolling poll which had been fairly accurate, if anything slightly down on the Tories, throughout the campaign and which was showing 42 to 36 per cent. They pointed out that the real test would not come until the following night (Thursday) when both Marplan and one of their own private Harris polls were due.

Lord Young, Tim Bell and Howell James had lunched on Tuesday for a preliminary discussion about their plans, which Bell and Young were now due to put to Mrs Thatcher a day early – when she returned from Scotland and the north-east on Wednesday night. Young was speaking in Southampton that evening and dashed back to London in his car afterwards, having only time to eat a hamburger on the way up. He and Bell spoke to each other about the Gallup poll from their respective cars and agreed that it was worrying, but almost certainly a 'rogue' poll. They arrived at Downing Street more or less together at 10 p.m. and went straight upstairs to the Prime Minister's flat, collecting Stephen Sherbourne on the way.

Mrs Thatcher was by now very tired and suffering considerable discomfort from her tooth. She said she did not have time to get it treated; it would have to wait until after the election. (She went to the dentist the following Friday morning.) The strategy put to her was that the message for the last few days should be more co-ordinated than anything they had done so far. The idea, said Bell, 'is to get everyone singing from the same hymnbook'. The message would be simple: 'Britain is a success again. Don't let Labour ruin it.' The Prime Minister's contribution in her concentrated appearances on television and in her speeches in the next six days would be to start giving this vision of how Britain was going to be, rather than allowing herself to be sidetracked into arid discussions of whether certain taxes were going up, or how the Housing Bill would work. The time for questions was over; here now was the whole story.

She reacted warmly to their proposals and made it clear that she was still not happy with either the advertising or the PEBs, a situation which would require yet more of her time next day. Also, from her talks with other people, she had gained the impression that her Party Chairman was appearing on television too often and she suggested his appearances be reduced. Young, who thought that this might cause problems – after all a Party Chairman was supposed to appear on television at election times – suggested that she choose the right moment and ask both himself and Tebbit to make way for the younger men for the last few days. She accepted this idea and added that she would also ask Tebbit to get out and around the marginals over the last few days, leaving Young to co-ordinate the office. Pleased with what had been achieved, she saw them out, promising that in the morning she would call a meeting after the press conference – with William Whitelaw, Lord Young, Norman Tebbit and herself – to go through all the proposals and set up the structure to co-ordinate all the appearances.

Lord Young and Tim Bell left just before one o'clock in the morning. 'Wobble Thursday' had begun. By the time it was over there would be more anxiety than on any other day of the campaign, more stress, more tensions, more anger and more anguish in the corridors of power. And the recriminations would go on long after the results of the election were known.

Wobble Thursday to Winning Thursday

Of all the conversations silently witnessed over the years by the portrait of Rudyard Kipling, Mrs Thatcher's favourite writer, which hangs on the wall in the tiny waiting-room sandwiched between a lavatory and the office of Stephen Sherbourne and Michael Alison on the ground floor of 10 Downing Street, few can have matched the drama of two that took place in the late afternoon and early evening of 4 June – 'Wobble Thursday'. In the first, the Prime Minister approved in outline the rough drawings for the two-and-a-half-million-pound advertising blitz which was to bring the Tories' campaign to a thundering climax, knowing that the material had been prepared by Tim Bell and not by Saatchi & Saatchi; in the second, Lord Young confronted Maurice Saatchi, who initially refused to accept the work – and ordered him to take it.

The two events were the climactic points of a day of high drama which left nearly all its participants emotionally drained and some deeply shocked. So charged was the atmosphere for most of the time – in both Central Office, where it started, and Downing Street, where it ended – that one of the key players in the drama said later that he had never known a day or events like it; nor did he ever wish to again. To understand what happened, and why feelings ran so high, it is necessary to go back over it in some detail.

Mrs Thatcher, her tooth still painful, arrived at CCO at 8.30 a.m. and went straight to her office for her morning briefing session. As soon as she sat down she turned to Norman Tebbit and, as agreed the night before, said that she thought he and Lord Young should not appear on television as much as in the

previous week; more of the time should be given to the younger
men such as Kenneth Clark and John Moore. The chairman
neither agreed nor disagreed, but said he would look at the
suggestion. For most of the hour the meeting lasted she seemed
tense and was questioning, but not irascible; nevertheless, only
four of the six items on the agenda were covered, and on one of
them, the opinion polls, there was not much good news. Norman
Tebbit did his best to allay fears about the previous day's Gallup
poll and to cast everyone's mind forward to the more reliable
result which could be expected that evening from Marplan.
There was no debate on the newspaper headlines of the day, nor
was the report from the media monitoring unit taken. It cannot
have escaped her notice, nor pleased her, that the numbers of
people present had risen above twenty again; consequently the
heat in the small room was almost intolerable.

A few minutes after Mrs Thatcher's meeting had started, Neil
Kinnock arrived at Transport House, just thirty yards away
across the square, from a highly successful early morning visit
to St Thomas's Hospital, where he had been filmed surrounded
by nurses and patients. He was in Smith Square for one of his
rare London press conferences the subject of which was health,
and the early morning film would provide the background to the
debate which the party planners hoped would, and which indeed
did, dominate the television agenda throughout the day. But
Kinnock had one problem: how to evade the barrage of questions
the 'big guns' – the political editors of the newspapers and the
TV commentators, who were crammed into the room – were
bound to ask.

He pulled a masterly stroke; knowing that most of them would
have to leave shortly before nine-thirty to be in time for the start
of Mrs Thatcher's press conference, he, Michael Meacher, the
Labour Health spokesman, and Margaret Beckett simply read a
series of statements until 9.27, by which time most of the big
guns had left. In these statements was raised the case of Martin
Burgess, the 10-year-old boy who had been waiting fifteen
months for a hole-in-the-heart operation. It was this case, when
it was raised at the Tory press conference a few minutes later,
which drew Mrs Thatcher away from her carefully prepared
brief on pensions into the minefield of health, and eventually

exploded the issue of her own private medical insurance into the campaign with her statement that she was covered privately 'to enable me to go into hospital on the day I want, at the time I want and with the doctor I want'. Thus, in less than two hours, the Labour leader had given the TV editors early and emotive film, grabbed the issue of the day and trapped Mrs Thatcher into a disadvantage. The week-long struggle to dominate the media with the next 'issue' looked like slipping from the grasp of the Tories. (There was also irony in Kinnock's statement at his conference: 'The huge increases in the cost of dental treatment mean that people are not visiting dentists as often as they should, or are not having the treatment they need' – for no one apart from Mrs Thatcher's close circle knew of her abscess.)

The pain in her tooth, lack of sleep, anxiety about her next speech the following night, the awareness that she had just made a slip and that she had been trapped on her most vulnerable point (the desire to refute the accusation that she did not 'care') – any one of these factors, or all of them, could have contributed to her mood during the next hour. There are two versions of how she expressed her anger and frustration. One is that she became increasingly bad-tempered and loud-voiced, until her questioning could be heard clearly outside her room where the arranged meeting with William Whitelaw, Lord Young, Norman Tebbit, Stephen Sherbourne and John Wakeham (who, though not on the original list, had turned up anyway) was taking place. The other does not deny that she showed great anger, but insists that it was expressed quietly, if occasionally vehemently. No one, however, denies that the object of much of her wrath during that time was the work of the advertising agency, Saatchi. Nor is there any doubt that, at no stage in the meeting, or subsequently, was the agency sacked or removed from the account.

The meeting started just after 10.15. First she raised yet again the matter of Norman Tebbit's and Lord Young's television appearances. Once again Young said he would step down, but Tebbit resisted. It was too risky, in his view, to put the younger men in at this stage, the safe 'old hands' would not be likely to make mistakes and, in any case, most of the programmes had already been planned around his presence. Thus thwarted, the Prime Minister became more cross. She then turned to the

proposed direction of the campaign for the last seven days and
said she did not like the PEB which was being prepared by
Saatchi for the last night of the campaign. She had been shown
the proposed opening five minutes which consisted of clips of
her speeches going back to 1979, and she objected strongly to
it. She ordered a meeting to be held that afternoon, while she
was away in the Midlands, to come up with fresh ideas for the
broadcast and added: 'What is more, I want Gordon Reece to
be there.' The chairman immediately welcomed the move and
insisted that he himself would invite Reece.

Mrs Thatcher then asked to see the advertising for the weekend. Michael Dobbs was summoned to the room and asked to
bring it. While he was away she expressed, once again, her deep
dissatisfaction with some of the advertisements that had been
running in the papers in the last few days, proofs of which were
lining the walls of the room. Lord Whitelaw, anxious to make
the peace, said he thought the picture of the surrendering soldier
was quite a good piece of work. She conceded the point, but
nevertheless her anger continued unabated, only increasing when
Dobbs reported back that the work for the weekend was on
its way from Saatchi and therefore not immediately available.
However he did explain that the concept of them was choice: a
choice between the Labour way and the Tory way, as demonstrated by the successes of the last eight years. Tebbit tried to
defend the advertising and pointed out that she had not been
shown the work already because she had been too busy to look
at it. She then gave a new brief: she wanted more positive
work establishing the good things the Tories had done, but also
containing a clear and simple contrast to what Labour had done,
or would do if they got in. The meeting closed after nearly an
hour. In silence the people in the room picked up their papers
and filed out. Lord Young, who had tried several times to induce
her to put him in charge of items (as agreed the night before) by
saying 'Tell me what you want me to do, Prime Minister', but
had been ignored, caught up with her and Sherbourne on the
first-floor landing and asked what was wrong and what he could
do. Wearily, she asked him to make sure the PEB meeting went
well and to take charge of the final broadcast. Then she walked
downstairs and out to her car to return to Downing Street.

Those who were at that meeting will no doubt speculate for ever as to what it was that caused her outburst. Having spoken to several people who were there, and who were with Mrs Thatcher later in the day, I believe that at the root of her behaviour was frustration, aggravated by the tiredness and pain. For nearly a month now she had been desperately careful, in her relationship with Norman Tebbit, to avoid overruling him on CCO matters; at this crucial stage she had been the more careful because she admired his political skills and judgement so much. She knew, too, that Lord Young had taken inordinate trouble to keep Tebbit happy, but, as one close associate of them both put it, 'it was like trying to stop the irresistible force meeting the immoveable object' – and the strain was beginning to tell on all three. Now, she felt frustrated and angry that there appeared to be no way of resolving this situation without the sort of confrontation which could be catastrophic both for herself and for the party.

In this context her anger could also clearly be seen as a sort of final warning that, unless matters improved swiftly, those very measures which she dreaded taking might yet have to be taken. Aware that a major crisis was at hand, Lord Young went back through the swing doors and into Michael Dobbs's office, where he found John Sharkey, who had arrived with Saatchi's work. He looked through it with them and told them that he did not feel that it would fit in with what the Prime Minister now wanted. He suggested that Saatchi work through the day on Mrs Thatcher's new brief and have it ready in time for her return from Alton Towers at about 5.30 in the evening. Shortly afterwards Stephen Sherbourne arrived back from Downing Street and he, Tebbit and Young went through the list of things which had been agreed the night before and which the Prime Minister had not raised at the meeting. Young then rang Tim Bell to tell him that things were finally back on course – but that the advertising was still not as required.

A few minutes later the telephone in Bell's office overlooking Hyde Park rang again. It was Downing Street, summoning him to the PEB meeting at 3.30 that afternoon. The significance of that phone call was clear to him. For a month now he had been very discreet about his contacts with the Prime Minister – he too was aware of the extent to which everyone concerned had been walking on eggshells. Now he was no longer being 'sneaked in past the dustbins' – he was being invited in through the front door. It was clear that the Prime Minister now regarded his contribution as essential. If there was a problem with the advertising, he as an advertising man should perhaps then help out. At 12.30, just as the first rumours were sweeping the City that the next day's Marplan poll would show the Tories with only a two per cent lead over Labour, he and the agency chairman Frank Lowe sat down and started to compose a series of advertisements. They worked through lunch and had eight finished and ready to be drawn up by art director Alan Waldie by the time Bell had to leave for Downing Street at 3.20 p.m. Still undecided as to how to introduce them there, he told Lowe that he would call later to check the work was completed and give instructions.

At Downing Street the first of a series of delicate manoeuvrings was taking place which were to give much of the day an air that one of those partaking in them described as 'more that of a bedroom farce than the corridors of power'. Saatchi's creative director Jeremy Sinclair was in Paris for the day and therefore could not attend the meeting to discuss the PEB – for that reason it was felt 'safe' to invite Tim Bell to contribute openly to the discussions. However another meeting, on an altogether different subject – of which more later – was also due to take place in Number 10 that afternoon (at 2.30 p.m.) involving John Banks, the chairman of another advertising agency, Young & Rubicam. One major figure from the world of advertising going through the door of Number 10, on a day when major jitters were fast developing all round, was explicable – two could have started a huge scare. The Banks meeting was therefore hastily switched to John Wakeham's office in Number 12.

The PEB meeting, attended by Stephen Sherbourne, Lord Young, Howell James, Tim Bell, Anthony Jay and Ronald Millar, lasted an hour and a half; as it came to an end Bell took Young aside and told him about the work he had done with Frank Lowe. Young expressed great interest and asked to see it, if possible, before Mrs Thatcher arrived back in Downing Street from her tour. Word about the Marplan poll had spread and the mood in Downing Street, as well as in CCO, was, to say the least, gloomy. It was agreed that Howell James should return with Bell to his office, go through the work with Bell and bring it back to Downing Street in case desperate measures were needed.

James arrived back at Downing Street at 5.30 p.m. in the middle of a thunderstorm and, as he struggled out of the car with the sixteen boards on which the rough artwork was mounted, he was accorded the privilege of the huge Prime Ministerial umbrella across the pavement. He took the material straight to Stephen Sherbourne's office, where the political secretary and Lord Young were waiting anxiously. The three of them hastily looked through the boards and agreed that this was the sort of material the Prime Minister had been looking for. The advertisements ran to a simple and well-tried formula: a large positive statement about a Tory government achievement (e.g. 'Income tax is down to its lowest level for 20 years') followed by a smaller negative statement about what Labour would do, or had done (e.g. 'Every Labour Government there has ever been has increased taxation'), and the same line at the bottom of each advertisement: 'Britain's a success again. Don't let Labour ruin it. Vote Conservative X'. It was based on a campaign the Saatchis and Bell had developed together in 1979, which was called 'The Facts' and consisted of a series of statements such as 'Law and Order: The Facts' and 'Employment: The Facts'. The slogan at the bottom was not original either – it had been borrowed from the Tories' own 1959 campaign, when the slogan was 'Life's Better with the Conservatives. Don't let Labour ruin it'. The simplicity of the approach and the bold typography were a stark contrast to the material which had been produced so far by the Saatchis – one of which the Prime Minister described as resembling more a building society advertisement than one for a political party.

Lord Young and Stephen Sherbourne hustled Howell James next door into the small waiting-room, which is lined with bookcases and therefore had sufficient shelving on which to prop up the work. He set about putting all the single-page layouts on one side of the room and the double pages on the other, while Young went outside and stood at the end of the wide corridor up to the front door so that he could see when the Prime Minister arrived. She came though the door while James was still at work. Young and Sherbourne approached her and asked her to come into the waiting-room to look at something they had to show her. She said she was busy and had only a short time to prepare for her appearance that evening on 'This Week' with Jonathan Dimbleby. 'Prime Minister, trust me,' Young said to her. 'Tim has done a whole campaign for you for the last week and I want you to see it. Just come in and have a look at it.'

Somewhat reluctantly, she entered the room as Howell James was putting up the last of the boards. She stood back and looked round them all quickly, then said: 'Excellent. This is excellent,' and started to go round reading each one. 'This is exactly what we need,' she added as she did so. 'Why haven't we had something like this . . . This is what we have been saying all along . . . This is good.' She particularly liked one on lower inflation and another which said: 'The Conservatives are spending three times as much on the Health Service as the last Labour Government. The only government to reduce spending on health was the last Labour Government.'

When she had finished she turned to Lord Young and asked the question that was in all their minds: 'What do we do?' 'Prime Minister, leave it to me,' Young replied. 'It is very simple. I will telephone Saatchi's. They will come over and we'll look at their campaign. If you prefer it, we'll go ahead and do it. If you don't, then all you have to do is to say that you don't and —' She cut him short: 'David, I don't have the time,' she said. 'I'm already behind and I've got to go and prepare for the Dimbleby interview. Could you *please* take it forward?' 'Leave it to me, Prime Minister,' Young replied. And she left the room and walked quickly up the stairs to her study above.

Lord Young immediately phoned Michael Dobbs, but was put through to Norman Tebbit. He told him the Prime Minister was back and the Saatchis should bring their work to Number 10 at 6.30, then asked Tebbit to come separately and five minutes early because he had something he wanted to tell him. It was still pouring with rain and Tebbit was held up in the traffic so, unfortunately, Maurice Saatchi and John Sharkey arrived first. They were asked to wait in the waiting area outside the room where the Tim Bell/Frank Lowe advertising was laid out, but

Saatchi seemed anxious to go up to see the Prime Minister and, after several moments the whole party decamped upstairs to the waiting area outside the Prime Minister's study, where, by now, she was already well into her briefing with John Whittingdale. When Young heard Tebbit arrive he moved swiftly back downstairs and intercepted him, drawing him towards the little waiting-room. Heated words could be heard being exchanged for a few minutes as Young sought to impress on the chairman that, although the work had been done by Tim Bell, it was nevertheless what the Prime Minister wanted – unless the Saatchi work was better.

For nearly ten minutes the two men argued until finally they came out of the room and went upstairs to where Maurice Saatchi and John Sharkey were waiting. 'All right,' Norman Tebbit said. 'Let's have a look at what you've got.' One by one he went through the advertisements saying: 'That's no good. That's no good . . .' Then he asked Saatchi to go downstairs with him, while Lord Young helped Sharkey pack up the material. Young then took Stephen Sherbourne aside and said, 'I think we can get this through without having to involve her,' to which Sherbourne replied, 'If you can take the strain off her it will be the greatest thing yet done in this campaign.' Young then asked him to get the Prime Minister out of her study and up to the flat, before she could be intercepted by either Tebbit or Saatchi.

He then went downstairs again and, at the foot, saw David Willets from CCO and Brian Griffiths coming towards him from the front door. Both were smiling and Willets held a piece of paper. 'You know the Marplan?' Young asked. 'Yes,' they answered. 'It's not two per cent. It's 44–34. It's ten per cent.' 'Thank God for that,' he said, and walked over to the little waiting-room, put his head round the door and gave the results to Norman Tebbit, who was visibly much relieved. Tebbit invited him in and Maurice Saatchi said: 'There is no way we can do this. We can't take this work. It's amateurish. We can't do it.'

Lord Young took him to one side and pointed out forcibly what would happen to his company's shares if Labour were to win: 'What do you think I'll be worth, or any of us, next Friday, if they win?' He added that it wasn't 'a matter of anyone's pride. We are here for one person – for her. If these ads are what she wants, then these are what she gets.' Saatchi said: 'I can't do anything with these ads. They're Tim's aren't they?' 'Forget they're Tim's. It's not Tim. It's the idea,' Young insisted. 'It's for her. She's the one thing that is going to win this election. But she has to really do it in the next five days. We've always planned to end up with a bang. Now she thinks these ads will give her that. They give her confidence.' He went swiftly round the room gathering the boards up, then added: 'You know the idea. Make it work.'

Maurice Saatchi left with John Sharkey and Norman Tebbit and Lord Young went upstairs. Tebbit went in to tell the Prime Minister, who was still in her study, about the poll result and she came out smiling. Young said to her quietly: 'It's all right Prime Minister. We've fixed it. You're going to have the whole campaign as you want. Go and sock it to Dimbleby.' He then scribbled a note for her, outlining what they had done. He went straight to Lord McAlpine's house, which had been lent to the 'exiles' for the duration and where Tim Bell, Gordon Reece and Howell James were waiting. It was some moments before he felt able to tell them what had happened. They watched the Prime Minister's television performance, in which she handled the health problem very well: she was beginning to make a strength of her weakness. She turned many of the questions round on Dimbleby. It was the performance of a Prime Minister. 'She looks serene,' said James. 'That's because she's tired,' said Bell. 'She should be tired more often,' James joked. They all agreed the tide had turned – even though all the news bulletins were still concentrating on health.

Next morning at 10 a.m. Maurice Saatchi and John Sharkey arrived once again at CCO. Lord Young had asked the Prime Minister at the 8.30 briefing if she wanted to see the new work. She had said no, could he handle it; and he and Norman winked at one another. The material, which was, as expected, perfectly acceptable, was 80 per cent the way Tim Bell and Frank Lowe had envisaged it. In some cases the wording had been altered slightly: where they had written 'The Conservatives are spending 3 times as much on the Health Service as the last Labour Government', the Saatchi version said 'Spending on the Health Service is up by 31 per cent more than inflation' and where they had written 'Income tax is down to its lowest level for 20 years', the Saatchi version said 'The basic rate of income tax is down to its lowest for nearly 50 years'. Two words had also been changed in the slogan: instead of 'Britain's a success again. Don't let Labour ruin it', the Saatchi one said, 'Britain is great again. Don't let Labour wreck it'. Bell later argued that 'Success' and 'Ruin' were 'people' words, whereas 'Great' and 'Wreck' were polemic words. Nevertheless the work was basically the same as what he and Lowe had produced the day before and, although it was later claimed that the advertisements did little more than take a number of assertions that had been made in previous ones, or in PEBs, and put them together in a particular formula, it was that formula that had caught Mrs Thatcher's eye. And, as one of the strongest Saatchi supporters said, 'If it made her happy, then so be it. The most important thing throughout the campaign is keeping the PM above all in a reasonable frame of mind.' But one person, closer to the Saatchi camp, saw the imposition of Bell's ideas as being a continuation of the 'rotten service the agency was getting from the client'. He added: 'I think the Saatchis have decided in the higher interests, and for the moment, to swallow all their personal feelings about it as best they can. But, if the advertising is not up to scratch, then that is a reflection, not on the agency, but on the client.'

Norman Tebbit and Lord Young went through the layouts one by one nodding approval, then Young asked what were they going to do with them. 'We've got three pages booked in all the Sunday papers,' Maurice Saatchi told him. 'Good,' said Young, then turned to Tebbit: 'What we'll do now is take three pages in every paper every day of next week including election day.' Tebbit looked aghast: the cost would be £2 million, on top of the £500,000 they were already planning to spend on Sunday. 'Don't worry,' said Young. 'I've already cleared it with Alastair and we have the money.' As one senior Tory said later: 'So much for the Tories' carefully planned advertising blitz – it was literally done on the spur of the moment – like that.' Young and Howell James, nevertheless, spent much of Friday and Saturday going round the newspaper editors promoting the big campaign that was about to start.

The advertising campaign may or may not have had an effect

on the election result, but it certainly affected the party. For the first time the Tories seemed to have come out of their corner really punching – for the first time also, as she went into her six bouts with the television programmes, Mrs Thatcher seemed to be imbued with the same spirit. The advertisements seemed to give her and the party confidence as they went into the last week. She now seemed to those around her to have found a way of coping with the personal attacks on her. In her speech in Edinburgh on Tuesday night she had held up a series of newspaper headlines from 1979 about unions closing cancer wards, the health dangers of rubbish in the streets because of the dustmen's strike, of patients being sent home – then she had turned on Labour with her most withering scorn: 'And these are the people who tell *us* they care.' she thundered. 'How *dare* they?' The confidence had come out in the Dimbleby interview, and on Friday it was there for all to see. However, many people in the upper levels of the party wondered, because garbled versions of the events of 'Wobbly Thursday' had been leaked, whether the issue might not be the last straw in the relationship between Lord Young and Norman Tebbit. Once again, after an embarrassing first fifteen minutes together that morning, the two of them appeared to have come to terms with what happened, in the interests of winning.

The third prong of the Tory toasting fork was also unveiled on Friday – and it was the one which was finally to skewer Labour's hopes. First defence, then the hidden threat of Labour, now taxation became the issue. In a concerted onslaught, which was to continue until polling day, the party – once again led by Norman Tebbit and this time ably assisted by Nigel Lawson – concentrated on how the nation would pay for Labour's expensive programmes. At first television more or less ignored the newspapers' lead on the story, but then, as the Labour leaders began to differ in their versions of who would pay what in tax, they were forced to take note of it. The *Daily Mail* started the story on Friday 5 June claiming that couples with an income of only £9000 would have to pay more tax. Next day most of the rest of the papers had picked it up and by Sunday it was well and truly running. Nigel Lawson ensured that the momentum was kept up by accusing Roy Hattersley of lying through his teeth. It was the perfect issue on which to end the campaign, for it not only assured the voters of the Tories' economic prudence, and of their success in cutting taxes, but also of Labour's profligacy with their money.

There were, however, still problems with the tour on Friday as there had been at Alton Towers the day before, when the entourage had arrived to find the weather appalling and very few people there – the children's half-term holiday had been the week before. Now they found themselves at one point visiting an empty building site in the north-west. However Mrs Thatcher's speech at Chester that night was reckoned to be her best of the campaign. It was bouncy and confident and once again it took her dominant personality, thought to be her greatest weakness, and made it into her greatest strength. 'Strong, clear consistent leadership – that is the only way to secure success at home and respect abroad,' she said. 'To the charge of providing that kind of leadership, I gladly plead guilty.' There was no hiding her, as she was now frequently pointing out, either from the media or behind glossy packaging. 'What you saw was what you got. And it talked right back at you,' said one amazed American reporter, more used to the set-pieces of Reaganite communication.

There was an interesting reason why the speech in Chester was so bouncy and almost spontaneous in its delivery. It had only just been written – most of it in a flat panic on the plane on the way up to the north-west and some of it at the last minute in Chester itself. The reader will remember that one of the causes of the tension between Mrs Thatcher and Norman Tebbit in 1986 had been the interest she was alleged to be, indeed was, showing in the work of the advertising agency Young & Rubi-cam. This research, called VALS – 'values and lifestyles' – centred on a new way of dividing the populace into various groups. Most Tories were in the so-called 'belongers' group, who were polled regularly and monitored for any significant changes in their attitudes.

Throughout the early months of 1986, Mrs Thatcher and several other senior Cabinet Ministers were 'offered' this re-search. The point of contact between Y&R and the upper levels of the Tory party was provided by Geoffrey Tucker, who had been a communications expert at CCO under Edward Heath.

Tucker now had a consultancy closely tied to the PR agency
Burson Marsteller, which was owned by Y&R. 'We got this free
offer of their research,' said one associate of Mrs Thatcher, 'so
we took it – with our eyes open, knowing that sooner or later
there would be a "bite". It was obvious that one day they would
make a pitch for the account. We took it for a while, principally
because we were not getting any material of this sort from the
Saatchi team.'

The arrangement continued until the Tebbit fracas in July
1986, when Mrs Thatcher stopped taking the material. It was,
apparently, not showing much that was not obvious anyway.
The Y&R team then switched their pitch to the rest of the
Cabinet – regularly sending them, particularly members of the
A-Team, copies of their latest reports. No more approaches were
made to Downing Street until just before the election, when,
once again, the reports started to arrive and were glanced at
cursorily by Stephen Sherbourne before being consigned to the
bottom drawer of his desk. At no stage before or during the
election campaign did Mrs Thatcher meet John Banks, until the
last Saturday when she bumped into him by accident and spent
a minute or two in casual conversation.

However, on 'Wobble Thursday' when the polls were looking
so bad, Banks had sent in to Downing Street a VALS report
which purported to show the underlying currents of feeling
among the populace which were being picked up and partially
shown in the traditional polls. If the polls were starting to slide,
then, it was felt in Downing Street, the research might help
pinpoint what was going on. It appeared that, among the 'belongers', there was a need for reassurance that they were safe and
that the government was not going to let them down. Banks and
Tucker, through Ronald Millar, asked for a meeting with Stephen
Sherbourne: Mrs Thatcher was unaware of the arrangement,
and knew only the merest outline of the research when she went
off to Alton Towers. This was the meeting that had to be switched
to 12 Downing Street, because of Tim Bell's imminent arrival at
Number 10. Sherbourne went to the meeting at 2.30 p.m. and
found Millar, John O'Sullivan (the *Times* leader writer seconded
to the policy unit) and Tucker there – Banks arrived forty minutes
late, shortly before Sherbourne had to leave for his meeting in

Number 10. He listened to their suggestion that the way to steady the 'belongers' was to talk to them in reassuring language, using certain key words and phrases. He left them to try to work this exercise on the first draft of the speech for Chester the following night.

Next morning Sherbourne took one look at the speech and was horrified, but not half as much as Mrs Thatcher was when she saw it. She almost literally tore it up and the two of them spent every available moment of the day desperately rewriting against the clock. On Saturday, Banks and Tucker arrived again with Millar in Downing Street – this time at Number 10 – and were ensconced in O'Sullivan's room, which is near the lift to the flat. There they proceeded to work on the speech for the Wembley rally on Sunday. In the afternoon, when Mrs Thatcher returned from her electioneering in north London, they waylaid her by the lift and she talked to them politely for a few minutes. In the final draft of the forty-minute Wembley speech, I am assured, there were 'a few' phrases of theirs: there was therefore considerable surprise, then anger, at all levels in Downing Street, two days after the election, when *The Times* carried a bizarre story claiming that Banks's 'Project Blue' had saved the Tory campaign. It was not to be the last story in which credit was rashly claimed, in what became a week of stranger and stranger tales about who had done what: one or two were true and accurately reflected the contributions made to the campaign, others caused hilarity, some caused anger – and even a writ or two.

With the climax of the campaign approaching the Wembley rally was one of a number of major events which were to place Mrs Thatcher, her personality and her style at the very centre of the election. While, a few miles away in the heart of what is humorously known as the Stalinist Republic of Islington, Neil Kinnock was being endorsed by the likes of Julie Christie and Glenda Jackson, Mrs Thatcher was getting the same treatment from Jimmy Tarbuck and Janet Brown. Once again in her speech she was confident and went straight on to the offensive: 'If planes and tanks and nuclear weapons could be stopped by moving a composite motion at a Labour Conference,' she said, 'there might be a grain of sense in the Labour leader's grand strategy. But they can't. And there isn't.'

If the Labour Party wanted to make her the issue, then she was now ready to be the issue. All her energies and drive were now concentrated into the next five days; many of those around her with none of the responsibility and twice the sleep were dead on their feet. Yet she rallied herself and them; she seemed to find reserves of energy which left many of them staggered. There developed a will to go on in CCO and the sort of oddball humour you find among the survivors of a terrifying, but nevertheless exhilarating ordeal.

Nowhere was Mrs Thatcher's seemingly inexhaustible energy better revealed than in the efforts she put in to getting the last PEB made to her satisfaction. Between Wednesday and midnight on Sunday, when she finally left the Saatchi headquarters in Lower Regent Street, there were eight meetings and more hours of writing and rewriting than in any other project of the campaign. On Wednesday she had been shown a compilation of clips of her old speeches, hastily put together against Holst's 'Jupiter' music – 'I vow to thee my country' – which, it was proposed, should be used as the opening five minutes of the broadcast. She had not liked it at all and told Saatchi to go away and do something better. At the meeting on Thursday afternoon in Downing Street, where Lord Young, Howell James, Tim Bell, Stephen Sherbourne, Anthony Jay and Ronald Millar gathered to discuss it (Gordon Reece was supposed to have been there, but he was not called until it was too late for him to manage), Bell had also argued that the opening clip might be wrong, because it was too much like Hugh Hudson's film of Kinnock in style; and, where the Kinnock film had then relied on third party endorsement of the man to boost him, it might be seen as colossal conceit to have Mrs Thatcher effectively endorsing herself. The meeting was inconclusive and adjourned until the following day, when Lord Young asked to see the offending clip of film. He watched it in silence, then said to the group with him: 'I now know why I work for her. That is the most moving thing I have ever seen in my life.'

However, it still had to be 'sold' to Mrs Thatcher. He told Saatchi to remove the first excerpt, which was from 1979, to reduce the volume of the music and to tidy up the quality of the video. The group met again after lunch on Saturday. This time, because Jeremy Sinclair was present from Saatchi, Tim Bell was absent; although Gordon Reece was there. The script for the second half was now primarily on defence and, if that was to be the subject, it seemed to be in order. Lord Young and Gordon Reece then took both film and script to Downing Street, where she accepted the film, but rejected the script on the grounds that to concentrate on defence would make it a one-subject election and there were many, broader things she wished to say. The team, now augmented by Stephen Sherbourne, Ronald Millar and John O'Sullivan, worked for a while on some ideas before going back to CCO, where they continued throughout Saturday evening. On Sunday afternoon, after the rally, she met Bell, Reece, Jay and Millar and rejected parts of the new script as well.

No one there was at all surprised by the Prime Minister's new suggestion that she wanted a more 'homely' approach – about the good management of the nation and how the improvement in the economy meant life was improving for everyone. Those who had been through it all before, knew that she regarded this as one of the most important parts of the campaign and that it had not been well prepared for, in terms of the reassurance and less frenetic build-up required to make the event go well. Bell and Jay now sat down in Number 10 to redraft yet again, while she went ahead to the studio to prepare. At 6.30 the team, minus Bell (there had been a phone call from Saatchi requesting Downing Street not to embarrass them by bringing him along), went to Lower Regent Street. Bell took the slight well and went home. In a sense he was lucky because Mrs Thatcher now proceeded to rewrite the script yet again with Jay and Millar, finishing at 10.30 p.m. At last she was ready.

The Saatchi team had brought in Terence Donovan to film the Prime Minister. His burly presence seemed to reassure her – she is always comfortable among professionals who clearly know their job. It was now too late for the massage appointment she had made for 9.30 in Downing Street – she had promised herself the relaxation of that and a good night's sleep in order to be on top form for the next day's 'Panorama' interview with Sir Robin Day – so she cancelled it and turned to concentrating on the filming of her script. Everyone, except the technicians, was asked to leave the studio and she began a long series of 'takes' until she got it absolutely to her satisfaction. It took fourteen in all; in none of them did she fluff her lines, but she simply felt the inflection was not right. One take was going perfectly when, to everyone's annoyance, the camera ran out of film. Finally, just before midnight, she got up from the chair where she had been sitting for ninety minutes, said a cheerful 'goodnight' and thanks to everyone and bustled out. As one of those present said: 'I'm not sure there was all that much difference in the script in the end from the one we started with today – but she was happy; so did it matter?'

Mrs Thatcher's happiness and confidence, however, were personal rather than electoral. She now felt that the campaign was, at last, beginning to come together, that she could now handle the television interviews, that both she and the party would put up a good fight in the last week. But neither she nor the party had the same confidence in the result itself. Away from the hothouse of CCO and Downing Street – in the constituencies – there was a growing feeling coming from the grass roots that all was not well with the national campaign. Many candidates had complained that they were not getting the help some of the Labour rivals were clearly enjoying. There were grumbles that the performance of the Tory leaders on television was lacklustre and the press conferences sounded dull. Angela Browning had none of these complaints, though she did fear she was losing the votes of teachers and pensioners. Her main worry at the weekend was that the SDP vote in Crewe and Nantwich seemed to be collapsing, but she had no idea where it was going. At the same time Tom Arnold in Hazel Grove was showing ahead of the Liberals in a local poll, but worried about tactical voting against him. Both candidates said the problems of London seemed a million miles away.

In CCO the reports from most of the agents were confident, but some were worrying. The east and west Midlands were bullish, but in the last week the north-west reported things not going as well as hoped. And in Scotland, though the people there were confident, the picture from the polls was very gloomy. Some comfort was taken from the fact that it is almost impossible to poll Scotland accurately – but since all the polls showed the

Tories slipping in what had now become a four-cornered fight (with the Scottish Nationalist Party involved) no one was very hopeful. The weekend's private Tory polls brought little cheer to anyone in CCO. The problem, once again, was what to believe. For the first time in this election, most of the major companies were conducting special polls of the marginal seats. The results of these had shown huge variations: some had forecast a hung Parliament, others only days later predicted a Tory majority of 141. However, the Harris private tracking study of the Tory target seats – all of which they must hold to secure a majority of 58 – had consistently been gloomy and now, on the last weekend, was gloomier still. In the 48 seats where Labour was second, the Tories were now three points behind them – and they were down also, though still ahead, in the 24 seats where the Alliance was second. If this were the same on election day the party would have a majority of only about ten.

Should they believe this? Or should they believe the national polls, which, even taking the bad result of the Gallup into account, still showed them eight points up on the week? And their own Harris of that weekend showed them nine points up at 44 per cent to Labour's 35 and the Alliance's 19 – the same as the week before. While everyone could see the logic of accepting the national picture, it was difficult to ignore the nagging worry planted by the marginal polls – a worry which was compounded in *The Times* on Monday morning when its final Mori poll of the marginals showed the Tories holding a lead of only 40–50 seats. At no stage, right up to polling night itself, did this anxiety, that the marginals might, after all, be showing an accurate picture, entirely leave any of the senior people in CCO – or the Prime Minister herself. Long after the other party leaders had started showing the first signs of impending capitulation, they remained nervous.

This last *Times* poll was also a contributory factor in a heated debate between the paper and Downing Street and brought to a head once again the simmering row about the overcrowding of the Prime Minister's diary. At the end of the previous week the paper had the firm impression that it was due to have a final week interview with her, along with the other leaders – indeed it advertised the fact in that weekend's *Sunday Times*. When its political editor Robin Oakley rang to find out when it would be, he was told that no interview was fixed, nor could it be. He then asked Lord Young to intercede on his behalf, pointing out that there had never been an election when *The Times* did not have an interview with the Prime Minister. When Young spoke to Mrs Thatcher early on Sunday morning she reluctantly agreed to be interviewed at 10 a.m. on Monday, just before the 'Panorama' filming. But that night, when she returned to Downing Street after finishing the PEB, someone had brought in a first edition of the paper. The main election headlines on the front page were: 'Labour piles on pressure in marginals', 'Gould in appeal to waverers', 'Thatcher keeps summit waiting' and 'Customs men start election week disruption early'. To rub salt into the wound, the main picture on the front page was not of the Wembley rally, but of a smiling, confident Neil and Glenys Kinnock waving to the crowds at their gathering. The questions now being asked, not very subtly, in Downing Street were: why should the Prime Minister, after all her government's legislation and support had done to help Rupert Murdoch in Wapping, now give up any of her valuable time to a paper which was clearly encouraging a late swing to Labour? And, if that swing became a reality, then how long did Mr Murdoch think his papers would last before the pickets were back at Wapping, unhampered by any legal restrictions on their behaviour?

In a series of late-night phone calls, the gist of these questions, somewhat toned down, was communicated to the paper's editor Charles Wilson, as was the news that the interview was off. The following day there was much pleading within CCO for its reinstatement, but now Mrs Thatcher's diary was severely overloaded and, it was pointed out, the chairman had promised Sir David English that the *Daily Mail* could also have an interview. In the end, two days later, the Prime Minister relented, agreed to *The Times* and personally telephoned English to apologise, pointing out that he had had a session with her at the beginning of the campaign.

The tax issue continued to dominate the rest of the media, with more Tory pressure being applied each day. 'It was simple, but effective,' one senior Tory told me. 'All the Labour talk had been about caring and spending, with no clear indication given of where they were going to raise the money – apart from soaking the rich. All we had to do was point out that if they were going to raise as much as they said then "the rich" was just about everyone above the poverty line. Suddenly people began to realise that it was not someone else who was going to pay for it – it was them.' It was not a sign of panic or worry when, on the Saturday of that weekend, Amanda Ponsonby, Stephen Sherbourne's secretary, made a provisional booking with removals men for the following Friday. It is done before every election. She also began to pack up her own things from her desk and filing cabinets – for the very good reason that Friday was her birthday and, as she said, 'I would rather spend the day unpacking than packing.'

Mrs Thatcher's performances throughout the six major television and radio interviews grew in stature – and, although the questioning was frequently very hostile (sometimes even hurtful), that in itself was a benefit, because the public could see and hear that she was demonstrably *not* a woman who dodged the issue or evaded questions. The Tory hierarchy in CCO could see their greatest strength emerging at last. 'At the end of the campaign, you did not know who Kinnock was, or what he believed in,' said one senior man. 'He was just a ginger-haired bloke, who had a pretty wife, smiled a lot and walked around the coast in his anorak. You couldn't be certain about anything else. But with her, like her or hate her, you knew what she was and what she believed in.' The hostile questioning was, perhaps, at its worst on Saturday morning, on the 'Today' programme on BBC Radio Four. John Humphries was so aggressive – frequently interrupting with 'but, Prime Minister' – that his producer had to tell him over the earphones: 'John, no more "buts", please.'

The 'Panorama' interview with Sir Robin Day was almost as aggressive, but Mrs Thatcher kept her head and repeated, before correcting herself with a wicked little smile, her mistake of four years earlier, when she had called him 'Mr Day'. It slowed him down a little and she improved rapidly towards the end. In 'Election Call' on Wednesday morning, her memory came to her aid when a nurse from Mold in North Wales came on the line. Before the caller could start Mrs Thatcher took the wind out of her sails by saying: 'Mold? Haven't we just built a super new

hospital there? Is that the one you work in? Isn't it terrific?' The
nurse was forced to agree. Later that morning, however, health
reared its head again, and for the last time, when the Prime
Minister gave 'wrap-up' interviews for BBC and ITN to David
Dimbleby and Michael Brunson. During Dimbleby's interview
she referred to people who 'drool and drivel' about the Health
Service. She instantly apologised and withdrew the remark. But
she came out of the studio fuming at her slip, furious with herself.
She thought at the time the BBC would make a greater issue of
it than they did.

The trip to Venice also helped her confidence. If nothing else
it served to show the gulf between her and the Labour leader in
almost as dramatic a way as had their respective trips to Moscow
and Washington in the spring. There was the Prime Minister of
a major world nation taking her seat at a summit meeting, where
she was clearly seen as a principal leader of the West. 'And there
was the Leader of the Opposition,' as one Tory put it to me,
'who with all the compendium of rich political put-downs at his
disposal, could only describe the trip feebly as "a sandwich, a
sermon and a photo session".'

When she came back on Tuesday it was straight into the
election campaign again – she had her last major speech to
deliver in Harrogate that night. Her jet landed at Gatwick at
3.30 p.m. and she transferred straight to the campaign plane.
The speech had been 'FAXed' to her in Venice and when Stephen
Sherbourne, who was waiting for her on the tarmac, saw Charles
Powell waving it at him, his heart sank. Not another Chester,
he thought. But she had only altered a few sentences. The speech
covered all the main themes of the campaign: defence, the
dangers of the Left and taxation. She won her biggest applause
when she described Labour as 'inflation addicts'. 'With every
Labour Government,' she said, 'financial prudence goes out of
the window. The pound goes through the floor. Prices go through
the roof. And their promises go up the chimney.' And she drew
her customary standing ovation when she closed with: 'We
are a forward-looking people, a lion-hearted nation, ready to
confront the twenty-first century and reach out for greatness
again. Let us continue our task on Thursday.'

On the way back in the plane, Mrs Thatcher and her husband

went to the rear section where the sixty travelling television, radio and newspaper journalists and photographers were, and, as in 1983, walked up and down the aisle, chatting and helping to pour champagne. The photographers, by prior arrangement, all put their cameras down – everyone had agreed it was not to be filmed or recorded. One 'snapper' asked how confident she was and she held up both hands with fingers crossed. For a second that section of the plane froze as they all waited for one of their number to crack and grab his camera. No one did, so they asked her to do it for them next day – the last day of the campaign. The gesture was a spontaneous reflection of her feelings: there was much less of the confidence this time than there had been in 1983.

True to her word, in Southend next morning, she put both arms up with the fingers crossed and the photographers got their picture. It was a happier day than many on the tour, although she did not get over her slip on health for some hours. The party went in five helicopters around the South of England, the sort of barnstorming finish she loved. The photographers all produced their T-shirts saying 'Maggie's Mystery Tour 1987' and gave her one saying 'Tour Leader '79, '83, '87' which she put on and posed with them for a picture. When she won and went to Smith Square the following night, they asked, would she then hold up three fingers – one for each term? 'I have to win first,' she said. She may not have been confident, but the other parties appeared to have tacitly conceded. The last Labour PEB started with an undergraduate level of satire, attacking her for wanting to be the Queen. It was a level from which, Tory observers in CCO noted, Neil Kinnock hardly rose for the rest of the week. On Wednesday he signed off his campaign by calling her 'arrogant and unfit to rule' (queens rule: Prime Ministers govern) and hopefully claimed: 'This is the last day of Thatcherism.'

While Mrs Thatcher was out finishing her tour a meeting took place in Smith Square, which, in its own way, tried to wrap up the campaign too, but from another point of view. After she had done her last-minute television interviews and seen Robin Oakley from *The Times* in CCO, she joked with Norman Tebbit and Lord Young that it was all very well their having drinks with journalists (a small party was being held) but she had work to do – then she left to catch her helicopter. The two men stayed talking for a while to the correspondents who had regularly attended the press conferences, then went upstairs to the chairman's office, where Maurice Saatchi was waiting for them. He produced a document called the 'Brick Wall' strategy, which outlined how the advertising campaign had been planned from the beginning. It had been designed to start late to allow Kinnock to over-expose himself, and to hold the big money advertising blitz back until the last week. It was to be the basis of a press briefing to be held for journalists after the election. There were those in the upper levels of the party, however, who were surprised by the document. They pointed out, for example, that the blitz had only been planned on the last Friday morning. Lord Young was unable to attend the briefing.

On Thursday, Mrs Thatcher voted early in Westminster, then spent most of the morning in Finchley, touring the polling stations and encouraging the party workers. She must have been asked a dozen times what she thought the result would be. 'We'll know tonight,' was all she would say. In CCO they thought it would be a 40–50 majority, but there were many who put it a lot lower than that. Yet another Vincent Hanna 'Newsnight' poll had stated that the Tory vote was dropping away in droves in the marginals. While not believed, this nevertheless caused the anxiety levels to rise in Smith Square. The nervousness was compounded by the awareness of the fact that a tiny switch in the votes could destroy even that lead, if it were to be true, and by the prevailing uncertainty about the marginals. A *Times* Mori national poll that morning had, optimistically, predicted a majority of 106. No one believed that.

During the afternoon and early evening of election day there is a curious lull for those who have been involved in the centre. It is a time when the worst fears tend to creep up on politicians. For the first time in four weeks, they have nothing to do. They have done all they can – it is now up to the electorate. The first to 'crack' was the Prime Minister. At 4.30 p.m. she rang CCO and asked if she could come over. Shirley Oxenbury told her there was virtually no one there apart from the chairman. Mrs Thatcher and Norman Tebbit then spoke for a few minutes, and less than an hour later he left the building and drove to Downing

Street. He stayed for two and a half hours and at one stage William Whitelaw joined him and the Prime Minister. Twenty-four hours later it became clear that the meeting had been the Prime Minister's last-ditch attempt to persuade Tebbit against resigning from the Cabinet. The smile on his face on 15 April had, in fact, been one of relief that at last he had cast the die and told her that he intended to return to the back benches when the election was over. There had been a slight but steady improvement in his wife's condition since before Christmas, and he felt his first duty was to her. 'A terrible dilemma that had been in his mind for months was now resolved,' a close friend said. 'That was why he was smiling. Win or lose, he was the only member of the team who knew what he was going to be doing afterwards.' In the hectic weeks since 15 April the Prime Minister had tried on a number of occasions to persuade him to change his mind and asked others to intercede. Whatever the difficulties between them during the campaign, she still had enormous admiration for her Party Chairman's talents in Cabinet and in Cabinet committees. She was desperate not to lose his political 'feel'. But her efforts and Whitelaw's were to no avail.

The Prime Minister eventually changed the subject and she and Norman Tebbit discussed what they thought the outcome of the election would be – including what she should do in the event of a hung Parliament. Since he was no longer a 'player' in the Cabinet stakes, she then sought his preliminary advice on how she might shuffle her team. He left shortly after eight and went off to supper with Michael Dobbs and on to the count at Chingford, where later that night, he stood, looking frail and the only candidate alone on the platform, to hear the news that his majority was up by five and a half per cent to nearly 18,000.

Lords Young and McAlpine dined at the fashionable San Lorenzo restaurant, with their wives and a group of friends. Michael Heseltine was also there, but the two parties were far apart and did not speak. McAlpine was confident that the majority would be more than 100. Young bet him £100 that it would not. He was still nervous. Just before the end of the meal – Young was due to go to the BBC for the start of its election programme – McAlpine was called away to the phone. When he returned it was with a big grin on his face. 'The ITN exit poll is going to be about 60,' he said. Young ordered a bottle of champagne and they drank: to victory. When Young and Howell James, who had come to pick him up, got to the BBC they were met by a producer who told them 'It looks grim for you. You could be 17 short of a majority – we're forecasting 26; but it could be worse.' For nearly an hour Young sat and watched as people in the studio earnestly discussed whether Mrs Thatcher would have to go, how would she cope with a hung Parliament and all the other gripping issues that this 'total Tory collapse' had involved. Then, when the Torbay result came in, showing a one and a half per cent swing to the Tories, he turned to Robin Day and asked him if he knew what ITN were predicting. 'No,' said Day. 'I'd find out if I were you, because I think you've got it all wrong here. They are saying above 60,' said Young. Day grabbed a phone and began talking urgently into it. Young left the studio with a smile on his face which only became broader as the night went on.

Mrs Thatcher went back to Finchley for the count. She heard at 2.30 a.m. that her vote had gone up by 2000 but her majority down by 401. She was going round the room individually thanking her party workers, when they told her the Tories had passed the 325 mark and were the next government. She had done it. She was the first Prime Minister since Lord Liverpool in the early nineteenth century to have won three times in a row. She drove back to CCO, through the cheering crowds in Smith Square. Norman Tebbit was waiting outside with 100 red roses. She saw the point immediately and laughed. When she entered the building she paused, as she had done twice before, half-way up the stairs to the first floor, thanked everyone who had made it possible and added: 'There's plenty for us to do now. There'll be no slacking!' As everyone laughed, Stephen Sherbourne, who was in Michael Dobbs's office, watching her on television, buckled at the knees and groaned, a rueful grin on his face. The pink champagne flowed on the first floor as Cabinet Ministers and other senior Tories, who lived near and whose results had been declared, began to arrive. No one could still quite believe what was happening – the Mori poll was coming true.

At 3.25 a.m. Mrs Thatcher walked through the surge of people in Michael Dobbs's office to the open window and, to a vast cheer from the crowd, acknowledged the victory. Good as gold, just as the photographers had asked, she remembered and held up three fingers. Two hours later she went home to Downing Street, where she dozed for an hour before getting up to start the third term.

The majority was 101. Forty-four per cent of first-time voters had voted Conservative. The Tories had lost eleven of their 21 seats in Scotland.

The Saatchis sent a coffin-sized bottle of champagne next day to each of the key figures in the campaign and issued the 'Brick Wall' strategy.

Tim Bell had specifically not been invited to the election night party. One Cabinet Minister later told me that the Prime Minister was very angry at this slight and had described his help in the campaign as 'invaluable'.

Michael Dobbs stayed at CCO assisting Norman Tebbit for a short while. Then he went on holiday, quietly content in the knowledge that at least the party had held 25 of the target seats which it would have lost on the national swing.

Tom Arnold, one of those target seats, won. Angela Browning lost.

Cecil Parkinson became Secretary of State for Energy. John Wakeham became Lord Privy Seal and Leader of the House of Commons and Lord Young became Secretary of State for Trade and Industry. Howell James went with him as special adviser.

Norman Tebbit's resignation from the Cabinet was accepted but he was asked to stay on as Chairman of the Party for the time being and stated that he wished to start the urgently needed overhaul of CCO. How far he would get and how long he would stay remained to be seen.

12 | Aftermath

Above all it was Her Victory.

It had been her date, her choice of people to fight it, her grounds of battle and, in the end, her personality which came to dominate it. If it had all gone wrong she would have been blamed for it. *The Times*, two days later, said: 'The election result is a triumph for two great, indomitable, predictable forces. One is Mrs Margaret Thatcher. The other is the good sense of the majority of voters.'

To deal with the second first: as even Michael Meacher conceded after it was over, eighty-seven per cent of the population have never been as well off as they are after eight years of Thatcher government. It was this which underpinned all the Tories' appeal to the electorate. It was this which was the counterpoint to the last week's barrage on Labour's tax plans. The fact, never argued over within the party, and accepted by the electorate, was that the Tories did have a good record, they had not run out of steam and they were worth another go. The line of improvement in the general economic wellbeing of the community had by 1987 visibly reached Wolverhampton and Walsall. What is more, people clearly believed that it was going to go on rising. The *Daily Express* aptly called the Tory economic recovery 'The National Wealth Service'. The other side of the coin was, of course, the fear the Tory party was able to generate in the electorate that they might lose all this if they voted Labour.

After a disastrous start, Mrs Thatcher changed strategy and went on the attack. It was then that both she and the party recovered their footing. An ITN poll showed that 22 per cent of the voters made up their minds during the campaign and 18 per cent in the last few days. With so much volatility and floating going on, it is well that, first, she did change tack and, second, she decided to meet the personality challenge head-on in the last week. It was the most concentrated series of appearances, speeches and interviews (interspersed with the hectic trip to Venice) that she had ever undertaken, but she won the battle single-handedly on television in that week. Each performance was underpinned by the blockbuster effect of the three pages of advertising in that day's newspapers. The public saw her on TV, then read the story in the papers.

Nothing can detract from this success, although it must be said that she was helped considerably by the lack of electoral appeal of the other parties. One Cabinet member went so far as to say, in criticising the performance of CCO: 'We owe our victory to Labour, more than to anything we did.' There was, indeed, as the events of the first week also showed, a common presumption among the Tories that the Alliance would come surging through past Labour, but that if Labour did stay ahead of the Alliance, then they would be easy to deal with. As it turned out, neither was true. David Owen and David Steel failed to sight the right target and remained on the sidelines throughout, while Neil Kinnock's packaging took a great deal of unwrapping. The common sense of the electorate was, to mix a metaphor, in danger of having the wool pulled over its eyes. But in the end, after the defence and tax debates, the voters clearly decided that Labour, in its present form, is unelectable. For all the gloss and the oratory, Kinnock only improved the Labour share of the vote by three per cent. While the 'loony Left' lurks beneath the surface, it is not likely to go much higher.

There is no doubt that, until Mrs Thatcher's progressive intervention in the planning, and later the running, of the campaign, the potential for a huge disaster was looming. She seemed just to avert it at every point right up to the last week. So far I have heard everyone, from the Prime Minister herself to the doorman at CCO, blamed for this near-débâcle; but, as I said at the beginning of this book, it is not for me to take sides in the great debate which will now either rage or seethe inside the party on this issue. Everybody knows it all very nearly went wrong, everybody has a favourite horror story, everybody names a

different guilty party. The tragedy will be if, in the end, the
party decides to use a neutron bomb on CCO – destroying the
personalities involved but leaving the systems intact. Both need
changing. Clearly there were immense difficulties between the
Prime Minister and Norman Tebbit, the manager – just as there
were none between her and Tebbit the politician. Her lack
of confidence in his ability to direct CCO and the appalling
relationship between the Downing Street team and the CCO
team were widely commented on at the time. It is a great
testimony to all three that they managed to make the Thatcher/
Young/Tebbit axis work.

That they managed to keep it working, throughout what was
probably the most politically fraught month of their lives, was
a miracle. 'It was,' said one close to all three, 'a month of
overwhelming and unrestrained fear and fright.' It is both a
blessing and a curse that the Prime Minister has greater faith in
people than she does in systems. It is a kind of entrepreneurial
approach to politics: you see a problem – you throw your best
people at it – they solve the problem. It can work marvellously,
and indeed often does. But you cannot always guarantee that
the right people are thrown at the problem, or that the underlying
fault in the system will thus be identified or remedied. In this
case, throwing Lord Young at it was probably inspired – and,
in that sense, his dinner with Tim Bell on 2 March could be said
to have been a principal turning-point in Tory fortunes.

For it was the 'exiles' who, in the end, did much to save the
Tory party's communications and presentation. It is for others to
argue the finer points of whose contribution was most valuable.
Success, indeed, has many fathers, and failure is an orphan.
It matters less what, in particular, they contributed than the
reassurance that contribution gave. It was they who primed the
Prime Minister's confidence throughout the campaign, particularly to go out and fight in the last week. Much of the argument
has centred on the Tories' advertising campaign and its agency,
Saatchi & Saatchi. As one Cabinet Minister said to me after it
was all over: 'The Labour party couldn't have presented their
message better, but the people didn't want it. Until the last week
the Tories couldn't have presented their message worse – luckily
the people wanted it.' No doubt, again, the personalities involved

at all levels inhibited as close a relationship between advertising agency and client as had existed in the previous two elections. No doubt there was fault on both sides. But when something is wrong, it must be put right: complaining solves nothing.

'Putting it right' is the role chosen by Norman Tebbit after the election. He has stated that he is to spend the next few months reorganising CCO. There are those, at all levels of the party, who are saying that he has already had two years to put it right before the election and achieved nothing, so what makes him think he can do better now? And there are those who predict that, if, as his defenders say, Mrs Thatcher did not allow him then to make the managerial changes he wanted, she is hardly likely to let him do so now. We shall see: what is without doubt is that a major reorganisation is needed. In the 1983 election the party machine creaked when it was required to go at little more than thirty miles an hour. This time, when it was forced up to sixty, it very nearly fell apart.

What held it together, as *The Times* so rightly pointed out, was Mrs Thatcher herself. She had the courage to make herself the issue at the end, and there is not, and never was, any comparison Neil Kinnock could make. She took all the questions and answered them. She did not make false promises. She stood as the one who had delivered. The election was indeed decided by those who did not like or admire Mrs Thatcher – there simply were not enough of them.

How did Mrs Thatcher herself see the campaign? Five days after the election I talked with her in her study on the first floor at Number 10. She was calmer now the hurly-burly was all over. She had reshuffled her Cabinet, placed all her junior ministers and was anxious to get on with unfinished business. She clearly did not wish to reminisce too openly about what had evidently been an emotionally, as well as physically, draining experience for her. Nor, having walked so carefully on eggshells for so long, was she now going to trample across them, disregarding the feelings of the personalities involved. Nevertheless, she was prepared to lift the veil on some of the tensions and heartaches of the previous five weeks.

It was, she admitted, 'the most intensive programme I think

I've ever had – particularly in the last week. It was fantastic pressure from Thursday to Thursday with all of the television and still some big rallies to do. I always prepare good speeches for the rallies. On Saturday morning, for example, I did a radio broadcast, then I went to do a Channel 4 question session, then I went up to my constituency for the rest of the day, then I had to come back here to work on the rally speech. The following morning I was on David Frost, then there was the Wembley rally speech to deliver in the afternoon, then I had to prepare and shoot the PEB in the evening. I staggered back about half-past midnight. It just went on all week. I did get tired sometimes but I would not have backed out of any of it. Supposing I had cancelled a rally and said, "I'm sorry, I can't come up tonight, I'm going to send my deputy." I would never have done it. I would have crawled on to that stage and mimed it if need be.'

To have backed out would have been to lay herself open to further criticism, and she felt there were enough personal attacks on her anyway. 'This was the most belligerent campaign I have ever known. I think in the end it was counter-productive. They were vicious personal attacks. I had thought they might do it, but that they might have more wisdom. However they didn't. The thing was not to reply in kind . . . ever. It was a bit much to accuse me of being uncaring personally. But then you look at the people who were doing it. It wasn't us who had the coal strike. We didn't support the teachers' strike. Really, when you get people who profess to care, who actually wanted to turn off all the heat and light and power and never at any stage told Scargill to have a ballot, never at any stage condemned the violence at Orgreave or at Wapping, when it's this sort of person who accuses you of not caring – you know how to assess it.'

What then had been the worst part of the election? Surprisingly, she nominated the moment at the end of the first week when the decision had to be taken to turn the whole campaign on its head and go on the attack. It had clearly been a disappointment to her and those working with her. 'When we made the reassessment, we felt the message was not getting across. Basically we are a very positive party, and had wanted to be positive, positive, positive. But we realised that if you just go on being positive when you are being attacked and attacked, then the best defence is actually to attack back. So we had to turn round and we attacked on defence and then in the second week we had to go on attacking but always trying to do the positive part at the same time. Coming up to the last week we were able to do both once again. But we would like to have been more positive.'

She was amused by the criticism that she might have gone too slowly at first. She got up and walked round behind her desk to pick up a framed cartoon from the *Daily Mail* at the end of April, the period when election fever was at its height. It shows her in running shorts calling 'On your marks, get set!' to the other three leaders. Then she is seen walking away, reading the polls in the papers, sleeping, making-up, having her hair done and finally re-joining the runners who are, by now, completely exhausted. In the last frame she shouts 'GO!' and sprints off down the track ahead of them. 'There,' she said to me, holding out the picture – 'that's going up on the wall in here so that people don't forget who may have started first, but who finished strongest.'

She was, however, anxious to praise rather than apportion any blame for failures. Norman Tebbit, her chairman was 'a great campaigner', she said. 'I thought he was very, very good on many a television programme – supremely good on all the press conferences, and supremely good out and about in the constituencies. I shall be very sad to see him go. He's very good in Cabinet, very, very good. He's got a fine analytical mind and he's a marvellous politician. Oh yes, I really shall miss him. His experience is invaluable. I was surprised when he told me he wanted to go, because I had hoped that we would go on together . . . I would have understood had he said: "Look I really can't take the burden of a whole department again," because it in-volves you heart and soul. I would have understood that . . . Now he has decided I really rather admire him in a way. As I said in my letter to him – it's a desperately sad day – but we will keep in touch. He's carried an enormously heavy burden on his own and we must never forget that he too was in that building for some time before he was rescued . . .' She paused for a moment before going on. 'It could have been the other way round. It could have been Denis and me. That's why I understand. That's why he's been absolutely fantastic.'

Lord Young's contribution, too, had been immense. 'David is

very quick to sum things up and he has a very decisive mind. Also, of course, he hasn't a constituency to fight, so he had a degree of freedom that the rest of us did not. His managerial skills are very considerable. He and Peter Morrison, who has a great capacity with people, were very good together. They were all at DTI together. David Young started as adviser to Keith Joseph there. Then later David, Keith Joseph, Norman Tebbit and myself cut through all the red tape to create TVEI – which we started here in this room. So we had all worked together for a long time and knew each other.'

But how did the relationship survive the stresses of an election campaign? 'We all knew one another well enough to be able to say, "This is the job we've got to do and the important thing is winning." We had to reassess from time to time, but we never lost sight of our objective. That was why we were here and that was the only reason. We all knew that. There were no toes to tread on. It was the work we had to do. People might say lesser men could not have behaved as well as that. Well, we haven't got any lesser men.'

It is for the family that she reserves the greatest praise. Denis Thatcher is 'absolutely marvellous' and Carol was a 'great help'. But do they enjoy it and what sort of contribution do they make? 'Do you know, I think Denis really rather does enjoy it all. He's become a bit of an institution. He's developed his own style. People love to meet him as much as they like to meet me. Carol is very helpful because she tells you how people are perceiving things. She gives me another view on things. For example I simply couldn't understand it when people said that I wasn't meeting people because I knew I was, right from the beginning. But it wasn't being shown on television. You need people to tell you when the message is not getting across. I have a number of friends who help me with this too.' (She included Cecil Parkinson, Tim Bell and Gordon Reece among them.) 'Oh yes, quite a number of people ring up at weekends and I ring up and ask how they see things. It is invaluable to have another perspective, because I get a much more rounded view of things, seeing as much as I do here all the time, then suddenly I switch on the news and I then see why people are perhaps perceiving things differently.'

Meeting ordinary people is more of a rarity than she likes —
particularly in an election campaign. However, she found it was
not security that prevented it as much as the press of cameramen.
'I went to people wherever I saw them. But it is the cameramen
who stop you from getting at them — that's the trouble. I found
I had to dive away to get ten or fifteen glorious seconds with a
person before they were all round me again. Then they were
the ones who came and complained I wasn't seeing people!
Sometimes I would get away for longer and those snatched
encounters were the most valuable to me. Wherever we went
people were very, very generous and welcoming — they really
were. All right, you get some people who are very much against
you, who are very vulgar in their language. But I found more
genuine affection this time. I think I have become a bit of an
institution — you know, the sort of thing people expect to see
around the place. And the place wouldn't be quite the same
without this old institution. People seem to think: "She's not so
bad is she; this Maggie?" They wanted their children to meet you.
It's an extraordinary thing. Americans, of course, are absolutely
amazed. They say: "We've never had a chance to meet a person
like this."'

Despite the warmth of the reception wherever she went, was
there ever a moment when she thought she might lose? She
answered carefully, not precluding the possibility that she might
have thought the worst. 'Oh, I'm always prepared for everything.
I don't know . . . in my heart I did not see myself packing up on
Friday. When I looked, intellectually, at the polls I thought our
vote would hold up, but the important thing was how the
Opposition vote would split. If you look at Scotland, that was
what happened. So there was all the time a great unknown
factor, but, as I said, in my heart I didn't think we would lose.
The question was whether we would win by a sufficient amount
to keep confidence.'

She was definitely not impressed by the performance of either
Labour or the Alliance. 'Labour was all packaging — merely
packaging politics like some washing powder. What an irony
that *they* were using capitalist tools like advertising and so on
and not getting down to the nitty gritty. In the end the British
people weren't taken in by it, I heard it looked very good but I

didn't see it. The difference was between Michael Foot – a man
of supreme intellect and content but caring little about the
outward and visible signs of success, and the present man, who
had all the outward and visible signs, but no content. Indeed
he'd run away from the content. I couldn't believe for one
moment people would be taken in by that.

'Then we realised that some people weren't actually seeing
that it was a con; and that's when we had to turn around and
show it up. I mean you have a positive duty not to let people get
into power on the basis of concealing things. It was the age-old
con trick: you present yourself with a nice smile and beautifully
turned out and people think: "Ahhh – what a nice guy." That's
the confidence trick, to conceal what you are really about. We
attacked it; but it was also we who had the best manifesto and
we who had the best record. It was never going to work for
them. Then they got personal. Supposing we had run a really
vicious personal campaign, we would have been crucified. Supposing we had run the packaging they did, we would have been
crucified. There were double standards of judgement. But I think
that tells you something – people expect better of us than the
other party. And long may they expect better of us than the other
party!

'The Alliance didn't collapse because of the way they attacked
the wrong target. No, I think it was something more fundamental
than that. It was realised fairly quickly that they hadn't got any
policies, and they didn't even get on very well together. There
was something of the Gilbert and Sullivan about them. The fact
is they never really succeeded so much in attacking Labour as
they did in attacking us. But then don't forget that David Steel
is virtually indistinguishable from some members of the Labour
Party. We were less confident this time than in 1983 – because
we just did not know how it was going to split. But as soon as
I got to Finchley on the day I could see the Conservative vote
was much more determined. Early on we were ahead. We were
polling ahead of the similar poll in eighty-three. There was a
feeling among our supporters that we must go to the poll. We
must vote.'

How then did she feel when she heard that the party had
passed the 325 mark and she had passed into the history books?

'I was actually with my constituents after the count. It was the first time I had been there with them. We were standing with them before the big television screen when we got the majority.' What did she feel at that moment? 'It was the first time I really could be certain. What mattered to me more than anything else was that this thing we had achieved so far — for our country — should continue. It was somehow terribly important to all the voters that we got back. Somehow, if we didn't get back the other party just wouldn't have the kind of policies that were right for Britain. It would no longer be the Britain we had known and the Britain we had been proud of. Therefore, when I saw we had got it I was just proud to know that we could take it on and govern and hold international confidence abroad and that the majority was going to be enough to give us a chance of winning next time — which matters.'

Was there a moment of personal reflection that Margaret Hilda Roberts had come an awfully long way? 'No, no — that was totally submerged. I have only been the instrument of this thing. It was, I suppose, Keith Joseph and I who started it in 1974. I did feel it was a pity that Keith wasn't there. But my overwhelming feeling was that Britain would now go on in the way our hopes and dreams for it were. Then, what struck me more than anything else, was that forty-four per cent of first-time voters were for us. That means that in spite of everything, in spite of being brought up in a Welfare State, they wanted opportunity — and they were looking for the excitement of opportunity and the chance of opportunity. That was terrific. It had been worth it all.

'I think the victory showed that the British people generally realised that things were being well run, that this is something of great value and that our reputation abroad is something of great value and that they would like it to continue. There is a second strand also. It showed that many of them were afraid of what would happen if the Labour Party, with its increasing number of extremists, were ever to get in. I never in all my life found so many people so anxious to get themselves to the poll and so early. They wanted to vote *for* us; but also they were frightened there would be no defence, they were frightened about the militant trade unionsim and the violence attached to it, frightened of secondary picketing, and frightened of what their children might be taught in the schools. They also believed in the positive side of all those things, good defence, common sense, law and order, good education. But above all they wanted to be proud of the country they live in.'

She believed that the single most important weapon in the victory was her concentrated blitz of media interviews in that last week; more so than the tour itself, which she admitted had received disappointing coverage. 'From the time of the Jonathan Dimbleby interview onwards, that was when the tide turned. Those interviews were the most influential thing of all.' She conceded communications had been at fault earlier in the campaign and that she needed the election to remind her, yet again, of the importance of informing people. Central Office, she also conceded, did need reform. 'I think from time to time it does, because you come into a new phase and it is necessary to keep abreast of new developments. But don't forget – we did win. And we won by the devotion and loyalty and experience of a lot of marvellous people there. Nevertheless we would like to win by 150 next time.'

She then turned to her immediate tasks – education and housing reforms, the inner cities, the Health Service – before outlining her long-term goals. But first, I asked her if she had thought about her successor. What qualities would he or she need? 'You need to know where you are going and you need to be determined not to be deflected,' she said. 'Every now and then you might have to do a slight by-pass of something, but you must always know that you are going in the direction you want to. And you must always keep the momentum going.'

So is he or she in her government? 'Oh, I think they're in it. But I don't know whether they are in Cabinet yet or not. I just don't know that. They will need to be different in some respects. It takes a different capacity to turn round a great ship of state going in one direction: first to turn the whole thing round and then get it going in another. So perhaps the one who keeps it going will not have to be quite so combative as me, because by then the ship will have its own momentum.' How then will she know when to go? 'I have no idea, but I shall know by a combination of experience and feel. But first we have to get lots of young people starting on the first rung of the ladder so they can be promoted upwards, so all the available talent is ready.'

And when the time comes, what would she like her political epitaph to be? 'I don't know — I've got a bit of time to think about that!' She laughed. 'We've been working to restore the political system to bring out all that was best in the British character. That's what we've done. It's called Thatcherism — it's got nothing to do with Thatcher except that I was merely the vehicle for it. But it is in everything I do. It's a mixture of fundamentally sound economics. You live within your means; you have honest money, so therefore you don't make reckless promises. You recognise human nature is such that it needs incentives to work harder, so you cut your tax. It is about being worthwhile and honourable. And about the family. And about that something which is really rather unique and enterprising in the British character — it's about how we built an Empire, and how we gave sound administration and sound law to large areas of the world. All those things are still there in the British people aren't they?

'For years my worry was that when we got it all back and got the ball at the feet of the people, they wouldn't kick it. I just did not know if the spirit was still there or not. But in the last year it's started to come right. And it *is* there. People know when they vote for me that what I have to offer is not empty promises. All I can do, all any government should do is to give people the opportunity to demonstrate their talents, for themselves, their families and for their country. It is a partnership between government and people.

'So perhaps my epitaph should say: "What she did was to restore Britain."'